WELCOME

I hope this book will be an enduring gift from Beautiful British Columbia or a titillating compilation of humour, recollections and panache for British Columbians to savour.

The birth of this B.C. All-Celebrity Cookbook took place on April 5, 1993 at 8:20 a.m. when Shane Nagel, the Burnaby Chamber of Commerce Sales Manager, pitched what he described as "just another idea." That was Monday. By Friday, the first sampling had been selected and solicited.

Thanks, Kevin Evans, C.B.C. News, your phone call was the first in a dizzying series of calls, letters and submissions. So, congratulations Shane, you've always been important to us but now you're a celebrity.

Enjoy,

Abby Anderson, C.A.E.
General Manager
Burnaby Chamber of Commerce

Volunteers are the heartbeat of non-profit associations.
To them we express our heartfelt thanks:

Ruth Kean

Shannon Clark

Taylore T. Fox – for her support and production of our gala fundraiser held at Hart House Restaurant

Rob Hazeldine – Hazeldine Press

Red Robinson – for his support, enthusiasm, and direction

Hart House Restaurant on Deer Lake – for hosting book release gala

B.C. Sports Hall of Fame – for assistance locating contributors

NOTE: If there is "Somebody" missing from our publication let us know. Some "somebodies" may have chosen not to participate; others, regrettably, we may have missed. It's your province, you be the judge for B.C. ALL-CELEBRITY COOKBOOK – VOLUME II.

CITY OF BURNABY
OFFICE OF THE MAYOR

October 15th, 1993

Ms. Abby Anderson
Chamber of Commerce
149-9855 Austin Ave.
Burnaby, B.C. V3J 1N4

Dear Abby:

Congratulations to you and your staff on the B.C. All-Celebrity Cookbook. It's not just a memento of British Columbia; it's a book that provides a real "Flavour" (shall we say) for those who are well known in the Province.

I hope your readers will enjoy my Chocolate Chip recipe on page 289. I've got another favorite ready to submit for Volume Two.

Best personal regards,

William Copeland
MAYOR

4949 Canada Way, Burnaby, British Columbia, V5G 1M2 ❖ Telephone (604) 294-7340 Facsimile (604) 294-7724

Celebrity Line-Up &

The Salvation Army
Territorial Headquarters
Canada and Bermuda
20 Salvation Square
(P.O. Box 4021, Postal Station A)
Toronto, Ontario M5W 2B1
Telephone (416) 598-2071
FAX (416) 598-5063
Office of the Chief Secretary

"Have you read The War Cry?"

October 8, 1993

Mr. Shane Nagel
Burnaby Chamber of Commerce
Suite 149-9855 Austin Avenue
Burnaby, British Columbia
V3J 1N4

Dear Mr. Nagel:

All Celebrity Cookbook

The thought (or is it taste!) of a new recipe holds excitement for all who choose to purchase this remarkable book produced by the Burnaby Chamber of Commerce. We are deeply indebted to them for their initiative.

The generous thought in making the Salvation Army the recipient of profits from the sale of this helpful reference is gratefully acknowledged.

We thank everyone who shares in this by purchasing a copy.

We trust that you will discover in its pages the new "tastes" which will make it special and rewarding!

To our greeting we add God's blessing.

With every good wish.

Yours sincerely,

Roy Calvert
Colonel
CHIEF SECRETARY

William and Catherine Booth Founders | **Bramwell H. Tillsley** General | **Wesley Harris** Territorial Commander

TABLE OF CONTENTS

Published by The Burnaby Chamber of Commerce
1st Printing November, 1993
Printed in British Columbia (Canada) by Hazeldine Press

CELEBRITY LINE-UP &

Breakfast Brunch

The Financial Post

333 King Street East, Toronto, Ontario M5A 4N2 Telephone (416) 350-6300 Fax (416) 350-6301

The world's finest Sunday morning omelette:

-2 eggs per person

- stir (never beat!) in large bowl

- simmer chopped green pepper

- simmer, slightly later, chopped onion

- mix into egg bowl Tabasco sauce

-- also a lashing of Heinz Chili Sauce

-- put into the mix slices of Gorgonzola cheese

-- also one can of smoked oysters

-- pour mix over peppers, onions

--serve over toasted whole wheat bread

-- a slice of papaya on the side

-- with bottle of champagne

-- go to bed and make love

Allan Fotheringham

FROM:

David Ingram ---------------------------------- (604) 657-8451
201-935 Marine Drive --------------------- FAX (604) 649-4759
North Vancouver, BC
V7P 1S3

TO:

Abby Anderson, C.A.E.
General Manager
Burnaby Chamber of Commerce ----------------- (604) 421-0064
149-9855 Austin Avenue ------------------ FAX (604) 421-3630
Professional Wing, Lougheed Mall
Burnaby, B.C., V3J 1N4

Dear Sirs:

Thank you for your invitation to submit to your recipe book. Unfortunately, the letter was addressed to "West" Vancouver rather than "North" Vancouver, but Her Majesty's Crown Corporation postal service did get it through to me.

Herein my belated "tongue in cheek" but very real recipe.

One Egg - Y U C K Y O M E L E T T E
(Sundays and Holidays)

FRESH Ingredients

- Mrs Dash - Fine Ground Herbs and Spices (no salt added)
- Mrs Dash - A Dash of Flavour (no salt added)
- Mrs Dash - Lemon & Herb (no salt added)
- Hy's of Canada Seasoning Salt (nothing but the best)
- Vege-Sal (a little bit different)
- Mad Dog Chili Smoke n'Fire Seasoning (smoke dried jalapenos)
- Naturally Cajun "Insanely Hot" Seasoning
- Club House Garlic salt
- Club House Celery Salt
- Ketchup (No Name)
- Barbecue Sauce (No Name)
- 1 dozen eggs
- 2 Large Spanish Onions
- Butter or margarine (cholesterol is not discussed here)
- Fresh Garlic
- Hot Dog Buns (for special occasions)

LEFTOVER Ingredients

Boiled potatoes and/or

Onions and/or

Rice and/or

Broccoli and/or

Asparagus and/or

Peas and/or

Ham and/or

Chicken and/or

Noodles and/or

Spaghetti and/or

Rice and/or

celery, cooked carrots, radishes, pepperoni, Bavarian Smokies, and anything else edible in the fridge such as Chinese Food, Pizza, Lasagna, or what have you.

Utensils - Depends on size of family

Minimum - 2 10 inch skillets - 2 eight inch crepe skillets - 2 small (1 egg) mixing bowls - enough plates, etc for family.

D E S C R I P T I O N

How does one describe a recipe for YUCKY omelettes?

I do not know. No two omelettes are the same. Even if made at approximately the same time.

That's why they are YUCKY omelettes - that's why they are good.

HISTORY.

Yucky omelettes have their origins in women's lib. The original women's lib from the time when men were men, and women looked after the house.

Growing up in that atmosphere of the 50's in Winnipeg, all the mothers and daughters in the neighbourhood did all the "house" things with two exceptions.

Fathers and sons loaded the coal stoker and looked after taking out the clinkers in winter and mowing the grass in summer and fathers always cooked Sunday breakfast.

I don't know why. It was just the way things were done.

That situation is true in our home today. Of course, I don't have to load the stoker and I intelligently made sure that there was not a blade of grass in our yard and our son takes out the garbage, but carrying on the tradition, I get to make Sunday breakfast and that is where YUCKY omelettes enter the picture.

It also took three weekends after the invitation to submit the recipe to come close to being able to codify.

There are only two absolutes in YUCKY omelettes.

1. The onions start sauteing in one of the skillets on medium with butter or margarine.

2. Only one egg per omelette.

D I R E C T I O N S

Turn all four burners on stove to medium.

Put a dollop of butter or margarine in each frying pan. The trick here is to keep the heat adjusted so that the margarine or butter does not burn. If it burns, turn that burner down a bit, dump out the burned butter, clean that pan, and put in another dollop of butter. All pans should be just at that level where the butter is sizzling hot, but is not turning colour.

Each burner will be different. Make a mental note or even write it down so that "next week", you will get off to a better start.

1. Slice your two Spanish onions. If you can't get or don't have Spanish onions, any old "large" onion will do. If you can't find "large onions (4" in diameter) use four or five small ones. If you don't like onions, leave them out and go to the next step. (turn off frying pan if such is the case and miss out this step next week as well). If you decide to keep the onions in, slice one thin and the other thick, or both thick, or both thin. It doesn't matter. Dump them in the frying pan. Add some more butter. Onions fried in butter are delicious. Some mornings, we stop here and just have fried onions.

1(a) Season to taste.

I like three or four cloves of garlic here. Slice into tiny diced squares, mix in with onions.

1(b) Carefully sprinkle MAD DOG CHILI'S Smoke and Fire Seasoning over the onions. The top of the onions should just be orange with lots of onion showing. You will likely want to add more later, but wait until you and your guests have tasted.

2. Arrange your leftovers in front of you. Observe the degree of cooking that they have already been exposed to and govern your selves accordingly.

Start adding your ingredients to the second skillet. Less cooked items first. For instance, if you are lucky enough to have some boiled potatoes, You will want to slice them fairly thin slices and throw them in first. Some left over "real" ham is nice (whatever you do, do not use sliced Black Forest ham from the

Parliament Buildings
Victoria B.C.
Photo Kharen Hill
Tourism B.C.

deli - Yucky omelettes do not tolerate wimpy foods). Chicken is good. Sometimes you might want to dice a Bavarian Smokey sausage here (in a pinch, you could use a garlic or pepperoni sausage but never, never, never use an ordinary wiener here). Stir fry the Ham, chicken, turkey, potatoes much as you would with a wok.

Watch your two crepe pans here as well. If the heat is too high, they might start scorching. Turn down a bit if so.

You have, of course, been stirring your onions in Skillet 1. This is a good time to taste and decide if a little more MAD DOG CHILI might be in order or if perhaps Naturally CAJUN should be added or perhaps a light sprinkling of garlic salt. If you can find one, dig out one of those little squares of diced garlic for a taste test.

3. To Skillet 2, add some Hy's Seasoning salt and One of the Mrs Dash seasonings. I suggest that the "lemon" be used sparingly. It is a specialist seasoning that only works occasionally. I haven't yet managed to write down what the magic combination was - if you figure it out let me know.

Add the noodles, or spaghetti or rice now. Not too much, but enough that the Skillet # two has a good inch to an inch and a half of goodies in it. Stir fry for about five minutes, tasting the odd ingredient and adding some Vege-Sal or Hy's or Mrs Dash as needed.

Add the "delicates"; the left over asparagus, peas or artichoke hearts.

4. Break an egg into each of the bowls. (i.e. one egg per bowl). stir the eggs until creamy yellow. Pour one into each of the 8" crepe pans. swirl pan to get egg over whole bottom. Put a streak of Ketchup or barbecue sauce (never both) directly across the centre of the egg at right angles to the handle.

5. Immediately dish out a "STRING" of onions across the centre and over top of the ketchup. (1/4" by 1/4" should do)

6. Next put about a 1/2 inch high by one inch wide strip of items from skillet # 2 on top of the onions.

7. sprinkle a little Mrs Dash on the egg which is not covered by our mixture.

8. Put another line of Ketchup over top of our mixture from skillet 2.

9. Cook one to four minutes (depending on heat).

10. Gently lift the edge of the egg closest to the handle and start "rolling" up the egg. It will get a little bulky at the centre, but it will roll. Roll it right out of the pan onto a dinner plate. This gives a rolled omelette up to 3 inches thick.

10a. FOR special occassions, birthday mornings, etc., toast a heavily buttered hot dog bun in one of the crepe pans - three minutes a side should do. put just a little filling in the egg and roll tightly. Voila! Yucky HOT DOG omelette. (Mitchell, the six year old's favourite).

11. Serve with slices of LARGE orange (oh yes - another Fresh ingredient) and some squares of hot buttered toast.

12. Enjoy - It is a criminal offence to use a knife. Forks only.

For the true aficionado, a small extra helping from Skillet #'s one and two "on the side" is in order.

SIGN OF A SUCCESSFUL YUCKY OMELETTE

When Peter, my nine year old asks for a second. and then a third.

When Jose, the wife has one.

When Jane, the 18 month old uses two hands to stuff it in and only leaves a bit on the floor.

David Ingram
President, David Ingram & Associates

MAX WYMAN

Editor, Saturday Review, The Vancouver Sun

Saturday morning. Leave your beloved in bed with *Saturday Review* and a pencil (for the crossword) and take yourself off to the kitchen. You're going to make breakfast-in-bed crepes.

Melt a quarter-cup of butter. In a blender, in this order, put: one and three-quarter cups of sifted all-purpose flour; four eggs; a cup of milk; a cup of water; a pinch of salt; a scratch of nutmeg. Blend it all, about as fast as the blender will go; stop from time to time and scrape the unblended flour from the sides into the mixture. Continue until it's smooth. Trickle in the cooling melted butter; blend some more. Pour the batter into a bowl and let it sit for half an hour or so. Get the coffee going.

Invent some fillings and sauces. Check the larder and the liquor cabinet. Find some *apricot* jam? Put some of it in a small pan with the juice of a lemon and a bit of the rind, add some sugar, a good glass of sweetish wine, simmer it all over low heat for 15 minutes. *Raspberry* jam? same process: jam, lemon, sugar, eau de vie or raspberry brandy. *Caviar* leftovers you're saving for sometime special? It's here: just splosh a little sour cream and vodka on the side. *Marmalade?* Simmer with Grand Marnier. *Fresh fruit* (grapes, plums, strawberries)? Chop them up, sprinkle them with sugar and rum. Be as creative or as simple as you like (plain lemon juice and sugar is sensational sprinkled on crepes). Put your sauces in little dishes and make them look pretty.

Make your crepes. Heat a crepe pan or a heavy-bottomed frying pan to medium-high; smear the bottom with butter, then tip in a good spoonful of the batter, just enough to put a thin coating over the bottom of the pan. Let it cook a minute or two, then loosen it at the edges with a spatula and turn it over. It should be lightly brown on both sides. The first will be a bit too thick and buttery; keep that one aside for the dog. Bring the heat down slightly and continue to cook the crepes, placing each face down as it's done on a plate in the warmed oven. This recipe will probably yield a dozen or more dozen good-sized, filigree-edged crepes (enough for a fine breakfast for two). Layer them so that the side with the even brown speckles is on the outside when they're rolled up: it just looks nicer.

Transfer the entire production - piled-up crepes, multiple sauces, coffee, spoons and spreading utensils - to the bedroom, where you'll be just in time to finish the crossword, sitting up beside your beloved, licking sticky fingers as you feed each other crepes.

The Vancouver Sun A Southam newspaper
2250 Granville Street, Vancouver, B.C. V6H 3G2 Telephone (604) 732-2111

Catch + Release Salal Pancakes

Get up early and go fishing.
Make sure you use a barbless hook and release your catch carefully.
On the way back to camp pick a cup full of ripe salal berries.
While the coffee is boiling, mix together:

3 cups flour
6 tsp. baking powder
3 tbsp. sugar
1 tsp. salt

Add to:

1 egg (whipped)
3 tbsp. oil
1½ cup milk
1 tsp. vanilla

After thoroughly mixing all ingredients add the cup of salal berries. Cook in a hot frying pan until lightly browned each side.

Mark Hume

BChydro 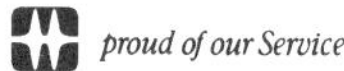

"Bunner Pancakes"

by Patrick Kelly
Training & Development Coordinator
Aboriginal Relations Department

This recipe is as much about love and caring as it is about hearty food. The basic pancake is enriched and turned into fun for you and your loved ones. A "Bunner," as my youngest daughter calls herself (ie. her version of bunny) came into being January 1988. She has two sisters, one now ten, the other fifteen.

Ingredients

1 1/2 cups sifted pastry flour, or
1 1/4 cups sifted all-purpose flour
2 teaspoons baking powder
3/4 teaspoon salt
1/4 cup medium unsweetened coconut
1/4 cup finely chopped walnuts (or your favourite choice of nut)
1/2 banana
1 egg
2 tablespoons oil
2 tablespoons pancake syrup
1 - 1 1/2 cups milk
1/4 cup finely chopped fresh berries (optional)

1. Measure the flour. Mix and sift dry ingredients.

2. Mix coconut and walnuts into sifted flour mixture.

3. Chop the banana (and fresh fruit, if used) into fine pieces and mix well into the flour mixture.

4. Into a well in the top of the flour mixture, add the egg, oil and syrup.

5. Add most of the milk into the well and mix into the dry ingredients, slowly to avoid lumps forming; stir and do not beat. Add as much milk to the mixture until the batter flows freely off the spoon but not too thin. (Note: a good consistency allows you to be creative with many fun shapes.)

6. Heat a griddle or heavy pan to a low medium heat; to test the temperature, sprinkle with a few drops of water; if they dance, the pan is ready. You may wish to add a small amount of oil to the pan to avoid sticking.

7. Before you begin cooking the pancakes, ask your loved ones, "What kind of pancake do you want?" Imagine one says, "I want a Bunner pancake!" Well, there you go with the challenge. You will need to use much of the surface of an average size frying pan.

British Columbia Hydro and Power Authority, 333 Dunsmuir Street, Vancouver B.C. Canada V6B 5R3

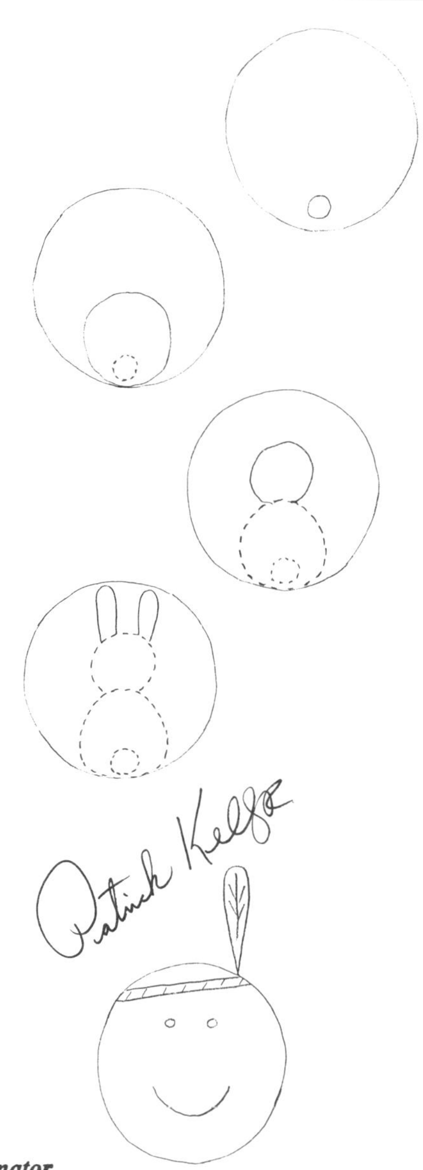

1. "**The Bunner Pancake**" - Using a tablespoon, place one small drop (about 1/2 tablespoon) of batter towards the bottom of the pan. This will be the bunner's tail.

2. Over top of the tail, and towards the centre of the pan, spoon about two or three generous tablespoons of batter to form the lower part of the bunner's body.

3. A little further up the pan and joining the lower body, spoon about two tablespoons of batter to form the bunner's head.

4. To the top of the bunner, add the mandatory "bunner ears." When bubbles begin to break on the surface of the pancake, flip the pancake. A good size flipper is recommended so you can get under as much of the bunner as possible. With a little practice, you will know when and how to flip your wildest creation.

5. After you flip the pancake, check out your creation and see how you like it. Think of other features you may wish to add and place them in the pan at the step you think would work best. I often put facial features on before the head.

6. You can experiment with many fine creatures and shapes. Facial and other features placed in the pan will brown first. As you cover them over with batter, the features stand out on the finished pancake. Serve and enjoy with your loved ones.

Patrick Kelly, *Training and Development Coordinator*

Patrick is the newest addition to B.C. Hydro and the ARD, having joined the corporation in late April of 1993. A member of the Lakahahmen Band of the Sto:lo Nation, Patrick has been an active community volunteer for many years. He is currently Second Vice Chair of the Vancouver Community College Board of Governors. He attended both Simon Fraser University and the Native Indian Teacher Education Program at University of B.C. Patrick was a Program Officer with the Canada Employment and Immigration Commission before joining the Department of the Secretary of State in 1982, where he spent ten years. Prior to assuming his role with B.C. Hydro, he was Executive Director of the Canadian Council for Aboriginal Business, B.C. Chapter. Patrick is a strong believer in life-long learning and continues to take training courses and read on a wide number of subjects.

Visual and Performing Arts in Education

THE UNIVERSITY OF BRITISH COLUMBIA
Scarfe Building · 2125 Main Mall
Vancouver, BC Canada · V6T 1Z5
(604) 228-4531 · (604) 228-5340

17th. Aug. '93

Dear Abby Anderson,

Thanks for your letter of the 11th. requesting a recipe. Well — I'm not at all sure that I'm a "celebrity", but I've written out a simple recipe of English Pancakes — a fond memory of my Mother's cooking so many years ago. If you wish to use it – fine!

Sincerely
Michael Foster
MICHAEL FOSTER

(I retired from U.B.C. in '89 and I now have the title of professor emeritus) My home address is 5715 Owl Court, North Vancouver, B.C. V7R 4V1

ENGLISH PANCAKES

(TO SERVE 4.)

2	EGGS.	2
$\frac{1}{4}$ pt	MILK	150 ml
2 fl.oz	WATER	60 ml
3 oz	PLAIN FLOUR	75 g
1 oz	CASTER SUGAR . . .	25 g
	VANILLA ESSENCE. .	
	PINCH OF SALT. . .	
$3\frac{1}{2}$ oz	BUTTER	100 g.

- Put eggs, milk and water into a bowl.
- Whisk or beat until creamy and smooth.
- Add to flour, caster sugar a few drops of vanilla and salt
- Whisk until creamy and smooth.
- Melt butter in a frying pan
- Pour in a little of the batter and spread in a thin layer over the pan.
- When the underside is cooked flip the pancake over to brown the other side.
- As soon as each pancake is ready, fold and place in a warm oven while other pancakes are cooked.
- Add more butter to the pan as necessary.
- Before serving sprinkle with white granulated sugar and a few drops of lemon juice. Then roll up the pancake for eating.

(Other than sugar and lemon juice jam is often preferred)

MICHAEL FOSTER

VANCOUVER
PORT CORPORATION

2760 Granville Square
200 Granville Street
Vancouver BC V6C 1S4
Tel. (604) 666-3841

SOCIETE DU PORT
DE VANCOUVER

2760 Granville Square
200, rue Granville
Vancouver C-B V6C 1S4
Fax (604) 666-8239

16 July 1993

POTATO PANCAKES

2 potatoes - peeled
2 heaped tablespoons flour
1 teaspoon each salt and pepper
2 eggs
olive oil

Grate potatoes on medium grater. Mix flour, pepper and salt. Then add 2 eggs, broken in one at a time. Beat all together into a rough purée. Lightly cover bottom of frying pan with olive oil and heat. Put 1 teaspoon of the mixture into the hot oil for each pancake. Spread out quickly with a spoon into thin ragged shapes. Fry until crisp on both sides. Serve hot with cold beetroot slices.

SALMON FISH CAKES

1/2 lb. fresh salmon - cooked and flaked
1/2 lb. potatoes - freshly cooked and sieved
salt
peppercorns - freshly ground
2 oz. butter
2 eggs - beaten
breadcrumbs
clarified butter for frying

Blend salmon well with potatoes. Season to taste with salt and pepper. Melt the butter and add it to the mixture, binding it with a beaten egg. Roll to 1-1/2 inch thick and cut to desired shapes. Dip cakes in the other beaten egg and breadcrumbs, shaking off any surplus. Fry on both sides until golden brown.

Patrick Reid, O.C.
Chairman

A member of Ports Canada *Membre de*

WATT
COMMUNICATIONS

Watt's Wonderful Waffles

You gotta get up pretty early in the morning to put this together for Sunday brunch, but if you do, they'll certainly leave you alone long enough for a delightful Sunday nap, which you'll need to sleep this feast off.

1 cup warm water
1 tablespoon brown sugar
1 tablespoon yeast

2 cups milk
2 tablespoons butter
2 cups flour
2 tablespoons brown sugar
3 eggs separated
1 teaspoon salt
1 teaspoon vanilla extract
1/2 teaspoon nutmeg

1. Combine the water, sugar and yeast and set aside to allow to rise.
2. Combine the milk and butter, and heat to the scalding point, and allow to cool.
3. Combine the yeast mixture with the scalded milk, making sure the milk is cool enough (you can just keep your finger in it) not to kill the yeast. Add the flour, sugar, egg yolks, salt, vanilla and nutmeg and mix to a smooth texture.
4. Cover the top of the batter with a sheet of waxed paper and place it in a warm place to rise. Rising should take about an hour. You can even place it in the oven at a very low heat.
5. When the batter is about twice its original volume, whip the egg whites until they "peak," and fold them into the batter.
6. Heat your waffle iron, and get cookin'. The waffles are best served right off the grill. If you store them in the oven they bet soggy, and there's nothing worse than soggy waffles. Serve with maple syrup, yoghurt and strawberries, or, my personal favourite, molasses.
7. Bask in the glow of glory reflected off your golden brown wonderful waffles.

Keith Watt

(Keith Watt is a veteran Vancouver writer and documentary maker. He's a two-time winner of the Jack Webster award for editorial excellence.)

305 - 1110 Hamilton Street, Vancouver, B.C. V6B 2S2 • Telephone (604) 683-2202

Phillips, Hager & North Ltd.
Investment Counsellors
17th Floor, 1055 West Hastings Street Vancouver, B.C. V6E 2H3
Telephone (604) 684-4361 Fax (604) 684-5120

July 9/93

Dear Abby,

The following is my favorite recipe:

Lazy Man's Porridge - serves one.

1/3 cup oatmeal
1 cup skim milk
some raisins

Microwave for about 5 minutes in a roundish bowl. (It will foam over the top if the bowl is too deep)

Serve without adding any milk or cream (ie low fat). It will taste creamy & stay hot.

Porridge connoisseurs will add a touch of honey rather than the traditional brown sugar.

A genuine lazy cook will appreciate that the porridge not only stirs itself in the microwave, but the bowl can be rinsed under the tap. No pot scrubbing. Bon apetit!

Sincerely

Art Phillips

THE UNIVERSITY OF BRITISH COLUMBIA

Department of English
#397 - 1873 East Mall
Vancouver, B.C. Canada V6T 1Z1
Tel: (604) 822-5122
Fax: (604) 822-6906

SOUTH VANCOUVER CINNAMON SWIRLS

1. Preheat the oven to 400° F.

2. Grease a large baking sheet and set aside.

3. In a large bowl, sift together:
   - 2 cups flour
   - 4 teaspoons baking powder
   - 1/2 teaspoon salt
   - 2 tablespoons sugar

4. Cut 4 tablespoons of vegetable oil into the dry mixture.

5. Add 2/3 cup milk, mix with a fork, and then knead quickly a few times until the dough forms a single ball. If the dough is too sticky, add a little more flour.

6. Turn the dough onto a floured board, and with a rolling pin roll the dough to about 1/3" thick (it will look like a rectangle roughly 12" by 8").

7. Spread the cinnamon-butter mix (see below) onto the flattened rectangle of dough:

   CINNAMON-BUTTER MIX

   mix together, in a small bowl, about half a cup of brown sugar, 3-4 tablespoons of soft butter, and 2-3 teaspoons of cinnamon

8. After the cinnamon-butter mix is spread on the dough, scatter a layer of raisins evenly on top of it.

9. Starting at the longer side of the rectangle, roll the dough into a log shape (as though you were rolling up a newspaper) and pinch the dough together as you finish so that the roll doesn't come apart.

10. Slice the roll into sections, each about 1/2" thick, and transfer each section (or "cinnamon swirl") onto the baking sheet.

11. Bake for 12-15 minutes, depending on the heat of the oven, until the tops turn slightly golden.

12. Serve warm or cooled, with or without butter.

W. New

W.H. New
Professor

HOUSE OF COMMONS
CHAMBRE DES COMMUNES
OTTAWA, ONTARIO
CANADA
K1A OA6

THE SPEAKER
LE PRÉSIDENT

JOHN FRASER'S

DUMPLINGS IN MAPLE SYRUP

1 3/4 cups maple syrup
3/4 cup of water
1 3/4 cups of flour
1/2 tsp cinnamon
4 tsp baking powder
dash of salt
2 tsp shortening or lard
2/3 cup homogenized or 2% milk

Place maple syrup and water in a wide saucepan and bring to a boil stirring often (the saucepan should have a lid for use later).

In a bowl, sift together flour, cinnamon, baking powder and salt. Cut in shortening or lard mixing by hand until mixture resembles oatmeal. With a fork, stir in the milk just until blended (the mixture will be lumpy).

With a large spoon, shape dumplings and drop onto lightly floured plate. Drop dumplings into boiling syrup leaving 2 or 3 inches of space between them. Cover tightly and boil gently over medium heat for 15 minutes without removing lid. Serve immediately on its own or with whipped cream or ice cream.

With the Compliments of

The Hon. John A. Fraser, P.C., Q.C.,
Member of Parliament
Vancouver South

Toad in the Hole

This is the stuff that made Britain great!

Ingredients:

1lb pure pork sausages (Nitrate and preservative free)

3 eggs ½ tsp sugar
1 cup Milk 1 cup flour (white)
½ tps salt 2 tbsp oil

Method:

Prick, and place apart, sausages in deep meat dish. Pre-heat oven to 350° and cook for 10 mins, turning once.

In medium bowl mix eggs, salt and sugar beat together, medium speed. Add flour and ½ cup milk, beat until smooth paste. Add remaining ½ cup milk, 2 tbsp oil, beat low for 1 min.

Pour over sausages in very hot pan, return to oven for 10 mins on 450°. Turn down to 350° for 20 minutes or until batter is lightly brown and puffed.

Serve with mashed potato and lashings of brown gravy.

David Hornblow
July '93

2327 Yew Street
Vancouver,
British Columbia
V6K 3H1
Telephone
(604) 734-0791
Facsimile
(604) 734-8613

Here's a recipe for Tea Biscuits copied out of Best Recipes This Side of Heaven: Home-tested recipes from Anglican Church ladies.

Tea Biscuits

2 cups flour
4 ½ tsp. baking powder
1 tsp salt
¼ cup margarine (or butter)

Mix together with pastry blender. Add 1 cup milk. Form biscuits and work as little as possible. Place on buttered pan. Bake 425° for 10 minutes

Scones: Add ¼ cup sugar and
½ cup currants.

St. Thomas Anglican
Church
Walkerton, Ont.

I add almond flakes, raisins, coconut shreds etc. Sometimes I substitute apple sauce for the margarine and use 4 tsp. instead of 4 ½ tsp. baking powder.

Joy Kogawa

Joy Kogawa
Award Winning BC Author

BRITISH COLUMBIA SPORTS HALL OF FAME & MUSEUM

777 PACIFIC BLVD. SOUTH, VANCOUVER, B.C., CANADA V6B 4Y8 • TELEPHONE: (604) 687-5520 • FAX: (604) 687-5510

Tattie Scones

For years my Scottish mother and grandmother have consistently turned out these wonderful scones. I must confess to having had much more practise eating them than baking them, but luckily they are quite easy to do.

8 oz flour
2 oz shortening
3 tsp baking powder
1/2 tsp salt
8 oz cooked mashed potatoes (slightly warm or cool)
1/4 pint milk

In a large bowl, mix together the flour, baking powder and salt.

Cut in the shortening until mixture resembles fine bread crumbs.

Mix in the potatoes (warm potatoes seem to make lighter scones).

Form a well in the centre of the mixture, add the milk and draw in the dry ingredients with a knife.

Turn dough out onto a floured board and divide into four equal portions.

Roll each ball out in turn to make a circle about 8" in diameter and no more than 1/4" thick.

Mark into quarters with a knife and prick with a fork.

Bake on a lightly greased griddle at a moderate heat until light to golden brown.

Makes 16 scones (never enough!). Best served warm and dripping with butter, but almost as nice cold.

Yours sincerely,

Patricia Armstrong
Curator

LOCATED IN B.C. PLACE STADIUM, VANCOUVER, B.C. • DONATIONS ARE TAX DEDUCTIBLE UNDER TAX NUMBER 0366872-50-27

Welsh Cakes

3 cups sifted all-purpose flour
1 ½ tsp. baking powder
½ tsp. soda
1 ¼ tsp. salt
1 cup white sugar
1 tsp. nutmeg
1 cup shortening (half butter)
1 cup currants
2 eggs
6 tablespoons milk

Sift dry ingredients into a bowl. Cut in shortening. Add currants. Beat eggs and milk together, and add to fruit-flour mixture. Mix well. Divide dough into 3 or 4 parts. Roll out about ¼ in. thick on lightly floured board. Cut into rounds with cookie cutter. Bake on heated griddle at 350° F (an electric fry pan works well) 10-12 mins. on each side, until cooked through + nicely browned. Makes 3 dozen cakes.

Eileen Kernaghan

Eileen Kernaghan
Leading BC author & owner of Neville Books

Skyline
Vancouver B.C.
Photo Ed Gifford
Tourism B.C.

The Coast Westerly Hotel

1590 Cliffe Avenue
Courtenay, B.C. V9N 2K4
Telephone: (604) 338-7741
Fax: (604) 338-5442

BREAKFAST PUFFS

5 TBLS. shortening
½ cup sugar
1 large egg
½ cup milk

1½ cups flour
2¼ tsp. baking powder
¼ tsp. salt
¼ tsp. nutmeg

Cream shortening and sugar together. Beat in egg. Add dry ingredients alternately with milk. Pour batter into greased muffin tin, filling each cup 2/3 full. Bake at 350^for 20-25 minutes.
Remove from oven, and while still hot roll each one first in 6TBLS. melted butter, then in a mixture of ½ sup sugar mixed with 1 tsp. cinnamon.

SALMON PATE`

1 pound canned salmon
8 oz. cream cheese
1 TBLS. lemon juice
2 tsp. grated onion

1 tsp. prepared horseradish
¼ tsp. salt
¼ tsp. liquid smoke

Mix all ingredients together -- form into a ball -- chill. Roll in mixture of ½ cup of pecans and 3 TBLS. parsley.

Sincerely

Linda Beech

Linda Beech
General Manager

Call Our Toll Free Coast Line 1-800-663-1144

Hongkong Bank of Canada
Suite 300, 885 West Georgia Street, Vancouver, BC V6C 3E9

WRP Dalton
President
and Chief Executive Officer

06 May 1993

Mrs. A. Anderson
General Manager
Burnaby Chamber of Commerce
Suite 149
9855 Austin Avenue
Professional Wing, Lougheed Mall
Burnaby, B.C.
V3J 1N4

Dear Mrs. Anderson:

Further to your letter of April 27th I am delighted to enclose a couple of my favourite recipes.

The first is for a Shrimp Cocktail Sauce and it is a "must have" recipe to enjoy the wonderful fresh shrimp we can get on the West Coast. I have just returned to Vancouver after a few years in Toronto and the thing I missed most was B C fresh shrimp. This wonderful West Coast Shrimp needs a special sauce to go with it and here it is. You can make it as hot as you want by simply increasing the appropriate ingredients.

The other recipe is for "Pioneer Muffins". Our West Coast pioneers had to be hardy, energetic people. Good food was part of ensuring strength and stamina needed to attack the West Coast wilderness. I honestly have no real idea whether or not these truly are pioneer muffins but they have everything but the kitchen sink in them and so they can't help but be healthy and tasty.

Thanks for giving me the opportunity to participate in your "All Celebrity Cookbook".

Best regards,

W.R.P. Dalton
Look for Mr. Dalton's shrimp cocktail sauce in volume 2!

Telephone: (604) 641-1850 Facsimile: 685-9712 Telex: 04-507750 answer back: HONGGROUP VCR
*member:*HongkongBank *group*

PIONEER MUFFINS

3	Eggs
1/3 Cup	Brown Sugar
2/3 Cup	Vegetable Oil
1/4 Cup	Molasses
2 Cups	Natural Bran
1 Cup	Grated Carrots
1 Cup	Applesauce, Mashed Bananas or Pureed Fruit
1 1/2 Cups	Liquid (Water, Milk or Apple Juice)
1 1/2 Cups	Whole Wheat Flour
1/2 Cup	Wheat Germ
1 Tsp	Baking Soda
2 Tsp	Baking Powder
1 Tsp	Salt
1 Tbsp	Powered Milk
1/2 Cup	Raisins (Optional)

If using applesauce, add 2 Tsp Cinnamon to dry ingredients and 1 Cup Chopped Walnuts.

Method

In large bowl, beat eggs. Add sugar, oil, molasses, bran, carrots, applesauce and liquid. Stir well.

In medium bowl, mix well whole wheat flour, wheat germ, soda, baking powder, salt, powered milk and raisins.

Add dry ingredients all at once to egg mixture, stirring only until moist.

Bake 375 degrees for 20-25 minutes. Makes 2 dozen muffins.

W R P Dalton
President & CEO
Hongkong Bank of Canada

TERRY GOULD is a magazine journalist, screen writer and author whose dramatically told articles have won him ten Western Magazine Awards, a Certificate of Merit for Excellence in Journalism from the Jack Webster Foundation, a National Magazine Award, and twelve additional nominations.

Mr. Gould's articles concentrate on the human lives at the center of often tragic tales of violence and corruption, and he has translated one of the most telling of those tales into the CBC-TV screenplay *Racing With Dragons*. Born in the rougher reaches of Brooklyn, New York, Mr. Gould moved to Vancouver in 1986, and has worked as senior editor and senior writer of the *Vancouver Sun's V Magazine*, and the consulting editor of *Vancouver Magazine*. He is currently a feature writer for *Saturday Night Magazine*, and is at work on several screenplays and documentaries based upon his articles. He is the author of the book of short stories, *How the Blind Make Love*.

Cheese Blintzes

Batter:

8 eggs beaten
1 cup milk
1 cup water
2 cups flour
5 teaspoons melted butter

Combine beaten eggs, milk and water. Gradually stir in the flour, then add melted butter. If batter is too thick, add 1/2 cup water.

Use 8" frying pan. Heat pan with a touch of butter. Use approximately 1/8 cup batter for each blintz. Move hot pan quickly. Do not let set until bottom of pan is covered. Brown on one side only. Place browned side up on clean towel.

Filling:

2 cups cottage cheese
2 egg yolks
1 tablespoon sugar

Mix filling ingredients together. Place about 1 tablespoon (scant) of filling on edge of pancake. Fold edges toward the centre and roll up. Blintzes can be refrigerated for later use at this point.

To serve: Fry lightly and serve hot. Top with strawberry jam or sour cream.

September 7, 1993

BIOSHORT

CREDITS

FOUR BOOKS : NOT SO SCARLET A WOMAN - LIGHT AND HUMOROUS POEMS red cedar press; CLOUDS EMPTY THEMSELVES - ISLAND HAIKU red cedar press; MOSS-HUNG TREES - Haiku Of The West Coast--REFLECTIONS PUBLISHING; BEYOND THE LIGHTHOUSE - OOLICHAN BOOKS MINIBOOK - WILD STRAWBERRIES - TRABARNI PRESS

OVER 300 POETRY APPEARANCES IN ABOUT 200 MAGAZINES.
ABOUT 20 ANTHOLOGIES LATEST VIRAGO BOOK OF WICKED VERSE & THE HAIKU MOMENT

INTERNATIONAL GRAND PRIZE WINNER OF HAIKU JAPAN 89 & NUMEROUS OTHER POETRY PRIZES

Winona Baker

Winona Baker,
606 First St., Nanaimo, B.C. Can.
V9R 1Y9

(604) 753-8417

Recipe

DON & MARY'S GRANOLA

1 CUP LIQUID HONEY
1 CUP COOKING OIL (NOT OLIVE)

MIX TOGETHER:

5 CUPS ROLLED OATS
1 CUP WHEAT GERM
1 CUP BRAN (OPTIONAL)
1 CUP POWDERED MILK (NOT INSTANT)
1 CUP SESAME SEEDS
1 CUP SUNFLOWER SEEDS
1 CUP NUTS
1 CUP RAISINS (OR DRIED FRUIT OF CHOICE)

(OPTIONAL) 1/2 CUP COCONUT

Gently heat the honey and oil together. Stir into all the other mixed ingredients except the coconut - add it in the last 20 min. of cooking. Spread on a large cookie sheet / broiler tray. Cook for 30 minutes at 300 degrees. When cool store in a plastic bucket or suitable containers.
Makes a good trail food, a stick to your ribs breakfast, can be sprinkled on fruit for dessert.

John Cashore, M.L.A.
(Coquitlam-Maillardville)
Parliament Buildings
Victoria, B.C. V8V 1X4
Telephone: (604) 387-1187

Constituency Office:
102, 1108 Austin Avenue
Coquitlam, B.C. V3K 3P5
Telephone: (604) 937-3516

September 9th, 1993

Abby Anderson,C.A.E.
General Manager
Burnaby Chamber Of Commerce
#149 9855 Austin Ave.
Burnaby, B.C.
V3J 1N4

Dear Mrs. Anderson:

This letter is in response to your request for a favorite recipe of John's. The following is one that John actually makes himself from time to time.

JOHN'S MUNCHY MUFFINS

1 cup flour
1 cup natural bran
1 tsp. baking soda
1 tsp. baking powder
3/4 cup sugar
6 tbs.. oil
3/4 cup raisins (or raisins & walnuts)
3/4 cup chopped dates
1 cup boiling water
1 egg

Mix flour, bran, soda, sugar and baking powder.
In a separate bowl combine oil, raisins, water, egg and dates. Add to bran mixture mixing well.
Line muffin pan with baking cups.
Place desired amount in each cup.
Bake at 425 F for 25 minutes.
Yield: 12 muffins.

Good luck with the book and please let me know when it's available.

Yours truly,

Angel Kirner

Angel Kirner
Constituency Asistant to
Hon. John Cashore, M.L.A
Coquitlam-Maillardville

The City of Revelstoke
Fax (604) 837-4930 Telephone (604) 837-2161
P.O. Box 170, 216 Mackenzie Avenue,
Revelstoke, British Columbia V0E 2S0

OFFICE OF THE MAYOR

T = tablespoon
t = teaspoon
C = cup

A. **Cheese and Onion Bread** (recipe for 4 loaves)

2	T	Fermipan Yeast			
2	t	Sugar	2	t	Tabasco Pepper Sauce
4	C	Water	1	C	Dry Shredded Onion
3	t	Salt (heaping)	1	C	Shredded Cheddar Cheese
3		Eggs (beaten)	1	C	Grated Parmesan
2/3	C	Oil	10–12	C	Flour

Mix the cheeses, yeast and 1/2 the flour in a big mixing bowl. Combine all other ingredients (not too warm) then add to flour mixture. Knead and add remaining flour as required to achieve proper consistency. Rise dough twice before baking in 375 degree oven for 35 – 40 minutes.

This is a great bread for sandwiches and the aroma when it is toasting makes it irresistible.

TIP RE: Rising –– Using Microwave

Place a slim container with 2 cups water in microwave and heat it on full power for 5 min. Move container to corner and place dough in plastic mixing bowl in microwave covered by moist towel. Rise for 20 min. on lowest power (#1 = 100–110 degrees F) For second rising, punch down and repeat.

B. **Bun Mixture** (makes 4 dozen large hamburger buns or 8 dozen 4" diameter Parker House rolls or use 1/4 of recipe to make a dozen large cinnamon buns)

1	T	Fermipan Yeast	1	C	Melted Lard
6	C	Water	2	C	Sugar (white granulated)
5		Eggs (beaten)	18–20	C	White Flour
1	T	Salt (heaping)			

Add yeast to 10 cups flour. Combine all other ingredients (no warmer than 100 degrees) and add to flour mixture. Continue to add flour and knead until dough is of soft, smooth consistency. Because of the small amount of yeast, this dough has to rise and be punched down five times. I usually start this recipe at 7:00 p.m. or so and using the microwave for rising, have the buns shaped and in their pans by 9:30 p.m. Leave buns to rise overnight and pop them in the oven in the a.m. at 375 degrees for 10 – 12 minutes.

Great morning aroma and great buns!

I trust these recipes are worthy of your cookbook and look forward to obtaining a copy of the cookbook on completion.

Sincerely,

Geoff Battersby

Geoff S. Battersby, M.D.
Mayor

BANANA BREAD

1-1/4 cups flour
1 tsp. baking soda
2 eggs
1/4 cup oil
1 cup sugar
2 ripe, mashed bananas
1/4 cup chopped walnuts
1 tsp. vanilla

Sift together flour & baking soda. Mix & add eggs, oil, sugar, bananas, walnuts & vanilla. Pour into greased loaf pan. Bake for 1 hour at 350 degrees F.

Brigitta Dau
Vancouver based actor currently starring in "Northwood" on CBC

Appetizers

SIMON FRASER UNIVERSITY

PRESIDENT'S OFFICE

BURNABY, BRITISH COLUMBIA V5A 1S6
Telephone: (604) 291-4641
Fax: (604) 291-4860

MR BOB'S CHICKEN WINGS

3 lbs chicken wings
1 cup honey
1/2 cup soy sauce
2 TABLESPOONS CATCHUP
1 Clove Garlic
2 TABLESPOONS peanut oil

Preheat oven to 375°
Remove wing tips AND cut into two pieces
place wing pieces in baking dish in single layer
salt and pepper to taste And sprinkle with oil
mix honey, soy sauce, catchup and garlic And pour over wing segments
bake for About one hour

Bob Brown
Acting President

oberto oberti inc.
architecture and urban design

300 - 1445 west georgia street, vancouver, b.c. v6g 2t3 phone (604) 662-7796 fax (604) 662-7958

Cold Beef with Tuna Sauce

This is a wonderful, light cold Summer plate that may be served both as an appetizer or as a main course. It is a traditional dish of Northern Italy, where it is commonly called "Vitel Tonné". It is best with white wine, such as Soave or a Chardonnay.

♦

Preparation Time: 20 minutes
Refrigeration Time: 2 or more hours

♦

ingredients: (serves 10)

Beef eye of the round in one piece (kg.1.2)
1 whole large carrot peeled
1 large onion cut in four
4 celery stalks
4 bay leaves
1 egg whole, plus one yolk
1 1/2 cup of olive oil
juice of two large lemons
50 grams of drained capers
1 can of flaked white tuna
1 teaspoon of Worcester sauce
salt and pepper

♦

Boil the meat in a large pot with enough water to cover the beef completely. Add celery, onion, carrot, bay leaves and a teaspoon of salt. Simmer for about one hour or until the meat is completely cooked. Drain the beef and set it aside until it reaches room temperature. Refrigerate, wrapped in foil, for at least two hours or overnight. Set the broth aside for later use, after having discarded the vegetables.

When the meat is cold, prepare the sauce. Put the egg whole plus one yolk in a food processor. Add a pinch of salt and the Worcestor sauce. Process at the highest speed for a few seconds. Add olive oil in a thin and constant stream a medium speed. Slowly add lemon juice. The sauce will have the consistency of a fairly liquid mayonnaise. Transfer it to a mixing bowl with the exception of a few tablespoons that you will leave in the food processor. Add to the processor all the capers and the tuna. Process for a few seconds at the highest speed. Transfer to the mixing bowl and with a wooden spoon amalgamate the sauce.

Cut the meat in very thin slices. Arrange the thin meat slices on a platter, allowing for some overlapping. Pour the tuna sauce on top to completely cover the meat. Decorate with fresh parsley and/or sliced stuffed olives. Cover the platter with plastic wrap and refrigerate until serving.

Yours truly,
OBERTO OBERTI INC.
ARCHITECTURE AND URBAN DESIGN

Per: Oberto Oberti, President
OO/vm

oberto oberti inc.
architecture and urban design

300 - 1445 west georgia street, vancouver, b.c. v6g 2t3 phone (604) 662-7796 fax (604) 662-7958

THE VANCOUVER
BOARD OF TRADE

World Trade Centre
Suite 400
999 Canada Place
Vancouver, B.C.
Canada V6C 3E1
(604) 681-2111
FAX: (604) 681-0437

July 28, 1993

Ms. Abby Anderson, C.A.E.
General Manager
Burnaby Chamber of Commerce
Suite 149 - 9855 Austin Avenue
Professional Wing, Lougheed Mall
Burnaby, B.C.
V3J 1N4

Dear Abby:

My contribution of a recipe is as follows:

"Golden Boy" Canapes (Winnipeg)

1) Lightly spread Winnipeg cream cheese on stoned wheat thins.

2) Apply flakes of smoked Winnipeg Goldeye (steamed).

3) Top with Manitoba Whitefish golden caviar.

4) Serve with *cold* Ukrainian vodka.

Kind regards,

Darcy Rezac
Managing Director

/aml

MPR Teltech Ltd

8999 Nelson Way
Burnaby, BC
Canada V5A 4B5

Tel 604. 294 1471
Fax 604. 293 5787

June 7, 1993

Cheese Fondue (Neuchâtel style)

Ingredients for 4 persons:
20 oz. finely grated Swiss cheese (half emmentaler, half Gruyère)
2 breakfast cupfuls dry white wine
1 clove of garlic
1 jigger of Kirsch mixed with
1 level teaspoon cornflour (thickened)
pepper, nutmeg, paprika and plenty of 1 inch crusty breadcubes (white)

Rub the fondue pot well with the peeled clove of garlic. Pour the white wine and one third of the grated cheese into the pot and place it on the stove. Start stirring in a figure 8 motion, gradually adding the rest of the cheese. Cook over moderate heat, stirring all the time until it starts to boil. Add the cornflour mixed with Kirsch (or water) bring once more to the boil. Quickly season with pepper and nutmeg or paprika and bring to the table. Place the pot on the Spring chafing dish. Adjust the flame so that the Fondue will simmer through out the meal. Now spear a cube of bread on your fork and dip it into the pot, giving a good stir each time.

With this Fondue serve a sparkling white wine or tea. During the meal it is customary to drink a jigger of Kirsch to help digestion.

Bon appetit!

Alan E. Winter
President
MPR Teltech Ltd.
Burnaby, B.C.

HUMMOUS

Hummous is a middle eastern staple. It is high in protein and fibre, contains iron and calcium, is cheap, easy to make and -- most important -- delicious!

It can be served as a dip with crackers or wedges of pita bread. It also serves as a side dish, salad bar item or sandwich filling.

Since this dish is strictly vegetarian it can be offered to all your vegetarian guests as well as those who restrict their diets for religious or health reasons. Finally, I have not yet met anyone who didn't like it.

To make:

Combine in food processor:

One 540 ml (19 0z) can of chick peas (garbanzos) , drained
Two tablespoon tahini (see note)
Juice of one lemon
one clove garlic, peeled
one small hot pepper, fresh or dried, or a pinch of cayenne
1/2 tsp cumin
salt to taste

Blend together to form a smooth paste. If desired, throw in a few sprigs of parsley at the end. Do not over blend at this point or your hummous will turn green.

To serve:

Spread on a flat plate and garnish. Garnishes could be a swirl of oil and a sprinkle of paprika, black olives, sliced pickles, or a handful of whole chick peas.

Note: Tahini is sesame seed paste and can be bought at Greek or other middle eastern grocery stores. If unavailable, substitute sesame oil or one tablespoon each of peanut butter and oil.

Roslyn Kunin
Executive Director of the Laurier Institute

3449 West 23rd Avenue
Vancouver, B.C. Canada V6S 1K2

Roslyn Kunin and Associates

Tel: (604) 736-0783
Fax: (604) 736-0789

George Bowering

2499 W. 37th,
Vancouver,B.C.
V6M 1P4.
Canada

Fax: 604-266-9000
E-mail:
George_Bowering@fraser.sfu.ca

GB's PICADILLO

My wife has always been willing to eat this one, but my daughter's face would go stony whenever she asked what's for supper, and the reply was GB's picadillo.

- 4 tablespoons extra virgin olive oil
- 2 pounds shaved beef (or hamburger, if you really have to
- 2 medium onions, coarsely chopped
- 1 or 2 cloves garlic, chopped
- 2 apples, peeled and cored and chopped
- 3 tomatoes, chopped (peeled if you are a peeler
- 4 jalapeños or serranos, sliced (remove the seeds, if you're chicken)
- some tomatillos, if you can get them, chopped
- 1/2 cup raisins
- 1/4 cup stoneless olives, halved
- corn niblets (heck, a small can of them)
- 1/8 teaspoon cinnamon
- 1/8 teaspoon cloves
- salt, if you are a salt person
- ground pepper
- 1/4 cup slivered almonds

Use a big skillet and heat the olive oil, and then brown the meat. Add the onions and garlics. When all this is brown, start adding the other stuff, except for the almonds. Simmer, uncovered as long as you want to (twenty minutes to a half hour usually does it), dabbing at it with a wooden spatula from time to time. Now sauté the almonds in a little olive oil till they are just turning brownish. Sprinkle the toasted almonds over the other stuff and let it all cook for a few more minutes without stirring. Serve with Dos Equis beer. The picadillo goes nicely in tortillas, if you like them. Use corn tortillas.

George Bowering
Governer General's award winner for poetry & fiction

Stanley Park
Vancouver B.C.
Photo Courtesy of Tourism B.C.

INTERFOR

Forestry and Logging Group

July 15, 1993 **CRAB DISHES**

1. **CRAB BALL**

2 cans crab
¼ cup mayonnaise
1 - 8 oz. Philadelphia Cream Cheese
Dash of Tabasco Sauce
2 tbsp. parsley
2 tbsp. finely chopped onion

Combine all ingredients until well blended. Shape into a ball and roll in chopped nuts. Wrap in plastic film and chill. Serve with assorted crackers.

2. **HOT CRAB DIP (Microwave)**

1 - 8 oz. package cream cheese
2 tbsp. milk
2 green onions thinly sliced
1 tbsp. chopped pimento
1 tsp. prepared horseradish
1 tsp. lemon juice
¼ tsp. salt
dash each of pepper and tabasco sauce
1 can crab

Microwave cream cheese in glass bowl 1/2 to 1 minute or until softened. Blend in milk until smooth. Stir in remaining ingredients. Microwave, uncovered, 1½ to 2½ minutes or until hot, stirring once. Serve warm with favorite crackers or raw veggies.

** Both of these recipes are much more delicious using self-caught west coast Dungeness Crab!

INTERNATIONAL FOREST PRODUCTS LIMITED

Fred Lowenberger

Fred Lowenberger, R.P.F.
Vice President,
Forestry and Land Use

International Forest Products Limited
P.O. Box 49114, 1055 Dunsmuir Street, Vancouver, B.C., Canada V7X 1H7 (604) 681-3221 Fax (604) 681-2924

The English Bay Café, Vancouver
with
Chef Heinz Ludwig

1. Scallops "Christian" for 6 persons

1 lb. sliced scallops
½ C. fine chop green pepper
½ C fine chop green pimento
½ C fine chop onions
1 oz. vegetable oil
3 oz. ketchup
dash of white pepper, salt
Tabasco, Worcestershire sauce
lemon juice

Defrost scallops, in running cold water. Drain. Slice scallops. Mix in all ingredients and chill. Serve in a cocktail glass.

Beach Avenue Restaurants Ltd. 1795 Beach Ave., Vancouver, B.C. V6G 1Y9 Tel. 669-2225 Fax 669-7375

THAI HOUSE

Downtown	- 1116 Robson Street,	Vancouver, B.C. V6E 1B2	Tel: 683-3383
Kitsilano	- 1766 West 7th Avenue,	Vancouver, B.C. V6J 4Z9	Tel: 737-0088
Richmond	- #129-4940 No. 3 Road,	Richmond, B.C. V6X 3A5	Tel: 278-7373
Metrotown	- #115-4600 Kingsway,	Burnaby, B.C. V5H 4L9	Tel: 438-2288

Easy Thai Garlic Prawns

Yield: 4 servings

500 g	fresh jumbo prawns
1	medium-sized leek or 50 g spinach/zucchini
4 tbsp	oil
1 tbsp	garlic, finely chopped
1 tsp	white pepper
1 tsp	sugar
1 tbsp	fish sauce

1) Peel and de-vein prawns; leave tails intact. Flatten slightly with back of a spoon into butterfly shape.

2) Boil vegetable. Place neatly to form a bed on serving plate.

3) Lightly stir-fry prawns in oil. Add garlic, pepper, sugar and fish sauce.

4) Place on to bed of vegetables and serve. Enjoy!

Meridian Inter. Trading Co. Ltd.
Thai House Restaurant
Sakura Karaoke Lounge
Houseco Homewares Canada Inc. (Toronto)
Manly Garment Company (Bangkok)

Patrick Chen

ANDRES
WINES (B.C.) LTD.

2120 VINTNER STREET, PORT MOODY, B.C. V3H 1W8
TELEPHONE (604) 937-3411 FAX (604) 937-5487

SHRIMP OR CRAB APPETIZER

1 lb. soft cream cheese (whipped Silverwoods)

1/2 red onion, chopped

1 tbsp. worcestershire sauce

1 dash tobasco

1 tbsp. lemon juice

Mix above, put in dish, add 1/2 bottle chili sauce on top, 1/2 lb. crab or shrimp. Sprinkle with parsley. Arrange crackers around the dip.

Bruce McDonald
Vice President and
General Manager

peter rolston

SHRIMP IN MELON RINGS

Ingredient	Metric	Method
1 honeydew melon		Peel and cut into 6 rings.
1/2 lb fresh, small shrimp	250 g	Clean and boil 3 minutes in lightly salted water. Cool and drain.
1/2 cup mayonnaise	125 ml	Combine and fold in shrimp. Chill for at least 6 hours. On individual plates spoon shrimp mixture into centre of melon rings.
1 tsp grated onion	5 ml	
1 Tbsp lemon juice	15 ml	
3/4 cup celery (finely chopped)	175 ml	
1/2 tsp salt	2 ml	
1/4 cup sour cream	50 ml	
1 tsp curry powder	5 ml	

P.S.

GEORGE SAYS, "TO ELIMINATE THE SMELL OF BOILING-SHRIMP, ADD A FEW FRESH CELERY LEAVES, TO THE BOILING WATER."

All the Best

Peter

2245 King Albert Avenue, Coquitlam, British Columbia, V3J 1Z8 • Phone (604) Bus: 936-5516/Res: 936-8118

ANGUS REID
Chairman and
Chief Executive Officer

#1100 - 1199 West Hastings Street
Vancouver, British Columbia V6E 3T5
Phone: (604) 893-1660 Fax: (604) 683-4888

Angus Reid's Rock and Roll Shrimp Appetizer

3 lbs large shrimp shelled and deveined
2 tsp butter
1 lemon

Spice mix:
1/2 tsp lemon pepper
1 tsp white sugar
1 tsp brown sugar
1/2 tsp ginger
1/2 tsp garlic
1/2 tsp onion salt
1/4 tsp cinammon

Saute shrimp in butter on medium high heat for one minute. Squeeze in juice of one lemon. Turn down heat and cover for 3 minutes. Add spice mix and serve on lettuce with cocktail toothpicks.

A SENSATIONAL APPETIZER FOR A PARTY
THIS IS A RICH HORS D'OEUVRE AND WILL SERVE
25 GUESTS WITH HEARTY APPETITES

BAKED CAMEMBERT TOPPED WITH JULIENNE PEPPERS & SUNDRIED TOMATOES

INGREDIENTS
- 1 KG WHEEL OF CAMEMBERT OR BRIE
- 2 TABLESPOONS OF OLIVE OIL
- 2 LARGE CORED RED PEPPERS CUT INTO THIN STRIPS
- 2 LARGE CORED YELLOW PEPPERS CUT INTO THIN STRIPS
- 1 CUP OF CHOPPED FRESH BASIL
- 1/2 CUP SUNDRIED TOMATOES - POACH FOR 1 MINUTE IN WATER TO MOISTEN
- 4 LARGE CLOVES GARLIC MINCED
- 1 TABLESPOON OF BALSAMIC VINEGAR

METHOD
- PEEL OFF THE TOP CRUST ON THE WHEEL OF CHEESE WITH A SHARP PARING KNIFE
- SET WHEEL INTO A CERAMIC OVEN PROOF DISH SLIGHTLY LARGER THAN THE WHEEL OF CHEESE
- QUICKLY SAUTE THE PEPPERS, GARLIC AND POACHED SUNDRIED TOMATOES IN OLIVE OIL UNTIL PEPPERS ARE TENDER
- REMOVE FROM HEAT AND STIR IN CHOPPED FRESH BASIL
- TOSS WITH THE BALSAMIC VINEGAR
- SEASON WITH SALT AND PEPPER TO TASTE
- PILE MIXTURE ON TOP OF CHEESE
- IF YOU WISH TO PREPARE THIS RECIPE AHEAD OF TIME, IT CAN BE ASSEMBLED TO THIS POINT AND REFRIGERATED UNTIL THE FOLLOWING DAY.
- AN HOUR BEFORE SERVING PREHEAT OVEN TO 350 DEGREES
- PLACE ASSEMBLED CHEESE IN THE OVEN FOR 30 TO 45 MINUTES, OR UNTIL CHEESE STARTS TO RUN
- REMOVE FROM THE OVEN AND SERVE IMMEDIATELY SURROUNDED BY FRENCH BREAD AND CRACKERS

RECIPE CREATED BY DEBRA LYKKEMARK
CHEF / OWNER OF CULINARY CAPERS CATERING

4075 Main Street, Vancouver, B.C. V5V 3P5

Canadian Enterprise Institute INC.

Best wishes on your entrepreneurial project – an excellent idea!

ARTICHOKE APPETIZER

1 cup mozarella cheese, grated
½ cup parmesan cheese
½ medium onion, chopped
1 clove garlic, minced
1 can (14 oz.) Artichoke Hearts, drained

Combine first four ingredients in a small bowl and mix together well. Quarter the artichokes and place evenly in a quiche pan. Cover with the cheese and onion mixture. Bake in oven at 350 for 30 minutes or until brown and bubbly. Serve on deli bread or crackers and ENJOY!

Variation: Add a small tin of flaked crabmeat or shrimp (drained) to the artichokes before adding the cheese mixture.

Submitted by Douglas Gray

Douglas A. Gray, B.A., LL.B.
President

Regards,
Doug Gray

☒ **Vancouver**
Suite 300 - 3665 Kingsway
Vancouver, B.C. V5R 5W2
Telephone: (604) 436-3337
Fax: (604) 436-9155

☐ **Calgary**
Suite 120, 100 - 1039 - 17th Avenue S.W.
Calgary, Alberta, T2T 0B2
Telephone: (403) 259-8026
Fax: (403) 244-2431

☐ **Toronto**
Suite 234 - 615 Mount Pleasant Road
Toronto, Ontario, M4S 3C5
Telephone: (416) 969-0630
Fax: (416) 322-5890

Memo
from Bill McCourt

Executive Office
Room 537
Tel: 661.6003
Fax: 661.6647

I am enclosing a couple of Mocktail recipes. I appreciate your following up and would be delighted to be included in the cookbook that is soon to be published.

These are recipes that I enjoy from the ICBC Drinking Driving CounterAttack brochure "Cool Ones for the road".

Bill

ROAD•WISE SURPRISE

serves 50

INGREDIENTS

Cranberry juice	**1.14 litre**
Unsweetened orange juice	**1 litre**
Almond extract	**15 to 30 ml (2 to 4 T)**
For tart drink: club soda	**2 litres**
For sweeter drink: ginger ale	**2 litres**

BAR EQUIPMENT • SUPPLIES

For mixing: one 8-litre (two-gal) container.
For refrigerating: a covered container or containers able to hold 8 litres (2 gal).
Punch bowl and cups, or highball glasses.

MIXING

Chill all ingredients for at least 3 days. Combine the juices in your mixing container and add almond extract to taste. Refrigerate at least three hours until needed.

Then try out the effects of different mixers. If a sample of the juice is too tart for your taste, double it by adding a 50-50 combination of ginger ale and club soda (e.g., 200 ml juices, 100 ml ginger ale, 100 ml club soda). You can achieve more sweetness still by doubling with straight ginger ale.

Before serving, pour the ingredients back into the mixing container and add mixer to double the quantity. Use either 2 litres club soda, 2 litres ginger ale, or 2 litres of a combination.

CRASH•FREE COOLER

serves 30 to 32

INGREDIENTS

For one day ahead

Sugar	**375 ml (1 ½ c)**
Water	**375 ml (1 ½ c)**
Ginger ale or 7-Up (optional)	**1 to 2 litres**

For day of serving

Chilled grapefruit juice	**1 litre (1 qt)**
Chilled pineapple juice	**1.4 litre (1.5 qt)**
Chilled orange juice	**1 litre (1 qt)**
Lemon juice	**200 ml (¾ c)**

BAR EQUIPMENT • SUPPLIES

Garnish
Ring mold or ice cubes
Punch bowl and cups

MIXING

A day before you mix the ingredients, boil the sugar in the water for 5 minutes and refrigerate the syrup. If you prefer a decorative ring to ice cubes, then freeze water, ginger ale or 7-Up in a ring mold.

On serving day, place the ice ring or cubes in a punch bowl. Add the syrup and the chilled juices, stir and garnish.

Cardamom Coffee

Meguido Zola

I grew up in Zanzibar—fabled spice island set in tranquil coral waters of the Indian Ocean.

Among the exotic foods and drinks of Zanzibar that linger with me still—African stews, Indian curries, Arab sweetmeats—were the aromatic coffees, variously spiced with clove, cinnamon, ginger, nutmeg, saffron and, even, fennel seed and fig.

Most fragrant was the cardamom coffee plied upon us by the Arab coffee sellers, carrying their conical brass pots on charcoal pans, as they wove in and out the crowds, clinking their porcelain cups. The recipe is simple:

- *Using the method you prefer, brew a strong, full-bodied coffee.*
- *Pour the coffee into a carafe, with ground cardamom powder at the bottom—roughly half a teaspoon for a 6-cup or 24 ounce pot.*

Or throw in the plump, green pods as the coffee brews.

Or do as the Sultan did: drink your coffee, black and without sugar, through a few cardamom pods held between your teeth!

Cardamom will lend your coffee a mellow aroma and a heady, camphorous flavour. . . and, as a nightcap, sweet, mysterious dreams—just as I try to recapture in the illustration below, from my children's book, BY HOOK OR BY CROOK: MY AUTOGRAPH BOOK.

Soups Salads

UMBERTO MANAGEMENT LIMITED 1380 HORNBY STREET, VANCOUVER, BRITISH COLUMBIA, V6Z 1W5 TEL.: (604) 669-3732 FAX: (604) 669-9723

CONSOMME DI POLLO
chicken consomme

Makes 8 cups/2 L

1 chicken carcass	Wash chicken bones under cold water. Chop carcass into large pieces and put in a pot.
1 small white onion, chopped 1 small carrot, chopped 1 stalk celery, chopped	Add vegetables to pot.
3 qts/3 L cold water	Add water to pot and bring to a boil. Skim froth from top.
1 bay leaf 1/8 tsp/pinch of fresh thyme, finely chopped	Season with bay leaf and thyme.
	Reduce heat and simmer on low heat for 2-3 hours. Strain through a sieve lined with a linen cloth.
salt white pepper	Season with salt and pepper to taste.

Chicken consomme can be stored in your refrigerator for up to 1 week.

CONSOMME DI MANZO
Beef Consomme

Makes 8 cups/2 L

1 beef knuckle bone, with a little meat on the bone, or equivalent weight of soup bones, with the meat on	Chop knuckle bone or soup bones into large pieces and put in a pot.
1 large white onion, finely 1 small carrot, ground 1 stalk celery, ground 1 small leek, washed and cleaned, then ground	Add vegetables to pot.
3 qts/3 l cold water	Add water to pot and bring to a boil. Skim froth from top.
1 bay leaf 1/8 tsp/pinch of fresh sage 1/8 tsp/pinh of fresh thymne	Season with bay leaf, sage and thyme.
	Reduce heat and simmer on low heat on low heat for 2-3 hours. Strain through a sieve lined with a linen cloth.
salt white pepper	Season with salt and pepper to taste.

Beef consomme can be stored in your refirgerator for up to 1 week.

HOLLINGER
INC.

2ND FLOOR, 1827 WEST 5TH AVENUE
VANCOUVER, B.C. V6J 1P5
(604) 732-4443
Fax: (604) 732-3961

FROM THE KITCHEN OF DAVID RADLER:

"A TASTE OF PARIS"

French Onion Soup

4 tablespoons butter
2 tablespoons olive oil
2 tablespoons brown sugar
6 medium to large onions, sliced, not chopped
2 tablespoons flour
3 cans beef consomme or broth
3 cans water
1/2 teaspoon dry mustard
Salt and pepper to taste
French bread
8 slices Gruyere cheese

Melt butter with olive oil in heavy kettle. Add sugar; stir until it dissolves; add sliced onions. Let rings separate and cook until onions are lightly browned and somewhat broken in half. Add flour and cook gently for several minutes until mixture begins to thicken and flour taste disappears.

Add beef consomme and water gradually, a cup at a time, stirring well after each addition. Add seasonings, cover and simmer slowly for 1 1/2 hours.

Make your soup early in the day and let it sit in the pot until ready to serve. This "resting" period in a cool place, not on the stove, develops flavour and gives the different ingredients a chance to blend thoroughly.

When ready to serve reheat soup and pour into individual bowls. Cover with a slice of French bread and Gruyere cheese. Place under broiler until cheese bubbles and browns.

The Uniglobe Building
900 1199 West Pender Street
Vancouver, BC
Canada V6E 2R1
(604) 662-3800
Fax (604) 662-3878

UNIGLOBE
Travel (International) Inc.

July 7, 1993

ONION SOUP

Take raw beef bones with some meat on them, roast them with carrot and onion pieces for about 30 minutes in a hot (450°) oven, turning the bones a few times while roasting.

Once roasted, place bones and vegetables in a large saucepan and throw away the fat. Deglaze the roasting pan with water. Add the glaze to the saucepan, cover the bones with water and simmer for 5 hours ----- this should be done the day before you make the soup.

The next day, take off any fat and put the broth through a sieve and set aside.

In a large saucepan add 3 tbs butter, 1½ tbs olive oil, 3 lbs of onions, ½ tsp salt, ¾ tsp sugar and brown the onions for 40 - 60 minutes over medium heat.

Once the onions are browned to a nice dark colour, spinkle with 2½ tbs of flour. Stir until flour is coked (about 3 minutes); take away from the heat; let this cool for a minute then add 2½ cups of hot beef broth (from the bones you roasted previously) - whisk while adding stock. Return to heat, add rest of the beef broth and 8oz of vermouth and let this cook very slowly for 2 hours.

Season to taste and before serving add 3 tbs of cognac and grated parmesan cheese.

Enjoy.

Yours truly,

UNIGLOBE TRAVEL (INTERNATIONAL) INC.

U. Gary Charlwood
Chairman of the Board and
Chief Executive Officer

GASTOWN - 53 WATER STREET

Gary Gibbons Kitchen Manager

SPIKY CHEESE SOUP

INGREDIENTS:

4 tablespoons oil

4 carrots

2 onions

4 stalks celery

1 or 2 green peppers,chopped

½ cup whole wheat flour

4 cups tamari bouillon or vegetable stock seasoned with 2 tablespoons tamari soy sauce

4 cups milk

3/4 lb cheddar and/or swiss cheese, cubed

sea salt and pepper to taste

DIRECTIONS:

HEAT A 4 QUART SAUCEPAN OR DUTCH OVEN. ADD THE OIL AND CARROTS. SAUTE FIVE MINUTES. ADD REMAINING VEGETABLES. SAUTE FIVE MINUTES LONGER. ADD THE FLOUR. HEAT GENTLY 3 TO 5 MINUTES STIRRING CONSTANTLY. SLOWLY ADD BROTH. COOK UNTIL THICK, STIRRING OFTEN. ADD MILK AND CHEESE. REDUCE HEAT, TO LOW. HEAT UNTIL CHEESE IS PARTIALLY MELTED. SEASON WITH SALT AND PEPPER TO TASTE. SOUP IS BEST WHEN SOME OF CHEESE IS STILL IN SOFT CUBES.

GARY GIBBONS

Province of British Columbia

Ministry of
Finance and
Corporate Relations

Parliament Buildings
Victoria
British Columbia
V8V 1X4

GARLIC SOUP

Ingredients:

Garlic cloves	40
Olive oil	10 - 12 Tablespoons
Pepper	
Chicken stock	6 Cups
White wine	a splash
Fresh thyme	

In a warm pot, add oil and peeled whole garlic cloves. Simmer but do not brown. Add a bit of wine and chicken stock. Cook for a few minutes. When ready to serve add pepper and thyme and a couple of drops of wine. Croutons and/or parmiaggino may also be added just before serving.

This is a delicious healthy soup that is quick, simple and inexpensive.

Jim Green
Community Development Coordinator

BEDWELL HARBOUR
Island Resort & Properties

ROAST CARROT AND DUNGENESS CRAB BISQUE

3 oz.	Unsalted butter
5 oz.	Onions, diced 1"
16 oz.	Peeled Carrots, diced 1"
1 oz.	Sugar
1 oz.	Flour
40 oz.	Dungeness Crab Stock
	Sea Salt, White Pepper
7 oz.	Creme Fraiche or Whipping Cream
5 oz.	Dungeness Crab Meat
	Freshly chopped chives

1. Preheat oven to 475 deg. F.
2. Melt half the butter in an oven safe pan over medium high heat.
3. Add the onions and carrots and saute; increasing heat to high. Stir occasionally until vegetables start to colour lightly. Sprinkle with the sugar and place in oven.
4. Roast for 20 minutes stirring once or twice as vegetables start to caramelize. Remove from oven.
5. Melt remaining butter in a medium size soup pot. Add roasted vegetables and flour. Stir well.
6. Slowly add crab stock while stirring to dissolve flour.
7. Simmer for 10 minutes.
8. Blend in a food processor until smooth.
9. Reheat with whipping cream, season to taste.
10. Garnish soup with crab meat and fresh chives.

ENJOY !

Geoffrey S. Couper
Chef de Cuisine
Bedwell Harbour Island Resort

9801 SPALDING ROAD, SOUTH PENDER ISLAND, B.C., CANADA V0N 2M0 TEL: (604) 629-3212 FAX: (604) 629-6777 1-800-663-2899

cooking carrot soup

with slow carrots thees ar
veree slow carrots

so i put them into th blendr
to speed them up i almost

brek th blendr so th slow
carrots go back into th pot

i keep having to replace th
watr its all boiling away

n th carrots arint dun yet
ther may b a leek in th pot

or thees ar th slowest carrots

th salmon thats going with
them was dun long time ago

ifs th carrots nevr get dun
ium going to eet th fish

its bin redee for hours

if yu get slow carrots
by mistake coz yr too

baked or groggd whn yu
get to th store ts ask

for fast wuns it can b
a long nite cooking

carrot soup

my favorit receipe

bill bissett

Bill Bissett
Prolific poet, artist & author of more than 50 books

David C. Bentall

June 29, 1993

Ms. Abby Anderson, C.A.E.
General Manager
Burnaby Chamber of Commerce
Suite 149 - 9855 Austin Avenue
Professional Wing
Lougheed Mall
Burnaby, B.C.
V3J 1N4

Dear Ms. Anderson:

Thank you for your letter of May 31, 1993 inviting me to submit one or two of my favourite recipes for inclusion in the ***All-Celebrity Cookbook.***

My wife, Alison, and I are enclosing two of our favourite recipes. If we can put smiles on our four children's faces, then we know we are guaranteed to please a crowd!

We would like to take this opportunity to wish you great success with the Cookbook!

Yours sincerely,

David + Alison Bentall

David and Alison Bentall

time 30 min
serves 8

Cream of Carrot soup

1 lb. young carrots
5. c. chicken stock
2 cloves garlic crushed
2/3 c. cream
Salt + pepper to taste
chopped parsley (garnish)

Wash + slice carrots 1/2" thick. Place in lg. saucepan with chicken stock + bring to boil. Reduce heat and simmer 20 min. Cool slightly Add crushed garlic and puree soup in blender. Reheat. Stir a cup of warm soup into cream and combine with remaining soup. Avoid boiling. Add salt + pepper to taste. Sprinkle with parsley for garnish.

DAVID AND ALISON BENTALL

TRADER VIC'S BONGO BONGO SOUP

2½ cups half and half (half milk, half cream)
10 ounces fresh oysters, poached (or 10 ounces drained canned oysters), whirled in a blender to puree
¼ cup strained creamed baby food spinach
2 tablespoons butter
1 small clove garlic minced or mashed
About 1½ teaspoons H.P. sauce
About ½ teaspoon salt
About 3/8 teaspoon freshly ground black pepper
Generous dash of cayenne
2 teaspoons cornstarch mixed with
2 teaspoons cold water
About 2/3 cup heavy cream, whipped

In a large sauce pan, heat half and half just to simmering. Add oyster puree, spinach, butter, garlic, monosodium glutamate, H.P. sauce, salt, pepper and cayenne. Heat to simmering, whisking until smooth; do not boil. Add cornstarch mixture, and heat and whisk until soup is slightly thickened. Correct seasoning. Ladle into heatproof serving bowls. Top each with a spoonful of whipped cream. Slip under broiler until cream is well glazed with brown.

Makes about 4 servings.

Raymond Chan

1601 W. GEORGIA STREET ▲ VANCOUVER, BRITISH COLUMBIA, CANADA V6G 2V4 ▲ (604) 682-3377 ▲ FAX (604) 687-3102

MUSSEL SOUP

Ingredients

1-1/2 lb.	fresh mussels
4 oz.	garlic, peeled and sliced
10 oz.	onions, peeled and sliced
20 oz.	whipping cream
50 oz.	clam juice, canned
50 oz.	white bread, crust removed
3 oz.	whipped cream
2 oz.	butter
1/2 bunch	parsley, chopped
To taste	salt and pepper

Method

1) Steam open the mussels in 10 oz. of the clam juice. Strain out the juice, cool mussels and reserve. Combine mussels with remaining clam juice, then set aside. Remove mussels from shell.

2) Sweat garlic and onions with butter in a Dutch oven over very low heat for approximately 30 minutes, stirring frequently. Do not colour. Add clam juice and bread. Bring to a boil. Add cream, and bring to a boil again. Taste and adjust seasoning.

3) In a blender, blend all the soup in small batches. Strain the soup through a fine mesh sieve.

4) Combine chopped parsley, 1/3 of the mussels (chopped) and whipped cream. Top soup with cream.

Sincerely,

Serves 6-8

Louis Gervais
Executive Chef

LG/fl

845 BURRARD STREET, VANCOUVER, B.C.
V6Z 2K6 CANADA — TEL.: (604) 682-5511
TELEX: 04-54230 — FAX: (604) 682-5513

TRAVEL COMPANION
OF AIR FRANCE

I've borrowed these recipes from a character in one of my books: Wanda Kettleman's mother, in Fall From Grace.

PORTUGUESE FISH SOUP

3 leeks
1/4 cup olive oil
2 garlic cloves, crushed
28 oz. can plum tomatoes, including juice
2 bay leaves
1 tsp each of leaf thyme and dried basil
1 tsp granulated sugar
10 oz. can chicken broth
1 cup water
2 medium potatoes, peeled and cut into 1 inch cubes
1 lb cod or halibut
1/4 tsp freshly ground black pepper
1 cup croutons
1/4 cup finely chopped black olives (optional)

1. Trim off roots and discard tough outer leaves from leeks. Slice off and discard dark green tops, leaving no more than 2 inches of light green portion. Slice leeks in half lengthwise. Gently spread out leaves and hold, root end up, under cold running water to remove grit. Slice into half-inch pieces.

2. Heat oil in a large saucepan over medium heat. Add leeks and garlic and saute until soft, about 5 minutes, stirring often. Add tomatoes and their juice, breaking up tomatoes with a fork. Add bay leaves, thyme, basil, sugar, chicken broth, water and potatoes. Bring mixture to a boil. Cover, reduce heat to medium-low and boil gently for about 10 to 15 minutes, or until potatoes are slightly tender. Stir often.

3. Meanwhile, cut fish into bite-size pieces. Stir into tomato mixture. Cover, reduce heat and simmer just until fish flakes easily with a fork, about 5 minutes. Stir in pepper. Taste and add more, if you wish. Remove bay leaves. Ladle soup into warm bowls, then top with croutons and black olives. Serve with pitas or a warm flat bread.

Per serving: 146 calories, 3.9 g protein, 57 mg calcium, 1.8 mg iron.

Bunny

Bunny Wright
Canada's leading female author of mysteries

PHIL REIMER
COMMUNICATIONS

July 19, 1993

Ms. Abby Anderson
Burnaby Chamber of Commerce
Suite #149 - 9855 Austin Ave.
Professional Wing
Lougheed Mall
Burnaby, B.C.
V3J 1N4

Dear Ms. Anderson:

I am delighted to contribute. I hope everything works well for you.

CHICKEN AND LEMON SOUP
An Albanian recipe.

Ingredients

- Chicken Stock
- Chevril
- Chives
- Eggs
- Brandy
- Minced Parsley
- Tarragon
- Heavy Cream
- Lemon Juice
- Cooked Rice or Vermicelli

To 7 cup rich Chicken soup, add 1 teaspoon minced parsley, 1/2 teaspoon each Chevril, Tarragon, and Chives.

Bring to a fast boil.

Lower heat and simmer 15 minutes.

In a bowl combine 1 cup heavy cream, 2 eggs, 1/4 cup lemon juice, and 1 tablespoon brandy.

Beating constantly, slowly blend in 1 cup hot soup. Add to soup pot - stirring constantly.

Reheat to just below boiling point. Serve. (Do not let soup boil after eggs have been added).

Optional: 1 or 2 tablespoons cooked rice or vermicelli per soup plate.

Yours sincerely,

Phil Reimer

P.O. BOX 2141 VANCOUVER, BRITISH COLUMBIA V6B 3T8
TELEPHONE: (604) 662-6953 FAX: (604) 662-6954

John Blatherwick, C.D., M.D., F.R.C.P.(C)
59 COURTNEY CRESCENT, NEW WESTMINSTER, B.C. V3L 4M1 • TELEPHONE (604) 526-0654

Turkey Bone Soup

In a 5 quart pot, place the bones from a turkey (from which the dressing has been rinsed) and cover the bones with water. Simmer for 3 hours and strain the broth. Pick the meat from the bones and add to the broth. Skim any fat off the top of the broth.

add:
- 1 cup celery
- 6 Sliced Carrots
- 1 cup Barley
- 2 Tbsp Salt
- 1½ cups Frozen Corn

Simmer until the barley is tender (about 1 hour)

Note: This soup is very thick, more like a stew. It will serve 10 or more servings. A great way to enjoy left over turkey.

John Blatherwick

HEAD OFFICE
4567 Canada Way
Burnaby, B.C.
V5G 4T1
Travel Services Tel: (604) 268-5000
Tours & Accommodation Tel: (604) 268-5022
Fax: (604) 268-5561

BCAA
Travel
Agency
CAA

Pumpkin Soup

1 can pumpkin (398 ml)
2 T olive oil
1 large onion, finely chopped
celery stock, finely chopped
small carrot, finely chopped
2 oz. prosciutto
4 T brandy
6 c chicken stock
6 T cream
1 egg yolk
salt and pepper
2 oz parmesan cheese
2 oz asiago cheese
2 oz old white cheddar

Heat oil, add onion, celery, carrot and meat. Saute until onion and celery are translucent and meat is crisp. Stir in brandy then cool for two minutes. Add chicken stock and pumpkin then bring to a boil. Reduce heat and simmer 35 minutes. Remove from heat. Mix together cream and egg yolk. Stir ladle of soup into cream and egg mixture. Slowly add to soup stirring constantly. Add salt and pepper. Grate cheeses together, mix and sprinkle on top, then serve.

Yours sincerely,

Dennis Cote
Director of Travel Services

A DIVISION OF B.C.A.A. HOLDINGS LTD.

HAZELBURGER SOUP
(so delicious!)

Ingredients:

1-1/2 lbs. lean ground beef
1 medium onion, chopped fine
1 - 28 oz. can tomatoes
2 cups water
3 cans consomme
1 can tomato soup
4 carrots, chopped fine
1 bay leaf
3 sticks celery, chopped fine
1 tbsp. parsley
1/2 tsp. thyme
pepper to taste
8 tbsp. pearl barley

Procedure:

Brown meat and onions. Drain well. Combine all ingredients in large pot. Simmer, covered, at least 2 hours or all day. Serves 10 people. Can also be frozen for quick meals at later date, eg. when I get home from a road trip.

Jack & Bob Hazeldine

With Compliments
Wilson Parasiuk
CHAIRMAN OF THE BOARD

PARTNERS IN EXPORT

BRITISH COLUMBIA TRADE DEVELOPMENT CORPORATION

Gazpacho

Ingredients:

7-8 medium sized tomatoes
2 medium sized field cucumbers
½ onion
2-3 cloves of garlic
1 green bell pepper
1½ cups cold water
3 Tablespoons olive oil
4-5 Tablespoons wine vinegar
3 Teaspoons salt
2 teaspoons paprika
2 Teaspoons cumin
2 teaspoons black pepper.
1½ slices of dried French bread

Quarter the tomatoes; seed the cucumbers; seed the bell pepper; dice the onion; press the garlic; cube the bread.

Blend all the ingredients but the bread in a food processor. Blend until smooth. Add bread to the mixture. Process.

The result is a cold, delicious, vegetable soup that can be served immediately. It improves after keeping it in the refrigerator for a few hours to allow the flavors to season.

A CROWN CORPORATION OF THE PROVINCE OF BRITISH COLUMBIA
Suite 730, 999 Canada Place, Vancouver, British Columbia, Canada, V6C 3E1 Telephone (604) 844-1900 Fax (604) 660-2457

SOUPS

Alan Askew
Film Producer

West African Peanut Soup

If you're a person who loves peanuts, but thinks they were made to eat at baseball games or on bread with jelly, think again and get ready for a culinary adventure.

This peanut soup is rich and spicy. The chopped scallions or chives are an integral element, not just a garnish.

SERVES 6 TO 8

2 cups chopped onions
1 tablespoon peanut or vegetable oil
½ teaspoon cayenne or other ground dried chiles (or to taste)
1 teaspoon grated peeled fresh ginger root
1 cup chopped carrots
2 cups chopped sweet potatoes (up to 1 cup white potatoes can be substituted)
4 cups vegetable stock (see page 685) or water

---

2 cups tomato juice
1 cup smooth peanut butter
1 tablespoon sugar (optional)
1 cup chopped scallions or chives

AFRICA SOUTH OF THE SAHARA

KABAN ENTERPRISES LTD.
1657 Nanaimo Street, Vancouver, British Columbia, Canada V5L 4Y9
Tel: (604) 251-2121 Fax: (604) 251-2323

GOOD LUCK TO THE BURNABY CHAMBER OF COMMERCE FOR YOUR EFFORTS TO ENHANCE TOURISM IN B.C.

MEATLESS RUSSIAN/UKRAINIAN BORSCHT

1) Pour two quarts of water in pot. Amount of water used in the making of this soup is to one's own preference.

2) Chop approximately 6 medium sized beets--boil until half done.

3) Add one large onion (diced).

4) Add 5 cups of chopped cabbage, boil till cabbage turns soft.

5) 1/2 cup of dill or to suit one's taste.

6) Add 3 medium chopped potatoes and one cup of peas.

7) 2 Tablespoons of vinegar to season with salt and pepper.

8) 2 Tablespoons of sugar (sugar will remove bitterness and enhance taste in any soup).

Remove 1/2 cup of hot soup and mix with 1/2 cup of sweet cream. Then pour back into the simmering soup. NOTE: Do not pour sweet cream into soup--it will curdle. Simmer for aproximately 15 minutes.

For a meat base, just boil beef or pork ribs or chicken, then add the above ingredients.

Enjoy!!!

AND REMEMBER OZZIE LOVES YOU!!!

OZZIE KABAN

KABAN ELECTRONICS LTD.
KABAN INTERNATIONAL INVESTIGATIONS INC.

Administration Office:
13379B 72nd Avenue, Surrey, B.C. V3W 2N5
Phone: **(604) 572-3883** · Fax: (604) 572-3993

CAESAR SALAD

(Serves four)

INGREDIENTS:

1 Head Romaine Lettuce
½ Tbsp. minced garlic
4 Anchovy fillets
2 Dashes Worcestershire sauce
½ Tbsp mustard
1 Dash tabasco
2 Egg yolks
½ Lemon (approximately 1 tbsp. juice)
1 Tbsp. red wine vinegar
4 oz. croutons
Cracked black pepper to taste

PREPARATION:

STEPS

1: In a mixing bowl, add anchovy fillet, minced garlic and Red wine vinegar. Blend to a point of paste.
2: Add Worcestershire sauce, mustard, cracked pepper, tabasco and egg yolks. Mix well.
3: Add lemon juice and while mixing in a fast motion, slowly pour in olive oil.
4: In another bowl, cut romaine and remove core. Clean and dry lettuce then place into bowl with dressing.
5: Sprinkle with paremsan and add croutons.
6: Toss and serve.

Sincerely,
RODAN JEWELLERS
SIMPLY CHARMING JEWELLERY STORES

Rob Davidson
President

Takakkaw Falls
Yoho National Park
Photo Courtesy of Tourism B.C.

#2400 - 555 West Hastings Street
P.O. Box 12089
Vancouver, B.C., CANADA V6B 4N5

Telephone: (604) 688-5044
Fax: (604) 681-8906
Telex: 495 9663

Good morning. Considering how much I like to cook and eat, its hard to belive that responding to your request can take this long! Finally, after great deliberation, here are two recipes which are easy, fun, so tasty and healthy (low fat.)

1. Viennese Potato Salad This recipe stems from my grandmother, an Austrian, and was transported to Canada by my mother who still makes it and has passed it along to me. Designating exact measures has been a challenge because we are so accustomed to doing this salad by instinct.

6 large potatoes
1 medium onion finely grated
¼ to ½ cup olive oil
¼ cup water
1/8 cup white vinegar
½ tsp sugar
½ tsp salt
freshly ground pepper
chopped chives

optional garnish: 3 boiled eggs
1 tomato in wedges

Boil potatoes in jackets, in a covered saucepan. Peel and slice while still hot (important.) Add finely grated onion and olive oil to potatoes. Heat to boiling point the vinegar, water, salt and sugar and pour over potatoes. Mix with large spoons (rather than forks) carefully to avoid potatoes either becoming mushy or breaking apart. Add pepper. If you feel that the salad is not quite moist enough then add more of the boiled dressing. Decorate with chives, sliced eggs and tomato wedges. Then watch the salad disappear!

Regards.

Lis Welch

*"The **only** name when service matters"*

The Salvation Army
Addictions and Rehabilitation Department
Wayburne Industrial / Thrift Stores

3451 Wayburne Drive
Burnaby, B.C. V5G 3L1

Telephone: (604) 298-8705
Fax: (604) 298-3509

"Have you read The War Cry?"

GERALD'S SALAD

35 oz Cool Whip
500 gm Cottage Cheese
2 packages Instant Tapioca Pudding (Jello - 3 1/4 oz box)

Mix Above Really Well.

Add:

Drained Pineapple Chunks
Drained Fruit Cocktail
Drained Mandarin Orange Segments

Refrigerate 1 Hour.

ENJOY!

Envoy Gerald Haggett
Executive Director
Industrial Centre & Thrift Stores

1455 Quebec Street
Vancouver, B.C.
Canada V6A 3Z7

TEL 604 . 687 . 8414
FAX 604 . 682 . 2923

Dear Ms. Anderson:

On behalf of Michael Francis, President, Science World, I would like to take this opportunity to thank you for considering his culinary skills are exemplary enough to be included in your cookbook.

After many hours of searching through his recipe files, he is very happy to submit the attached recipe for "Asian Noodle Pasta Salad". Apparently, it brings a smile to his face each time he thinks of it.

Thank you for the honour of being included with such a distinguished group of chefs.

Enjoy!

ASIAN NOODLE PASTA SALAD
1/2 LB DRIED FLAT RICE NOODLES
3 TBLSP OLIVE OIL
3 LG CLOVES GARLIC, MINCED
2 TBLSP FERMENTED BLACK BEAMS, CHOPPED
2 TSP MINCED GINGEROOT
2 MEDIUM SHALLOTS,MINCED
1/2 TSP RED PEPPER FLAKES
S&P
1/4 CUP BASIL
1/4 CUP CILANTRO
3 PLUM TOMATOES PEELED, SEEDED & CHOPPED
3 MEDIUM SCALLIONS SLICED THINLY
BRING 1 QT WATER TO A BOIL. ADD RICE NOODLES - REMOVE FROM HEAT & LET STAND UNTIL TENDER - ABOUT 5 MIN. DRAIN
HEAT OIL IN WOK - ADD NEXT 5 INGREDIENTS & STIR FRY UNTIL SHALLOTS ARE TENDER - ABOUT 2 MIN. ADD DRAINED NOODLES & STIR FRY TO BLEND FLAVOURS - ABOUT 2 MIN.SEASON WITH S&P
TRANSFER TO BOWL & COOL TO ROOM TEMP ADD REMAINING INGREDIENTS & TOSS TO COMBINE

BChydro

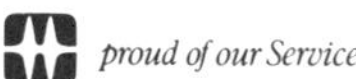

R.H. Hunt
President and
Chief Operating Officer

SHRIMP AND ALMOND SALAD

Set aside in refrigerator:

1 head lettuce (bite size pieces)
1 leaf lettuce " " "
1 bunch green onions (chopped)

Mix together and set aside:

1/2 cup oil
1/2 cup vinegar
1/2 cup sugar
Seasoning mix from Mr. Noodle's Chicken Soup

Lightly brown: 1/2 cup slivered almonds
Add: 4 tbsp sesame seeds
Break up: 1 packet Mr. Noodles Chicken Soup Mix
Mix together and set aside

Drain: 2 tins of shrimp
(or use equivalent quantity of fresh shrimp)
Set aside

Mix all together just before serving.

Yours truly,

British Columbia Hydro and Power Authority, 6911 Southpoint Drive, Burnaby, B.C. V3N 4X8

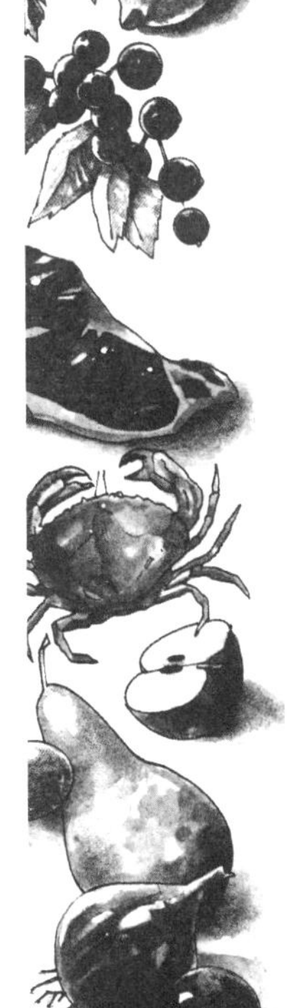

WARM SCALLOP SALAD WITH HONEY LIME VINAIGRETTE

Ingredients

2 - 3 Scallops per person
Buy wholesale, Canadian 40/60 count or Australian 40/60 count
- you will get a better price

For julienne of vegetables:
2 Red Peppers
2 Leeks
½ lb Snow Peas
3 lg Carrots
Vegetable Oil
Lettuces, assortment

Preparation

Thaw scallops and sauté in vegetable oil.
Prepare the assortment of lettuces, eg. red leaf, green leaf, romaine, endive, chicory, radicchio, watercress or anything fresh.

HONEY LIME VINAIGRETTE

¼ cup White Wine Vinegar
⅛ cup Lime Juice
1½ Tbsp Dijon Mustard
½ L Vegetable Oil
¼ cup Honey
Salt & Pepper to taste

Yield: ¾ Litre

K. Anne Milne
Executive Chef

1277 Robson Street, Vancouver, B.C., Canada V6E 1C4
Tel. (604) 688-0461 Telex 04-55150 Fax (604) 688-4374

Dawn Black, M.P.

New Westminster-Burnaby

HOUSE OF COMMONS
CHAMBRE DES COMMUNES
OTTAWA, CANADA K1A 0A6
TEL: (613) 992 9105
FAX: (613) 992 5501

800 12TH STREET
NEW WESTMINSTER, B.C.
V3M 4K1
TEL: (604) 666 7380
FAX: (604) 666 7389

4732 IMPERIAL STREET
BURNABY, B.C.
V5C 2H1
TEL: (604) 666 3094

Dear Ms. ~~Anderson~~ Abley:

In response to your request for recipes for the cookbook to be produced by the Burnaby Chamber of Commerce, I am pleased to send you two recipes.

I wish you all the best with the preparation of the cookbook and look forward to getting a copy myself!

AUNT NANCY'S SHRIMP SALAD

Ingredients

1 small package chow mein noodles
1 cup raw rice - cooked
1 small package frozen peas - cooked
1/2 cup chopped celery
1/2 cup chopped green onion
1 pound fresh shrimp

Dressing

1/2 cup oil
3 tbsp malt vinegar
1 tbsp soya sauce
1 tsp sugar
1/2 tsp MSG (optional)
1/2 tsp celery seed
2 tsp curry powder
1 tsp salt

Method

Cook rice and frozen peas. Add celery, green onions, and shrimp, then chill.

Mix dressing ingredients. Chill separately.

Just before serving, add dressing to rice and shrimp mixture, add chow mein noodles, then toss and serve.

Dawn

Dawn Black, M.P.
New Westminster-Burnaby

Saffron-Laced Orzo Salad

1/4 teaspoon	ground saffron
1/2 cup	olive oil
2	cloves garlic, finely minced or pressed
3 tablespoons	freshly squeezed lemon juice
1/4 teaspoon	ground cumin
2 teaspoons	ground turmeric
1 teaspoon	granulated sugar
	salt
	freshly ground pepper
1 pound	orzo
2/3 cup	pine nuts, lightly toasted (see note)
1/2 cup	currants, plumped in hot water for about 20 min. and drained
1/4 cup each	chopped fresh mint and parsley
3 tablespoons	chopped fresh coriander (cilantro)
	fresh mint sprigs or leaves (garnish)

Dissolve saffron in olive oil and let stand about 15 minutes. Add garlic, lemon juice, cumin, turmeric, sugar, and salt and pepper to taste. Set aside.

Cook pasta in 3 quarts of boiling water until very "al dente". Drain and rinse well in cold water, then drain again. Place in a large bowl and toss with saffron-flavored oil. Cool to room temperature, occasionally stirring the pasta to coat thoroughly.

Add pine nuts, drained currants, chopped mint, parsley, and coriander to pasta. Serve at room temperature garnished with mint sprigs.

Serves 10 to 12 as a salad or side dish.

NOTE: To toast pine nuts, place them in a small heavy frying pan over moderate heat. Stir until they begin to turn golden. Remove from heat and pour onto a plate to cool.

Tony Parsons

BCTV, A Division of Westcom TV Group Ltd.
Box 4700, Vancouver, B.C. V6B 4A3 (604) 420-2288 FAX: (604) 421-9427

Entrees: Fish Seafood

744 - 1055 Dunsmuir Street
P.O. Box 49292
Bentall Centre
Vancouver, B.C.
V7X 1P5
(604) 669-5657
Fax: (604) 669-3061

SALMON WELLINGTON

1 (397-g) package frozen puff pastry, thawed
1 5-pound (2.25 kg.) salmon, boned and skinned
Beaten egg for glazing
Stuffing:
1 pound (500 g) sole (or other white fish)
2 medium eggs
1 small onion
1 cup (250 ml) parsley sprigs
Salt & pepper
1/4 cup (50 ml) whipping cream

For stuffing, place sole, eggs, onion and parlsey in cuisinart with salt and pepper and blend until smooth. Add whipping cream and blend together. (Mixture should be of icing consistency.) Roll out pastry on lightly floured surface until large enough to enclose salmon. Place pastry on a large cookie sheet with a rim.

Place one side of the salmon towards one side of the pastry. Spread with sole filling, then put other side of the salmon on top. Brush pastry edges with beaten egg. Fold pastry over salmon to completely enclose. Pinch pastry edge to sea. Brush with egg yolk. Cut a few pastry fins out of any remaining pastry for decoration and attach with beaten egg.

Bake at 350 deg. F (180 deg. C) for 40 to 45 minutes. (If pastry browns too quickly, cover with foil.) Serve on a platter garnished with lemon slices and parsley. Cut into one-inch (2.5 cm) thick slices and serve with Hollandaise sauce. Makes 10 servings.

Barbara J. Rae

Jurock's Real Estate Investor

2nd Floor, Viva Tower, 1311 Howe Street, Vancouver, B.C., Canada V6Z 1R7
Phone: (604) 691-1718 (604) 683-1111 Fax (604) 669-3688

- Jurock Investments
- Jurock Real Estate Management Consultants
- Jurock Publishing Group

Believe it or not - as an old Maitre d'hote I can actually cook this !

SALMON WELLINGTON

2 lbs. (1 kg) salmon fillets

BECHAMEL SAUCE
1/4 cup two per cent milk
1 tsp. butter/margarine
1 tsp. flour

MIXTURE
1/2 cup two per cent milk
1/2 cup chopped onions
1/2 cup mushrooms/sliced
2 tsp. lemon juice
1 tbsp. butter/margarine
salt/pepper as desired

2 (215 gram) packages puff pastry
3 hard-cooked eggs, halved lengthwise
1 egg, beaten

Head north, catch a wild salmon and fillet it. If that's not possible, angle down to your nearest fish shop and find a (relatively) lively fish. (A fresh salmon should have clear eyes, firm flesh and a pleasant smell....justlike any good dining companion.)

Preheat oven to 400 F (200 C).

Divide salmon into two portions of 1.5 and 0.5 lbs. (750 and 250 grams). Finely chop or grind the small portion and blend into the milk. Season with salt/pepper. Thinly slice the large piece of the salmon.

Prepare a bechamel sauce: melt 1 tbsp. butter, add 1 tsp. flour and blend in the milk. Set aside.

Saute onions until soft (but not brown) in 1 tbsp. butter (or margarine). Add in the mushrooms and lemon juice. Stir in the bechamel sauce and simmer for five minutes. Season with salt and pepper to taste. Remove from heat and set aside.

Divide pastry into two portions, one slightly larger than the other. Roll out the smaller piece (12 by six inches or 30 by 15 cm for the stoutly metric) and place on a greased baking sheet.

Place half the salmon slices along the centre of the pastry. Top with half the onion/mushroom mixture. Cover with the minced salmon/milk mixture. Top with two rows of egg halves. Spread on remaining onion/mushroom mixture. Cover with remaining salmon slices.

Roll out remaining pastry 14 by eight inches (35.5 by 20 cm). Brush the edges with beaten egg and place it atop the salmon. Take a fork and punch steam holes into the pastry. Be artistic.

Bake for 25 minutes and accompany with either a mushroom creme or hollandise sauce.

Serves eight to 10 people. If you're clever (or lucky), try to invite at least a few people who claim they aren't partial to fish. Either this will convert them otherwise....or you'll get seconds.

Adapted from Canadian Living receipe.

Friendly regards,

Ozzie Jurock
JUROCK'S REAL ESTATE INVESTORc

RUSS'S SAVOURY SALMON

U. TV

2 CUPS FINELY CHOPPED SUNDRIED TOMATOES....

1 CUP CHOPPED PARSLEY...

1/2 CUP CHOPPED GARLIC

1/4 - 1/2 CUP EXTRA VIRGIN OLIVE OIL..

FRESH CRACKED PEPPER (TO TASTE)

FILLET SALMON —
MAKE BAKING TRAY OUT OF TIN FOIL. (MAKE SURE TO CRIMP SIDES INTO A RIM — SO JUICES WON'T SEEP.)
PUT SALMON SKIN DOWN ON TINFOIL AND PLACE IN B.B.Q.
MIX INGREDIENTS TOGETHER AND BASTE SALMON WITH GENEROUS PORTION.
COOK AT MEDIUM HEAT UNTIL MEAT IS FIRM. (YOU CAN TELL WHEN MEAT TURNS COLOUR & JUICES SHOW.
IT'S NOT GOING TO TAKE LONG.
PLACE WHOLE THING ON SERVING DISH & WAIT FOR COMPLIMENTS —

RUSS F.

Russ Froese

W.C. Brown
President
and Chief Executive Officer
BC Sugar

Salmon Barbeque

Ingredients: 1- cup vegetable oil
½- cup (light) soya sauce
2- tbsp rye whisky
2- tsp Rogers Demerara sugar
2- crushed cloves garlic

Mix ingredients well and marinate salmon fillets 4 to 6 hours in a shallow pan, turning every hour or two

Barbeque over medium heat, skin side first, about 6- minutes depending upon thickness of fish. Turn and cook the other side for approx. 2- minutes.

Bill Brown
June 16/93

P.O. Box 2150 Vancouver, B.C., Canada V6B 3V2 Telephone (604) 253-1131 Fax (604) 253-2517

NORTHWEST SPORTS ENTERPRISES LTD.

ARTHUR GRIFFITHS' FAVOURITE SALMON BARBECUE

You need:

Filet of Salmon (de-boned)
1 Onion
1 Lemon

Place salmon, skin side down, on a sheet of tin foil. Turn up edges of foil so that juices will cook into salmon. Thinly slice lemon and place slices on top of salmon. Thinly slice onion and layer over lemon slices. Add salt and pepper to taste.

Place salmon on barbecue (medium heat). Cook until fish turns white.

Serve Salmon with:

- Fresh corn on the cob.
- Scrubbed new potatoes boiled with a pinch of fresh mint. Serve potatoes with butter and English Salad Cream Dressing
- Joanne Griffiths' Caesar Salad (recipe below)
- Suggested dinner wine: Lindeman's Bin 45 (white)

Arthur R. Griffiths
President

ARG/mk

Suite 410 - Marine Building, 355 Burrard Street, Vancouver, British Columbia V6C 2G8
Telephone: (604) 681-2226 Facsimile: (604) 681-3871

James Douglas

Barbecue Salmon: Any size to fit the occasion.

Cut down back, bones from inside don't pierce skin.

Lay flat on double thickness foil making a lip all around. Sprinkle salt & pepper all over dot with butter or margarine. Sprinkle liberally with brown sugar. Drizzle all over with sauce.

Sauce recipe

1 c. mayonnaise

½ c ketchup

2 tbsp lemon juice or vinegar

mix & pour on fish

Put on hot barbecue or can be cooked in 400° oven. Put a piece of foil over top of fish. As fish is cooking spoon sauces from foil on salmon. It is cooked when back bone comes away easily.

James Douglas
Actor & Director
Principal Actor in " Street Legal" in 1992

Mr. Justice Wallace T. Oppal
Commissioner
Richard C.C. Peck, Q.C.
Commission Counsel

June 23, 1993

Ms. Abby Anderson, C.A.E.
General Manager
Burnaby Chamber of Commerce
149 - 9855 Austin Avenue
Professional Wing, Lougheed Mall
Burnaby, BC V3J 1N4

Dear Ms. Anderson:

All-Celebrity Cookbook

Thank you for your letter of June 2 inviting my participation in the above project. Having gone through my extensive volume of gourmet recipes, I have come up with the following:

SALMON TERIYAKI

Salmon Fillets

Combine:
1 cup light soy sauce
1/4 cup Sherry
2 T. sugar
2 garlic cloves, crushed
2 T. grated ginger

and marinate salmon fillets for a minimum of 30 minutes.

Put in a greased casserole dish and bake in an oven at 450°F. for approximately 10 minutes (10 minutes for each 1" of fish) or until flaky.

Garnish with parsley or fresh cilantro.

With my best wishes for a successful venture,

Sincerely,

Mr. Justice Wallace T. Oppal
Commissioner

H:\CES\WP\RECIPE.WTO

Room 155 (Plaza Level), 800 Hornby Street, Vancouver, BC Canada V6Z 2C5 **Telephone: (604) 775-1452** ▪ **Facsimile: (604) 660-9032**

Pacific Salmon with Maple Butter Sauce

Yield: 4 appetizer portions

For the sauce:

1 lemon
1 bayleaf
1 clove
1 tbsp white wine
3 tbsps maple syrup
2 tbsps 35% cream
3 tbsps cold butter

Squeeze juice of one lemon into saucepan, add bayleaf, clove white wine, and maple syrup. Reduce to 1/4, add 35% cream and reduce by half. Remove from heat and whisk in cold butter.
Keep on a warm, but not hot, surface.

For the salmon:

4 x 100 g fresh Pacific salmon (skin on)
sea salt
fresh ground white pepper
2 tbsps olive oil

Heat oil in pan, season the salmon and place in pan, skin-side down. Cook on medium heat on one side only- do not turn over. Cook for approximately 6 minutes or until the top becomes transparent. Remove salmon and place on towel to remove oil. Skin should be nice and crispy. Place salmon on plate, drizzle with sauce and serve.

E n j o y !

Wolfgang von Wieser
Executive Chef
Four Seasons Hotel Vancouver

FOUR SEASONS HOTEL · VANCOUVER

791 WEST GEORGIA STREET, VANCOUVER B.C. CANADA V6C 2T4 TELEPHONE (604) 689-9333, TELEX 04-55289, FAX (604) 684-4555

FOUR SEASONS HOTELS - Canada: Montreal · Toronto · Toronto (Inn on the Park) · Vancouver · England: London (Inn on the Park) · United States: Austin · Boston · Chicago · Chicago (The Ritz-Carlton) · Houston · Houston (Inn on the Park) · Los Angeles · New York (The Pierre) · Newport Beach · Philadelphia · San Francisco · Seattle · Washington DC
FOUR SEASONS RESORTS - Canada: Minaki, Minaki Lodge · Caribbean: Nevis, West Indies · United States: Dallas at Las Colinas · Maui at Wailea · Santa Barbara Biltmore
UNDER DEVELOPMENT: Japan: Tokyo · Carlsbad at Aviara · Singapore · Hawaii at Kona · Mexico City · Paris

CHARLES LILLARD

2450 Central Avenue * Victoria * V8S 2S8 * Canada *

KNUDSON COVE MOULDED SALMON WITH CUCUMBER SAUCE

1 cup canned salmon
1 tblsp flour
1/2 tsp salt
1 tsp mustard
cayenne to taste
1 tlbsp sugar
11/2 tblsp butter
3/4 cup canned milk
2 egg yolks
1/4 cup vinegar
3/4 tblsp gelatine
2 tblsp cold water

Flake salmon. Mix dry ingredients, add yolks, butter, milk and vinegar. Cook over boiling water, stirring constantly until mixture thickens. Add gelatine soaked in cold water. Strain and add to salmon. Put into mould, chill, and serve with sauce.

Cucumber Sauce: Beat 1/2 cup heavy cream until stiff. Add 1/4 tsp salt, dash of cayenne, a few grains pepper, and gradually 2 tblsp vinegar; now add 1 cucumber that has been pared, chopped, and drained through cheesecloth.

LOY LOWTHER'S BLACK BEAR FRICASSE

Using any cut, put meat through the mincer, using none of the fat. Add pork fat to taste. Put on stove in saucepan, add juice from bones cooked with some water to moisten well. Simmer at low heat until meat is well softened. Cook two diced onions in small amount of water until tender. When done add meat and gravy and cubes of cold, cooked potatoes and carrots. Simmer gently for 1/2 to 3/4s of an hour.

Your letter of 18 August only reached me on Friday. Attached are a couple of 'tried and true' recipes.

All best wishes,

Charles Lillard

Charles Lillard
Noted Poet, Historian & Editor

Vancouver Island Salmon

1/2 cup unsalted butter
1/3 cup wildflower honey
1/3 cup (packed) brown sugar
2 Tbls. fresh lemon juice
1 Tsp. natural liquid smoke flavouring
3/4 Tsp. crushed dried red pepper flakes
1/4 Tsp. ground allspice
salmon fillets (4-6)

1. Combine butter, honey, brown sugar, lemon juice, liquid smoke, red pepper flakes and allspice in a saucepan. Cook over medium heat, stirring, until smooth. Cool to room temperature.
2. Arrange the salmon in a dish just big enough to hold it. Pour the cooled marinade over it, and let it stand for 15 minutes. Turn and baste with marinade. Let stand for another 15 minutes.
3. Prepare hot coals for grilling.
4. Oil the grill well and cook the salmon, skin side up, over medium heat for 5-7 minutes. Then turn it over and cook for another 5-7 minutes.
5. Transfer the fish to a platter and serve at once.

4-6 portions

Susan Musgrave
Writer

Charlie & Darlene White's Salmon BARBECUE Marinade

Of all of the marinade recipes we have tried for barbecuing salmon, our guests like this one the best. You can also bake the salmon using this marinade, and it comes out very nicely.
The recipe is large because we barbecue salmon a lot - however, it can be easily cut down. It keeps well for weeks in the fridge.

1 cup vegetable oil
1 cup soy sauce
lemon juice from one lemon
1 tsp salt
1/2 tbsp garlic - crushed or chopped
1/2 cup brown sugar
1/2 cup scotch whiskey

Blend together. Put salmon pieces (skin on) in heavy duty plastic freezer bag, pour in enough marinade to cover salmon well, seal bag, place in fridge for 4-6 hours, turning occasionally. Barbecue, skin side down (This holds the salmon together)..watch it carefully as it is best when just barely cooked.

Charlie White

Charlie White
Well known salmon expert & author

Salmon in Puff Pastry.

4 boneless salmon fillets.
2 tbsp. green onion.
1 cup grated swiss cheese.
1/2 cup mayonnaise
1/2 lb. fresh shrimp or crab meat
2 tsp. chopped parsley.
salt + pepper.
1 tbsp butter melted.
3 pkgs. frozen puff pastry.

Cut salmon fillets in half.
Mix green onions, cheese, mayonnaise, shrimp, parsley + salt + pepper together in a bowl. Roll out puff pastry cut to size for 8 pieces of salmon. Place salmon on pastry, top with some shrimp mixture. Fold pastry over salmon and seal edges. Place on baking sheet, brush with butter. Bake at 400°F temp. for 20 to 30 minutes.

GEORGE MCLAUCHLIN
VANCOUVER PARKS BOARD

Lisa Hobbs Birnie

Bowen Island, B.C.
V0N 1G0

Heavenly Herbed Halibut Steaks

Ingredients for four steaks.

4 oz. (1/2 carton) semi-soft natural cheese with garlic and herbs
1/4 cup bottled tartar sauce
12 cucumber slices
1/2 cup (2 oz.) shredded Cheddar cheese
1 tablespoon snipped chives
4 6 oz. halibut steaks (3/4 inch thick)

Whisk semi-soft cheese and tartar sauce together. Arrange halibut in a microwave baking dish, placing thicker portions towards outside of dish. Spread steaks with cheese mixture and cover with vented plastic wrap. Microwave at HIGH for 7 to 8 minutes, until center of fish flakes when tested with a fork. Give dish a half turn during cooking time. Top steaks with cucumber slices. Sprinkle with Cheddar cheese and snipped chives. Microwave, uncovered, at HIGH for 2 1/2 minutes. Let stand five minutes, covered. Serve.

My best wishes in achieving your goal of enhancing the growth of tourism in our unique province.

Yours sincerely,

Lisa Hobbs Birnie

Lisa Hobbs Birnie

Lisa Hobbs Birnie
Award winning journalist & foreign correspondant

THE PAN PACIFIC HOTEL
Vancouver

John Williams
Regional Vice President and General Manager

Monday, August 2nd, 1993.

Ms. Abby Anderson, C.A.E.,
General Manager,
Burnaby Chamber of Commerce,
Suite No. 149,
9855 Austin Avenue,
Professional Wing,
Lougheed Mall,
Burnaby, B.C.,
V3J 1N4.

Dear Ms. Anderson,

Re: All-Celebrity Cookbook

In response to your letter of June 22nd, I am delighted to enclose two of my favourite recipes for enclosure in the above, and wish you great success in this exciting and enterprising venture.

Yours truly,

PAN PACIFIC HOTELS AND RESORTS.

John Williams.

JW/JIS

Enclosures:

300-999 Canada Place, Vancouver, British Columbia, Canada V6C 3B5
Telephone (604) 662-8111 Facsimile (604) 669-5748

AAA Five Diamond Award · A Member of The Leading Hotels of the World®

THE PAN PACIFIC HOTEL
Vancouver

John Williams
Regional Vice President and General Manager

GRILLED HALIBUT WITH GREEN PEPPERCORN SAUCE

Ingredients to prepare 4 portions

4 pcs	halibut filets(180 gr. or 6 oz)
25 gr	shallot - chopped fine
15 gr	garlic - chopped fine
20 gr	green peppercorn
25 ml	olive oil
50 ml	champagne vinaigrette
50 gr	butter, unsalted, cubed and chilled
80 ml	fish stock
80 ml	white wine
	tomato concasse - diced
	parsley - chopped
	salt & pepper to taste

Method

1. Panfry the halibut until golden coloured and finish in the oven at medium heat (375 °F approximately). Remove to platter and keep warm.
2. Add shallots, garlic and green peppercorns to the pan with a little olive oil. Sautée lightly and then deglaze with champagne vinegar, add fish stock and white wine and reduce by half.
3. Remove from heat, cool slightly until warm to the touch, then add butter, a little at a time, stirring constantly to ensure the butter does not break. Keep the pan warm enough only to melt the butter slowly.
4. Finish with tomato and parsley and season to taste.
5. Spoon over or serve under the halibut fillet.
6. A selection of fresh local vegetables finishes the dish.

300-999 Canada Place, Vancouver, British Columbia, Canada V6C 3B5
Telephone (604) 662-8111 Facsimile (604) 669-5748

AAA Five Diamond Award • A Member of The Leading Hotels of the World®

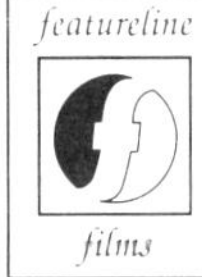

Featureline Films V.C.C. Inc.
137 South Oxley Street, West Vancouver, B.C., Canada V7V 1G9

September 13, 1993

Burnaby Chamber of Commerce
Ms. Abby Anderson
Suite #149 - 9855 Austin Avenue,
Professional Wing,
Lougheed Mall,
Burnaby, B.C.
V3J 1N4

Dear Ms. Anderson,

We are delighted to share one of our favorite recipes with you for the All-Celebrity Cookbook.

We are sending a recipe that we have used and loved for many years. By the way, this recipe was a big hit with the Black Sheep star Robert Conrad when we stayed at his home in California two years ago.

I hope your readers love it as much as we have. Good luck with your new Cookbook.

Best Wishes,

Susan and Aerock Fox

Susan and Aerock Fox
Featureline Films

Featureline Films V.C.C. Inc.
137 South Oxley Street, West Vancouver, B.C., Canada V7V 1G9

The Fox's

HALIBUT STEAKS WITH HOLLANDAISE
- for 4 -

- Ingredients -

(2) 1/12" halibut steaks
1 cup hollandaise sauce (your favorite recipe)
Salt and pepper to taste
1 large lemon
parsley

- Tools -

Skillet or large pot
Fish poacher or rack
poaching paper
Spatula
Paring knife

Place the fish poacher in skillet and fill with water to 1/12" above the poacher and heat to a boil.

Reduce heat to a simmer and place fish in water. Cover with poaching paper and simmer for approximately 10 - 15 minutes.

Remove paper and , while fish is still in the water, run a paring knife gently under the skin. If the fish is done, the skin should easily slip away.
Next, remove the bone the same way. If the fish is not done, the bone will seem to cling to the fish. Wait a few minutes more and the bone should come away in one piece.

We like to prepare this dish on large plates, in an artistic french style, and present to our guests at the table.

To serve, remove the fish from the water using a spatula and before putting on the plate, touch the bottom of the spatula on a cloth or paper towel to remove excess water. Pour a ladle of hollandaise sauce over each steak and garnish with parsley. Serve with baskets of warm french bread , small new red potatoes, steamed jullienned carrots and snow peas and garnish plates with lemon and tomatoe wedges and parsley.

Enjoy!

Susan and Aerock Fox

WHITE SPOT LIMITED

1126 S.E. Marine Drive
Vancouver, B.C.
V5X 2V7
Telephone: (604) 321-6631
Fax: (604) 325-1499

Dear Ms Anderson:

Thank you for providing me with the opportunity to contribute to the Burnaby Chamber of Commerce Cookbook. You will note by the letterhead and enclosed card that I am now with White Spot Limited, however I continue to serve as Chairman, Financial Institutions Commission. I trust the attached will prove to be worthy additions to the Chamber's efforts to promote tourism within the province via the Cookbook.

I want to take this opportunity to wish you and your colleagues every success.

HALIBUT WITH ORANGE MANGO SALSA

Halibut fillets	- 1 lb
Flour	- ½ cup
Salt & pepper	- To season
Orange juice (fresh squeezed)	- 8-10 oz
Mango salsa	- 8 oz (1 cup)
Vegetable oil	- 1 tbsp

MANGO SALSA

Mango, peeled, diced finely	1
Red onion, finely diced	½ cup
English cucumber, finely diced	½ cup
Lime juice	2 tbsp
Vinegar	1 tsp
Lime zest, grated	½ tsp
Cumin	¼ tsp
Tabasco	4 drops
Worstershire	2 drops
Pepper	To taste
Chili peppers (optional)	1 tsp

PREPARATION (Halibut with Orange Mango Salsa)

1. Season flour lightly with salt and pepper. Mix well.
2. Slice Halibut fillet into four equal portions, then dredge through seasoned flour on both sides. Shake off excess flour.
3. In a non-stick skillet, heat vegetable oil over medium heat.
4. Add Halibut fillets and saute for 1-2 minutes, then turn and saute remaining side until golden brown in colour.
5. Add in orange juice, then salsa, and mix well. Cover and cook a further 2-3 minutes, or until sauce is slightly thickened and fish is slightly translucent in the centre of the thickest point.
6. Carefully place fish fillets onto a heated plate, reduce sauce slightly, then pour a ribbon on top of fillet.
7. Serves 4.

PREPARATION (Mango Salsa)

1. Combine diced mango, red onion and English cucumber in a large mixing bowl.
2. Add lime juice, vinegar and seasonings and mix well. Season to taste.
3. Refrigerate for 1½ hours prior to serving.

Sincerely,

WHITE SPOT LIMITED

Dale Parker
President

SHRIMP CREOLE
Serving of four

1 lb of fresh shrimp
quarter cup of flour
one third cup light virgin oil
one 14 oz. can of tomato sauce
one quarter cup fresh parsley
one quarter cup fresh green pepper
4 small garlic bulbs diced
one half table spoon or sea salt and fresh ground pepper
4 slices of fresh lemon
heat slowly while adding one cup of still mineral water

In separate pot cook 2 cups of converted rice.
In separate pot boil shrimp in water and then drain.

When all ingredients are ready mix together and serve with fresh French bread and vegetables and bottle of chilled bottle of Chardonnay, Fortant de France, 1992.

Best wishes,

George S. Athans Jr. C.M. B.A.

Three time World Water Ski Champion

Member of Order of Canada and Canadian and B.C. Sports Hall of Fame.

President of Athans Communications a television and commercial production company in Montreal.

Michael Coney

2082 Neptune Road, R.R.3
Sidney, B.C. Canada V8L 3X9

31 August 1993

Abby Anderson, C.A.E.,
Burnaby Chamber of Commerce,
Suite #149 - 9855 Austin Avenue,
Professional Wing, Lougheed Mall, Burnaby, B.C.
V3J 1N4

Dear Abby:

Thank you for your letter re the cookbook; it sounds an interesting project.

I have a recipe I often use for company I want to impress. We call it Woodstock Shrimp Curry, because it was first fed to us in Woodstock near Blenheim Palace, England, by a nephew who was in the process of turning vegetarian but felt he could eat shrimp without violating his new creed. It works equally well with chicken. This is how you do it:

Fry in olive oil:
- 1 medium onion
- 3 cloves garlic

until golden, then add:
- 4 oz grated ginger root
- 2 bay leaves
- 4 jalapeno peppers, sliced and de-seeded
- 2 teaspoons coriander
- 2 teaspoons fennugreek

Fry lightly.

Put into a pot and add:
- 250 ml canned tomato puree
- 150 ml yogurt

Simmer for one hour, stirring occasionally. Near the end, add:
- 1 1/2 pounds shrimp
- 100 grams solid coconut cream
- 2 teaspoons salt.

The result will serve four; pour it over basmati rice. If you use chicken instead of shrimp, cut it into small pieces and put it in the pot earlier in the simmering process.

Sincerely,

Mike Coney

Michael Coney
Renowned science fiction & Arthurian author who has had 16 books published in 7 languages

Vancouver 86ers Soccer Corp.
1126 Douglas Road, Burnaby, British Columbia, Canada V5C 4Z6
Telephone (604) 299-0086 Facsimile (604) 299-1886

Shrimp in Tomato Sauce

A dieter's delight.

2		**onions, sliced**	**2**
2	**Tbsp**	**butter**	**30 mL**
½	**cup**	**instant non-fat dry milk**	**125 mL**
2	**Tbsp**	**flour**	**30 mL**
1		**can (19oz/540mL) tomatoes**	**1**
		salt and pepper to taste	
		curry powder (optional)	
1	**lb**	**shrimp, fresh or frozen**	**500 g**

In a medium saucepan sauté onions in butter. Thoroughly combine the next 6 ingredients and add to onions. Cook and stir until mixture thickens. Add shrimp and heat through. Serve with rice or pasta. Note: This dish can be prepared with any lean fish.
Serves 4.

BOB LENARDUZZI
VANCOUVER 86ER'S

PRAWNS

Ingredients

2	lbs. unshelled prawns
1/2	cup unsalted butter (melted)
1/2	cup olive oil
1	teas. salt
3	large cloves garlic (chopped)
1	tbls. lemon juice
1/4	cup minced parsley
2	shallots
	white wine (optional)*

Method

Put prawns in colander and rinse - let drain.

In saucepan, gently melt butter, oil, and all other ingredients.

Put prawns in pan or bowl; cover with this marinade and let stand in refrigerator for about 6 - 8 hours.

When ready to cook use hot frying pan.

If you want, now you can add a few dashes of white wine*.

Florence Paterson
Stage, Cinema & Television Actor

Skiing Blackcomb Mtn.
Whistler B.C.
Photo Randy Lincks
Tourism B.C.

Vancouver City Savings Credit Union
HEAD OFFICE: 515 W. 10th Avenue, Vancouver, B.C.
MAILING ADDRESS: P.O. Box 2120, Vancouver, B.C. V6B 5R8

Robert D. Quart, *Chief Executive Officer*
Tel. 877-7666 Fax: 877-0855

SEAFOOD PAËLLA

1 large onion
2 cloves garlic
olive oil
1 28 oz. can of tomatoes
8 chicken thighs, browned
1/2 lb. squid, sliced in rings
1 lb. peeled shrimp
1/4 lb. diced summer sausage
1 small can of baby clams
8 large mussels (in shell)
3 cups rice, uncooked
saffron
pepper to taste
1 cup frozen peas
2 lemons
4 eggs, hard-boiled
1 small can of red pepper

Chop onion and garlic. Fry in olive oil with tomatoes. Add browned chicken thighs and roast in oven at 350 F until chicken is cooked (approximately 40 minutes).

Use some of the sauce from the chicken, onion and garlic, to saute the shrimp and squid.

Dice the summer sausage.

Boil clams and mussels (save mussel shells for garnish).

Cook rice with saffron. When ready, add frozen peas, sausage, shrimp, squid, chicken, onions, and garlic. Squeeze 1/2 lemon over mixture to prevent rice from sticking. Mix well.

Spread in a large paëlla dish.

Garnish

Cut hard boiled eggs in half. Prepare 8 slices of lemon. Cut red peppers in narrow strips.

Dress up using hard boiled egg halves and lemon slices around perimeter of dish. Stick mussel shells into rice and lay out red pepper in strips like spokes from the centre of the pan.

Serve hot with a full bodied Spanish red wine and a side salad and french bread.

Serves 8.

ROYAL BANK

H. (Anne) Lippert
Vice-President & Area Manager
Vancouver Downtown

Royal Bank of Canada
Main Branch - Royal Centre
1025 West Georgia Street
Vancouver, B.C. V6E 3N9
(604) 665-5200
(604) 665-0315 (Fax)

Burnaby Chamber of Commerce
Suite #149 - 9855 Austin Avenue
Professional Wing
Lougheed Mall
Burnaby, B.C.
V3J 1N4

Attention: Abby Anderson, C.A.E.
General Manager

Dear Abby:

Thank you for your letters of June 24th and July 22nd and I apologize for not responding sooner.

As requested, I am enclosing herewith one of my favorite recipes to add to your production of an "All-Celebrity Cookbook". I am honoured that you thought of me and to be included amongst such distinguished names. I think this is a great idea to promote tourism.

Yours sincerely,

PAELLA
(Spain)

Serves 8 to 10

3 tbsp.	olive oil
1 1/2 lbs.	chicken pieces
1	medium onion, chopped
2	cloves garlic, crushed
1/2 lb.	tomatoes, chopped
3 cups	water or chicken broth
1 tsp.	salt
1/4 tsp.	pepper
1 1/2 cups	uncooked rice
1/8 tsp.	saffron or turmeric
1/2 lb.	lobster meat
1	10 oz. package frozen peas
2 oz.	pimentos
8	cooked mussels or clams in shells

Heat oil in Dutch oven and fry chicken until brown on all sides. Remove chicken; fry chopped onion, garlic and tomato pieces. Return chicken to pan, add water or broth and season with salt and pepper. Simmer gently for 15 minutes.

Add rice and saffron, blended with a little broth and cook for a further 10 minutes.

Stir in lobster, shrimp and peas, and cook for 10 more minutes or until all liquid is absorbed and meat is cooked and tender. Adjust seasonings.

Serve garnished with pimentos and mussels or clams in shells.

Spanish Paella

Paella is best cooked close to servingtime
Preferably 5 minutes before is completly cooked

* Opcional : chiken or pork ribes, can be added to fish.
(Serves 4 to 6)

- 1 pound of medium uncooked King prawns. Shelled with heads
- 1 cuttelfish (400 gr.)
  ^ (save the marrow bag inside the cuttelfish, as a ingredient for the tomatoe sauce)
- 2 Squids
- 6 small lobsters (save heads)
- pound of mussels
- 1/2 pound of clams
- 3 cloves of garlic
- 1 pound of crushed tomatoes
  (6 branch of parsely)

* 6 branch of Saffron
1/4 liter of olive oil
Salt
1/2 pound of green peas
1 red pepper
4 artichokes
3 cups of medium size white rice
6 cups of water

Wash and clean everything, fish, prawns without separating their heads, cut the squid, chicken, fish and pork ribes in small pieces. Save the heads and marrow bag inside the cuttelfish as a ingredient for the tomatoe sauce. Using a medium frying pan over high heat for 3 minutes, heat olive oil, add chicken and cooke it over medium heat,

gradually stir, until browned all over; remove chicken from frying pan and place it on a different plate.

Using the same oil add the shell prawns, leaving heads and tails intack. Cut almost though backs of prawns, remove dark veins. Press prawns upon gently along cut side with knife. Cooke over medium heat for about 4 minutes until prawns are almost cooked. Do the same process with the pork ribes, squid, lobster and once they are done place them in separate dishes.

Keep using the same oil as needed. Use the same oil to cooke the crushed tomatoes, at the same big frying pan, over medium heat, when the oil is separating from the tomatoes add the 3 cloves of crushed fresh garlic; the marron bag from the cuttelfish and parsley.

After 5 minutes add the rice into the sauce that we have prepared and stir for 3 or 4 minutes. In a different container boil the water that needs to be added into the big frying pan with the tomatoes sauce. Once is been added, put the fish, chicken, ribes, artichokes, cut in small pieces; red peppers in long pieces.

Add the squid, lobsters, mussels, clams, saffron and salt.

Let it cook for 15 minutes bring to boil, with high heat, preferably on a gas stove, and ¡¡ is very important not to stir while the rice is boiling!!. Remove from the heat and let it sit for 5 minutes.

* Spanish Paella would be served dry.

* Optional: lemon and white wine from Alella (Barcelona)

Tony Sagastizado
Actor, Singer, Dancer

ROYAL BANK

G.R. (Greg) Bright
Vice-President - Retail Banking
British Columbia & Yukon

Royal Bank of Canada
1055 West Georgia Street
Vancouver, B.C. V6E 3S5

Tel.: (604) 665-6782
Fax: (604) 665-6465
Cel.: (604) 657-3472
(604) 328-1472

SEAFOOD SUPREME

2 - 5 oz. cans	Canned Lobster
2 - 5 oz. cans	Canned Crab
2 cans	Canned Clams (drained)
1 lb.	Scallops, fresh or frozen
1 lb.	Shrimp, fresh or frozen
1 tin	Cream Clam Chowder
1/2 cup	Butter
1/2 cup	All-purpose flour
1/2 teaspoon	Dry mustard
1/2 teaspoon	Salt
1 1/2 cups	Milk
1 cup	Low-fat yogurt
1/2 cup	White wine
2 tablespoons	Butter
1 cup	Bread crumbs
1/2 cup	Grated Cheddar
1/2 cup	Parmesan

Put lobster, crab and drained clams into large bowl. Break into bite-size pieces.

Cover scallops with water. Boil 5 minutes. Drain. Then cook shrimp. Drain. Let cool.

In saucepan, melt butter. Stir in flour, mustard and salt. Add milk. Cook, stirring until mixture is thick, then add clam chowder. Let cool then add yogurt and wine. Then add cooked scallops and shrimp. Pour this over contents in bowl. Stir to combine. Pour into casserole.

Melt butter in saucepan. Remove from heat. Stir in crumbs and cheeses. Spread over casserole. Bake at 350 for 30-40 minutes or until it bubbles.

WEDGEWOOD
HOTEL

June 28, 1993

Ms. Abby Anderson, C.A.E.
General Manager
Burnaby Chamber of Commerce
Suite #149 - 9855 Austin avenue
Professional Wing
Lougheed Mall
Burnaby, B.C.
V3J IN4

Dear Ms. Anderson:

Further to your letter of June 2nd, 1993, I am enclosing my recipe for Cioppini for Two.

1 small lobster (previously cooked)
8 clams
8 mussels
4 scallops
4 shrimps
2 oz. Halibut
2 oz Salmon

2 oz. chopped tomato
2 oz. chopped onion
1 Tsp. chopped garlic
1 Tsp. chopped basil
1/2 tsp. chili flakes
1/2 pint fish stock
1/4 pint white wine
1 oz chopped fennel
1 oz virgin olive oil
Salt and pepper

- saute onion, tomato, garlic, basil, fennel, chili flakes.
- add stock, white wine - boil.
- add clams and mussels, cook for 1 minute.
- add Salmon and Halibut - cook for 1 minute.
- add rest of fish - cook for 2 minutes.
- take out all fish and put into dish.
- reduce sauce slightly and pour over fish.
- it's ready.

Yours truly,

Alan M. Groom

Alan Groom
Executive Chef

/gm

845 HORNBY STREET, VANCOUVER, B.C., CANADA V6Z 1V1
TEL: (604) 689-7777 TELEX: 04-55234 FAX#: (604) 688-3074

RUY PAES-BRAGA
Regional Vice President
General Manager

BOURRIDE

Provençal Fish Stew with Garlic Sauce

Of all the great fish soups and stews, this one is a favourite. The fish retains its distinct flavour more than in many other dishes of the type, and the creamy garlic sauce is a delight: a Provençal dish with the aroma and flavour of fennel, orange, olive oil, bay leaves, and garlic. The delicately poached fish is served on rounds of crisp French bread, surrounded by a rich garlicky sauce and topped with garlic mayonnaise--exciting to prepare as well as to eat.

FOR FOUR

2 lb. bass, mullet, whiting, haddock, or halibut fillets

COURT BOUILLON

1 medium-sized onion quartered
2 small bay leaves, broken up
2 strips orange zest, 3 inches long by about ¼ inch wide
1 tsp. fresh lemon juice
1 tsp. fennel seed, crushed with a mortar and pestle
1 tsp. salt
¼ tsp. freshly ground black pepper
1 ½ Tbs. white wine vinegar
3 c. cold water

AÏOLI (GARLIC MAYONNAISE)

makes 1 ½ cups, approximately

4 large or 7 small garlic cloves, pounded to a paste with a mortar and pestle
2 large egg yolks
¾ tsp. salt
½ c. olive oil combined with ½ c. peanut oil
¼ tsp. freshly ground white pepper
1/16 tsp. cayenne
½ tsp. dry mustard
1 ½ Tbs. white wine vinegar
4 tsp. fresh lemon juice

FOUR SEASONS HOTEL · VANCOUVER

791 WEST GEORGIA STREET, VANCOUVER, B.C., CANADA V6C 2T4, TELEPHONE (604) 689-9333, TELEX 04-55289, FAX (604) 684-4555

SAUCE

6 Tbs. aïoli
2 large egg yolks
½ c. strained court bouillon

---

8 slices toasted French bread, 1 inch thick (bake on a rack in a 350° F. oven for 4 minutes on each side)

Combine the ingredients for the court bouillon in a large heavy sauté pan or skillet. Bring to a boil, then simmer for 10 minutes. Strain the court bouillon, return to the pan, then poach the fish for 8 to 10 minutes depending on size and texture. Remove the pan from the heat. Carefully lift the fillets out of the pan with a large slotted spatula, allowing the liquid to drain off. Place the fish in a shallow baking dish, cover loosely with aluminum foil, and set in a 175° F. oven to keep warm.

To prepare the aïoli, combine the garlic, egg yolks, and salt in a mixing bowl. Beat with a whisk or an electric mixer until the yolks are thick and lemon-colored. Begin adding the oil, a scant teaspoon at a time, until the aïoli begins to thicken. Add the pepper, cayenne, and dry mustard and beat to mix. Add a bit more oil, then about 1 teaspoon of the wine vinegar, beating. Repeat the addition of some oil, then some vinegar, until all the vinegar has been incorporated.

The sauce should be quite thick at this point. Increase the amount of oil being added to about 1 tablespoon at a time, followed by a scant ½ teaspoon of lemon juice. The sauce will continue to thicken. Toward the end of the mixing, when the sauce is very thick, the oil can be added in a constant slow stream. Complete the sauce by beating in any drops of lemon juice still remaining, then beat for about 20 seconds more.

To make the sauce for the Bourride, in a small stainless steel or porcelain bowl combine 6 tablespoons of the aïoli with 2 large egg yolks. Beat to mix with a whisk, then gradually pour in ½ cup of the strained, still-warm court bouillon. (If the court bouillon has cooled too much, warm it briefly.)

To serve, place 2 slices of toasted French bread side by side in the bottom of each of 4 preheated wide soup bowls. (Italian spaghetti bowls are ideal). Pour ⅛ of the sauce over each portion of bread, then top with the pieces of poached fish. Pour the remaining sauce over the fish, then top each portion with 2 to 3 tablespoons of aïoli. Serve immediately.

Any leftover aïoli can be refrigerated, covered. It will keep for 4 to 5 days.

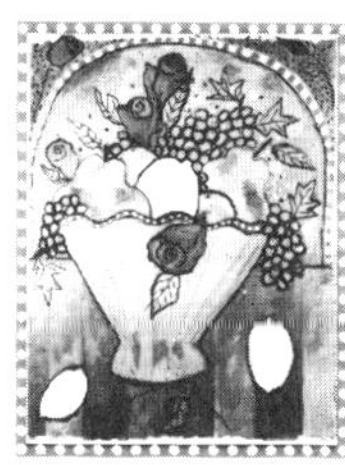

R A I N T R E E

A Uniquely Vancouver Restaurant

NORTHWEST SEAFOOD BOWL

1/2 package rice noodles (soak in cold water)

1 whole dungeness crab (cooked, cleaned, cut into four)
1 lb fresh mussels or clams
1 lb fresh spot prawns (head & shell removed)
250 grams squid (cleaned)
1 lb fresh halibut
1 lb fresh salmon
1 lb smoked Alaskan black cod
1 cup fresh tomato (chopped)
1/2 cup green onion (chopped)
fresh cilantro

MISO BROTH

4 tablespoons olive oil
1 onion (finely chopped)
2 cloves garlic (crushed)
1 cup dry white wine
1 bunch cilantro (chopped)
5 cups fish stock
1 1/2 cups brown rice miso (available from health food store)

Heat olive oil in heavy based pan. Saute onion, garlic & cilantro. Add wine and fish stock and bring to a boil. Add the miso & dissolve. Simmer until liquid is reduced by 1/3. Cool.

Divide rice noodles into 4 medium size chinese sand pots. Divide the seafood equally into pots. Add the miso broth, tomato & green onions to seafood. Place pots on stove and bring to a boil. Place lids on pots and bake at 400 for 10 minutes. Remove lids, garnish with cilantro and serve immediately.

Serves four.

JANICE B. LOTZKAR

RAINTREE RESTAURANT • 1630 Alberni Street, Vancouver, B.C. Canada V6G 1A6 • Tel. (604) 688-5570 • Fax (604) 689-7334 • LEON'S 685-5306
HARVEST MOON CAFE • 1218 Wharf Street, Victoria, British Columbia, Canada V8W 1T8 • Telephone/Fax (604) 381-3338

Svend Robinson
M.P.

Community Office:
4453 East Hastings St., Burnaby, B.C. V5C 2K1
(604) 299-4022
Ottawa Office:
Room 386, Confederation Bldg.
House of Commons, Ottawa K1A 0A6
(613) 996-5597
No postage required

ADA'S COOKED OCTOPUS

If you have caught your own octopus, you must first remove the tentacles and clean it. If you buy it already cleaned then you simply cut it into little chunks. Once it is cut up, pound the octopus a little bit with a steak hammer. Then, in a mixture of flour, salt and pepper, roll the octopus pieces. When coated, fry in a pan until brown.

Once the octopus has been fried, put it in a casserole dish along with a chopped onion and add water until the octopus and onion is covered. Let the casserole simmer in the oven until tender. Keep turning and stirring the octopus as it cooks. If you make this in the morning it should be cooked by the afternoon. The oven should be about 300 degrees but you should keep checking the octopus to make sure it is cooking slowly.

Dear Abby,

I am pleased to enclose a recipe for "Ada's Cooked Octopus", a traditional Haida dish for your Burnaby Chamber of Commerce cookbook. Best personal regards.

Sincerely yours,

Svend J Robinson, MP
Burnaby-Kingsway

Entrees: Meats

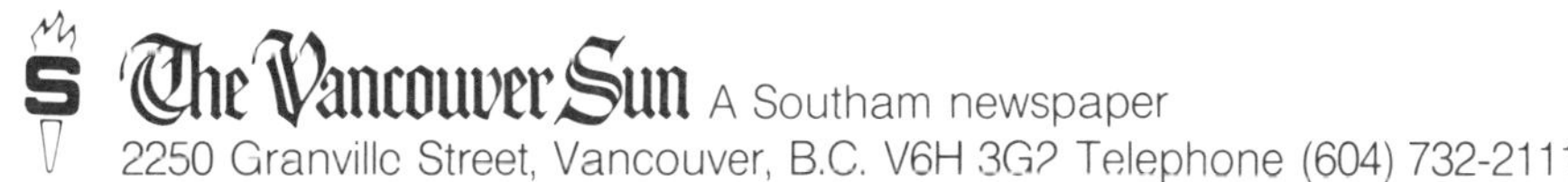

A SUPER LAMB RECIPE FROM EDITH ADAMS COTTAGE AT THE SUN — A PERSONAL FAVOURITE. SERVE WITH CRUNCHY ROAST POTATOES, FRESH PEAS AND CARROTS, SOME OKANAGAN RED, AND FIND HEAVEN!

IAN HAYSOM
EDITOR-IN-CHIEF.

CRUSTY RACK OF LAMB

- 2 racks of lamb (about 1¼ pounds or 625 g each)
- Salt and fresh ground black pepper
- 2 tablespoons (30 mL) olive oil
- ⅔ cup (150 mL) fine fresh bread crumbs
- ¼ cup (50 mL) unsalted butter, softened
- 1 teaspoon (5 mL) dried tarragon, crumbled
- 2 tablespoons (30 mL) Dijon mustard
- Watercress for garnish

Sprinkle lamb all over with salt and pepper. Brush completely with oil. Place, meat side up, in shallow roasting pan.

Roast, uncovered, at 450 F (230 C) for 10 minutes.

In small bowl, combine bread crumbs, butter and tarragon.

Remove lamb from oven and brush tops and ends with mustard; then spread with bread crumb mixture. Reduce heat to 350 F (180 C) and continue roasting about 25 minutes or until thermometer inserted into meaty part of rack registers 140 F (60 C) for rare. Allow five or 10 minutes more for medium or well done lamb.

Let stand, loosely covered with foil, for about 10 minutes before serving. Garnish with watercress.

Makes four servings.

August 12, 1993.

Abby Anderson, C.A.E.,
Burnaby Chamber of Commerce,
Suite #149 - 9855 Austin Avenue,
Professional Wing,
Lougheed Mall,
Burnaby, B.C.,
V3J 1N4.

Dear Abby,

I wish you the best of luck in your endeavours to help tourism in BC - a goal which benefits all of us.

My recipes are attached - I've avoided such traditional newsroom delights as the "City Editor's Lunch" (beer and chips), or the "Copy Editor's Snack" (French fries with Tabasco) in favor of some more conventional goodies.

Thanks for the invite to take part!

Neil Graham,
Managing Editor.

ROAST LEG OF LAMB

For the sauce:

- *one cup of (cheap!) dry-to-medium red wine;*
- *quarter cup of vinegar;*
- *teaspoon of crushed garlic (two if you like!)*
- *teaspoon of crushed fresh ginger;*
- *teaspoon of dried chervil;*
- *teaspoon of paprika (make it two if you like it spicy; I do)*
- *teaspoon of rosemary (fresh is best);*
- *two teaspoons of chopped fresh mint leaves;*
- *salt to taste (it takes more than you'd expect; I use about a teaspoon);*
- *a dozen peppercorns;*
- *two fresh chopped chili peppers (optional)*

Put the wine and vinegar into a small saucepan, add the herbs and spices, and bring to a brisk boil, stirring occasionally.

In the meantime, lightly score the leg of lamb, making cuts half an inch apart. Make sure you cut through the skin, but by no more than a quarter of an inch or so.

Put the scored leg of lamb into a casserole (use foil if you don't have one big enough) and pour the boiling sauce over it. Cover the casserole with foil and let it marinate for a few hours. (I usually prepare the lamb at breakfast time and cook it in late afternoon).

Put the lamb and sauce into a 325 to 350-degree oven for about two hours or until there's no blood coming out when you poke it deeply with a fork. Cooking time seems to vary, but err on the safe side if you don't like your meat bloody. The slower you cook it, the more tender the lamb becomes. Open for the last half hour or so to brown.

I usually partly boil some potatoes and carrots, and pop them into the sauce when I open the foil.

Great with salad and chunks of sourdough bread to dip into the gravy.

Neil Graham,
Managing Editor.

Lamb Marinated in Balsamic Vinegar and Cilantro with Curry Sauce

INGREDIENT

Lamb Chops or Racks	8-10 oz per person
<u>Marinade (for four)</u>	
Balsamic Vinegar	3 oz.
Fresh Cilantro minced	1/2 bunch
Olive Oil	1 and 1/2 cup
Dijon Mustard	1 oz.
Garlic (minced)	2 cloves
<u>Sauce</u>	
Curry Powder	1 oz
Lemon juice (squeezed)	1/2 lemon
Mayonnaise	1 cup

PROCEDURE

1. Prepare sauce : Mix lemon juice with curry powder. Add mayonnaise.
2. Prepare marinade : whisk olive oil and vinegar, then add cilantro, garlic, and mustard.
3. Place lamb in marinade for 4-6 hours
4. Grill or baked Lamb to medium doneness.
5. Place lamb on plate and pipe sauce over plate in diagonal pattern using squeeze bottle.
6. Garnish with grilled red peppers and asparagus.

ACKEEU LEE
CHEF

6695 Nelson Avenue, Horseshoe Bay, West Vancouver, B.C. V7W 2B2 Tel. 921-8188

Dal Richards' Orchestra

Orchestras • *Artists* • *Entertainment*

BUTTERFLIED LEG OF LAMB

1 cup dry red wine
3/4 cup soy sauce
4 large cloves garlic, crushed
1/2 cup chopped fresh mint leaves
2 tablespoons slightly bruised fresh rosemary leaves
  or 1 tablespoon dried
1 tablespoon coursely ground black pepper
1 butterflied leg of lamb (4 to 5 lbs.)

1. Combine the wine, soy sauce, garlic,mint, rosemary and pepper in a small bowl and mix well. Place the lamb in a nonreactive baking dish. Pour the mixture over the lamb, cover and refrigerate for 6 hours, turning the lamb frequently.
2. Prepare hot coals for grilling.
3. Drain the meat, reserving the marinade. Grill the lamb 4 inches above the hot coals, basting frequently with the marinade, about 20 minutes on each side. Check the lamb for doneness frequently after 30 minutes grilling.
4. Cut the lamb into very thin slices, and serve immediately.

Serves 8 with leftovers.

7 - 2, 550 BEATTY STREET, VANCOUVER, B.C. V6B 2L3 TELEPHONE (604) 669-2313 or 681-6060

INDONESIAN VEAL CURRY

10 oz. veal striploin, cleaned and cubed
2 Tbsp. olive oil
1 oz. calvados brandy
1 cup whip cream
3 Tbsp. coconut nectar
1-2 Tbsp. Madras curry powder
1 small Granny Smith apple, peeled, cored and diced
1/4 cup raisins
toasted coconut
2 cups hot cooked rice

Heat olive oil in a fry pan over medium heat. Add veal and saute 3-5 minutes until lightly browned, stirring occasionally. Add Calvados Brandy and flambe'. Add whip cream and simmer until reduced by half, 8-10 minutes.

When sauce is reduced to desired thickness add coconut nectar.

Mix in 1-2 Tbsp. curry powder, depending on how spicy you want the dish.

finally stir in the chopped apple and raisins and simmer 3-5 minutes, then remove from heat.

Split the cooked rice between 2 plates. Top with the veal curry and sprinkle with toasted coconut. Serve immediately.

Serves 2.

Patrick Corbett
President, Council of Tourism Association

RANCH OFFICE: C-26, 108 Ranch, British Columbia V0K 2Z0 • Tel: (604) 791-5225 • Fax: (604) 791-6384

ORCA BOOK PUBLISHERS

Orca Ribs

Start with the best ribs you can find, preferably baby back ribs (that way you avoid getting stuck with that slab of meat that has no bone in it and nobody wants to eat anyway).

Start at least a day before you want to eat. Gently boil the ribs for about 45 minutes in a pot of salted water along with an onion studded with cloves.

Drain and dump the ribs into the marinade. Cover and let sit in refrigerator overnight, turning from time to time. Cook at 350° or over fairly low heat on barbeque until nicely browned (about half an hour).

Marinade

1½ cups beer
½ tsp salt
1 tbsp dry mustard
1 tsp ground ginger
3 tbsp soya sauce
¼ tsp hot sauce (more or less to taste)
½ tsp worchester sauce
2 tbsp sugar
4 tbsp marmalade
2 cloves garlic

R.J.C. (Bob) Tyrrell
Publisher

P.O. Box 5626 Station B Victoria, B.C. Canada V8R 6S4
telephone: 604-380-1229
fax: 604-380-1892

SUNSHINE BAR-B-Q RIBS

2 LBS. OF YOUR FAVOURITE CUT OF RIBS (FAT REMOVED)
1/4 TSP. EACH: SALT, PEPPER, PAPRIKA & CINNAMON
1 LARGE CLOVE GARLIC (CRUSHED)
1 CUP BROWN SUGAR
1/2 CUP CRUSHED PINEAPPLE OR APPLESAUCE
1/4 CUP KETCHUP
3 TBLSP. LEMON JUICE

TO MAKE MARINATE

MIX ALL INGREDIENTS TOGETHER, HEAT UNTIL COMBINED. COOL. POUR OVER RIBS, COATING ALL RIBS WELL. COVER (SEAL) AND REFRIGERATE OVERNIGHT.

COOKING BAR B-Q STYLE (SUMMER):

REMOVE RIBS FROM MARINATE. SEAR AT HIGH HEAT TO SEAL IN JUICES FOR 2 MINUTES. LOWER HEAT TO MEDIUM - COOK FOR 20 MINUTES TO 1/2 HOUR, TURNING AND BASTING WITH MARINATE OFTEN.

BAKED STYLE (WINTER)

REMOVE RIBS FROM MARINATE. PLACE IN BAKING DISH AND BAKE FOR APPROXIMATELY 2 HOURS AT 300° F. TURNING AND BASTING WITH MARINATE OFTEN. ENJOY!!!

WINE: L'AMBIANCE RED WINE
C.S.P.C. # 160879

Cartier Wines & Beverages
Western Region
2210 Main Street
Penticton, B.C.
V2A 5H8
(604) 492-0621 · Fax 492-6990

UNIVERSITY OF VICTORIA
P.O. BOX 3050, VICTORIA, B.C., CANADA V8W 3P5
TELEPHONE (604) 721-7327, FAX (604) 721-6216

DEPARTMENT OF GEOGRAPHY

8 September 1993

Ms Abby Anderson,
General Manager,
Burnaby Chamber of Commerce.

Dear Ms Anderson,

Thank you for your letter of 18 August 1993, asking me to submit one or two of my favourite recipes. I am sorry for the late reply because I was not in Victoria during the month of August.

One of my favourite recipes is the

Five Figures Spare Rib

(A) Seasoning:
- ONE tbsp vinegar
- TWO tbsp white wine
- THREE tbsp sugar
- FOUR tbsp soya sauce (2 tbsp light and 2 tbsp dark)
- FIVE tbsp water

(B) Ingredients:
- 500 grams spare rib
- 2 tbsp chopped garlic

(C) Method:
1. Chop spare rib into pieces of about 2" long.
2. Brown garlic and spare rib with 2 tbsp oil. Sprinkle with white wine. Add soya sauce, vinegar, sugar, and water.
3. Stew with low heat for about 25 minutes until not much liquid is left.

Yours sincerely,

David C.Y. Lai

David Chuenyan Lai, C.M., Ph.D.
Professor

HENRY YOUNG

BIOGRAPHY

For over 25 years, guitarist Henry Young has been involved with crafting music of the highest calibre. As a former principal member of Nina Simone's band, he has received international critical attention, having performed at the prestigious Montreux, African and Newport Jazz Festivals. He has also worked with the likes of Almeta Speaks and Bobby Taylor & the Vancouvers. Henry is currently working on the lower mainland as guitarist, arranger and musical director for the Miss Vancouver Chinatown Pageant. Here is his original recipe for "jazz" ribs.

HENRY'S JAZZ RIBS

(Eaten and endorsed by renowned jazz vocalist, Joani Taylor)

Ingredients:

4 lbs. (1 slab) ribs (beef or pork)
Cut slab in half (approx. 2 lbs. per slab)
Add 2 tbsp. salt to pot of boiling water
Add 2 oz. white vinegar
Add ribs to boiling water, cook 5 - 7 minutes
Drain, then rinse ribs with cold water
Drain and pat dry

Prepare sauce:
(Henry's secret jazz sauce, prepared in the key of Eb while listening to jazz)

1, 5-1/2 oz.tin of tomato paste (concentrate)
2 - 3 tbsp. of worchester sauce
1, 10 oz. tin of orange juice (concentrate)
1 - 2 tsp. of cayenne pepper powder
1 - 2 oz. of dry wine (red or white)
1 - 2 tsp. of freshly ground black pepper
3 tbsp. of mustard (prepared)
1 med. yellow onion (finely chopped)
3 tbsp. of brown sugar
1 tbsp. of dry mustard
6 - 8 cloves of fresh garlic (minced)
1 - 2 tbsp. of red wine vinegar

**Do not add salt to sauce.

Mix ingredients well, cover ribs liberally and marinate for approx. 2 hours, continuously turning ribs over.

Put ribs in baking pan with sauce. Completely seal pan with tin foil.

Cook in preheated oven for 2-1/2 - 3 hrs. at exactly 250 degrees.

Ribs must be completely sealed during cooking in order not to let out any juices (so no peeking!). Check after 2-1/2 hours. Meat should be tender and almost falling off the bone.

** Please note: After eating ribs, should you and your friends have the urge to listen to jazz music; this is normal (do not panic). May I suggest running out and purchasing the latest CD by Ms. Joani Taylor, entitled "Absolutely", this would complement Henry's Jazz Ribs.

Enjoy! Bon Appetit!

BRITISH COLUMBIA CHAMBER OF COMMERCE
Suite 1607–700 West Pender Street, Vancouver, B.C. V6C 1G8 (604) 683-0700 Fax. (604) 683-0416

June 23, 1993

Abby Anderson
General Manager
Burnaby Chamber of Commerce
Suite 149 - 9855 Austin Avenue
Professional Wing, Lougheed Mall
Burnaby, BC
V3J 1N4

Dear Abby:

Got your note regarding your All-Celebrity Cookbook project. I'm delighted you asked me to participate and I enclose two of my favorite recipes.

The first is a childhood favorite I brought from my mother into my family. I still enjoy it and have used it in large quantities at camp.

SPANISH BEEF

In a casserole dish, mix together:
1 1/2 lbs ground beef
1 cup cracker crumbs
1/2 cup grated cheddar cheese
1 small onion, chopped

Add water to moisten and season to taste.
Bake at 350 degrees for 45 minutes,
stirring every 15 minutes.

ADD
1/2 cup cooked macaroni and
1 can tomato soup

Bake another 15 minutes

Kids ***love*** it!

Yours sincerely,

Dean Cooper,
President
BC Chamber of Commerce

Blanche Howard

3866 REGENT AVENUE. NORTH VANCOUVER. B.C. V7N 2C4

September 14, 1993

Abby Anderson, General Manager,
Burnaby Chamber of Commerce,
Ste. 149 - 9855 Austin Ave.,
Lougheed Mall, Burnaby, B.C. V3J 1N4

Dear Abby Anderson,

Thank you for your invitation to submit recipes, and I'm sorry you had to send all the way to Regina to get my address from my publishers when we're within shouting distance.

Here is an old favourite. When my son was small, he liked it so much I used it for medical diagnosis: if he wasn't well enough to eat it, he really was too sick for school.

MEAT LOAF

Oven to 350

1 1/2 lb. hamburger
1 cup oatmeal
1 egg
small onion, chopped
1 tsp. sage
1 can tomato soup

In a greased casserole, mix everything together except the soup. Spread the undiluted soup on top, and bake for one hour.

And a bit more sophisticated, and better for the weight:

Blanche Howard
Award winning fiction novelist

To maintain the vision and principles of Terry Fox while raising money for innovative cancer research in an annual event known as The Terry Fox Run.

Mission Statement of
The Terry Fox Run

SWEET AND SOUR MEATBALLS

Yield: 6 servings

Quick, easy and the kids love it!

1 1/2 lb. ground beef
2/3 cups cracker crumbs
1/3 cup minced onion
1 egg
1 1/2 tsp. salt
1/4 tsp. ginger
1/4 cup milk
1 tbsp. shortening
1 tbsp. cornstarch
1 can (13 1/2 oz) pineapple tidbits, drained (reserve syrup)
1/2 cup brown sugar
1/3 cup vinegar
1 tbsp soya sauce

Mix thoroughly beef, crumbs, onion, egg, salt, ginger and milk. Shape mixture into meatballs. Melt shortening in large skillet; brown and cook meatballs. Remove meatballs and keep warm. Remove fat from skillet. Mix cornstarch and sugar. Stir in pineapple syrup, vinegar, and soya sauce until smooth. Pour into skillet; cook over medium heat, stirring constantly, until mixture thickens and boils. Boil and stir 1 minute. Add meatballs and pineapple. Heat through. Serve with rice.

Dear Abby,

To follow two of my families favorite recipes.

Thank you for excluding me in your cook book.

Regards

Betty Fox

Paul St. Pierre
Moccasin Telegraph Co.
Box 964
23214 St. Andrews St.
Fort Langley, B.C.
V0X 1J0

FILET DE BOEF
AU MALE CHAUVINIST PIG

In the days when differences between men and women were more noticeable, I attended a union meeting where one member said to his debating opponent, who was a weedy little chap:

"Hell, man, one good drink, one good screw and one good steak and you'd be dead."

He, and many of us then, would doubtless have supported the statement that real men don't eat quiche, if we had known what guiche was. Of course, sensible men enjoy both but sensible people also recognize that there is a vast difference between the two and that nothing is worse than to cook quiche like steak or try to cook a steak in a teflon quiche pan. The whole approach must be different, as well as the end product.

The cooking of a steak is actually uncomplicated. People have done it more or less by accident while looking at a John Wayne movie on TV. The important features of steak cooking are found far from the stove.

FIRST, THE MEAT

Don't thoughtlessly grab Calgary grainfed beef even though supermarkets say you should. A lot of it is veal trying to act grown up.

At least try to find meat from a fully mature animal. A baby beef is no more interesting to the palate than a woman under 30 is in bed. Your steak should have the flavor that only comes with maturity.

Some of us believe that only grass fed aged beef is good. You can tell grass fed by the hard, yellow fat on it. However, it is rare to find any and in any case most people prefer the grainfed with the fat marbled throughout the meat. If you want that style, at least try find some from a big boned animal which lived long enough to see the duck ponds freeze and thaw more than once.

GET THE RIGHT CUT

You can't do much with a steak which is less than two centimeters (about 3/4 inch) thick. A full 2.5 cms is better.

One can get into endless argument about steak cuts and it would not profit us to trot them all out now. I happen to prefer T-Bone but I am often wrong about things.

Almost any the steak cut from the loin is good. This excludes shoulder steaks, round steak and flank steak. The flavors may be excellent, as the Orientals showed us in the case of the once despised flank steak, but they are used in other ways than what we are talking about which is (will trendy folk please shut their ears?) FRIED MEAT. Sorry to say a thing like that and apologies to all the people who write French menus, but a steak cooked in a pan is fried meat and nothing else. (Barbecued steaks are a different story; different cuts of meat, different treatment throughout. This recipe is for pans and skillets.)

Of well known steak cuts, the sirloin, which comes from the weak side of a New York steak, is usually tenderest. However tenderness is not the main objective. If it is, make yourself oatmeal porridge, which is truly tender. Our objective -- remember? -- is flavor.

THE FRYPAN

Steaks hearken back to the days of heavy and solid feeding and the cooking utensils were the same. The only pan which will properly cook a steak is made of cast iron and weighs abut as much as a manhole cover. No one can cook a decent steak on a pan made of aluminum or stainless steel.

A castiron pan or griddle has to first be seasoned by cooking oil in it for three quarters of an hour. This only has to happen once or twice in a generation. Once seasoned, soap and water never touch it again and the flavor of every meal cooked upon it carries over to meals yet to be cooked.

THE RECIPE (FINALLY)

Funny thing about cooking steaks is that once you have the right meat and the right frypan the rest is so easy.

1. Heat the pan until salt dances on it when sprinkled. Put no grease or oil in it. Do not even think about letting water touch the meat.
2. Sear one side of the steak. It must smoke.
3. Turn the steak over and turn the heat off or take the pan off the hot part of the stove.
4.. Put a tablespoon of garlic butter on the top of each steak. When it melts into the meat, out of which red juice will be oozing, the steak is done rare. For well done steaks, cook longer under low heat after the first turnover.

5. Serve with no sauces. Sauces are for poorer cuts of beef which can't make it on their own. A steak seems to taste better served on a wood plank. This is an illusion, but so are many of life's finest moments.

A MYTH IS GOOD AS A SMILE

For a hundred years and more people have said that searing seals the juices in the steak. We now know that this isn't so. However the searing is important because it puts little sticky bits of crusty meat on the steak and vastly improves the final flavor.

The macho man is expected to demand his steak be rare. "Just polish the horns, wipe its ass and lead it in!" There isn't much to support this prejudice. A steak cooked blue (practically raw) will have very little flavor because raw meat is almost tasteless. Don't take my word, try some. On the other hand too much cooking will reduce the finest meat to a black, hardened, evil thing that eats like the tongue of an old boot. Wise steak eaters trust their own palates and do not let other people tell them whether their meat should be red or brown.

Don't believe that beef and the other red meats are bad for you. Medical fads change almost as often as Paris fashions. The Argentines eat almost three pounds of beef each every day and they haven't done so badly. True, they have screwed up their economy, but we're accomplishing the same thing on a diet of chicken and yogurt.

yours truly

Paul St. Pierre

Paul St. Pierre
Noted BC author whose works include a new book on
the Mexican drug trade entitled " In the Navel of the Moon"

DUNCAN A. McNAUGHTON

SPICY BEEF BRISKET

1 BEEF BRISKET
1/2 TSP SALT
PEPPER AS DESIRED
1 SLICED ONION
2 WHOLE PIECE OF CELERY SLICED
1/2 CUP OF HEINZ RED CHILI SAUCE
1 CAN OF BEER
1/4 CUP CHOPPED PARSLEY

METHOD

SEASON AND COVER MEAT WITH ONION, CELERY AND CHILI SAUCE, SALT AND PEPPER.
ADD 1/4 CUP OF WATER, ROAST UNCOVERED AT 350 UNTIL BROWN.
REMOVE FROM OVEN AND POUR BEER OVER THE MEAT.
BAKE FOR 3 MORE HOURS UNTIL TENDER.

Dear Abby;

Duncan thanks you for your invitation to participate in the All-Celebrity Cookbook.

He is unable to see very well due to Macular Degeneration so I have enclosed two of his favorite recipes.

The Spicy Brisket is a recipe that was served in the famous Dallas Neiman Marcus lunchroom.

The pudding is referred to as "Peach Pud" around here and we all know that it means "real good".

I hope your recipe book is a great success. We certainly would like the opportunity to purchase one or more when it is available.

Sincerely
Eileen McNaughton

Duncan McNaughton
BC Sports Hall of Fame
Gold at the 1932 Olympics in high jump with a height of 6'5 5/8"

KIRIN
MANDARIN RESTAURANT
1166 ALBERNI STREET, (DOWNTOWN) VANCOUVER, B.C. V6E 3Z3 • TEL. (604) 682-8833
FAX (604) 688-2812

HONEY AND GINGER BEEF

8 OZ (250gr) BEEF TENDERLOIN

4 TBSP (60ml) HOISIN SAUCE

1 TSP (5ml) CORNSTARCH

10 OZ (300ml) VEGETABLE OIL

1 TBSP (15ml) VEGETABLE OIL

3 CLOVES GARLIC, MINCED

4 THIN SLICES GINGER, MINCED

1 SCALLION, WHITE PART ONLY,CUT INTO THIN SHREDS

2 TBSP (30ml) HONEY

2 TBSP (30ml) DARK SOYA SAUCE

FRESH CHINESE PARSLEY SPRIGS

STEAMED CHINESE BUNS

Slice beef paper thin,across the grain. Marinate 15 minutes with hoisin sauce and cornstarch; Heat 10oz (300ml) oil in wok to 360F (185C); Deep-fry marinated beef 1 minute, lift out at once with a strainer, and drain. Set aside; Discard oil, wipe wok clean, and return 1 tbsp (15ml) oil to wok and heat; Have ready combined garlic,ginger and scallion, and stir-fry 1 minute; Add honey and soya sauce, cook 15 seconds, and return drained beef to wok; Stir-fry 1 minute until beef is glazed; Serve on a platter, garnished with sprigs of Chinese parsley; Accompany with warm steamed buns.

余正平
Matthew Yee
General Manager

Butchart Gardens
Victoria B.C.
Photo Courtesy of Tourism B.C.

Juan M. Sanchez

"Milanesa"
Breaded Steak or Steak Milanes.

8. thinly sliced beef steach, medium sized. (approximately 1/2 kilo).
3. eggs, beaten with a little salt.
1. teaspoon chopped garlic and parsley mixture
2. cups bread crumbs
oil for frying, salt and papper to taste
1. lemon, sliced or in wedges

Season thinly sliced beef steaks with salt and pepper to taste, then pound them with a meat maller over a kitchen board to bring them to about the same thickness. Mix eggs with garlic and parsley mixture. Dip steaks in eggs, dredge with bread crumbs, pat and press to fix crumbs onto steak, and fry in hot oil. To fry milanesas use a very little oil, never more than about 1 cm. deep, adding more as needed as you go on frying. Oil should ~~there~~ be heated to keep steaks frying steadily, but not over the needed temperature so as to avoid scorching the crumbs wich will always be falling off. steaks.

As soon as browned lay on absorbent paper and keep warm. Take to the table along wich lemon wedges or lemon slices, serve with mashed potatoes or fried sweet potatoes, sauteed vegetables or fresh salad.

Juan Sanchez
Noted BC Artist

Gladys Blyth

Country Fried Steak.

Round steak cut 1/2 inch thick
1 egg, beaten
Dash of pepper
1/4 teaspoon ground ginger.
1 1/2 teaspoons salt.
1/2 cup fine dry bread crumbs
3 tablespoons oil
2 tablespoons flour
1 1/2 cups water.

Cut round steak into four pieces and tenderize with a mallet.
Combine egg, pepper, ginger and 1 teaspoon of salt.
Dip meat into egg, then into bread crumbs.
Heat oil in large skillet over medium heat.
Add meat and brown on both sides.
Remove meat and stir the flour and 1/2 teaspoon of salt into fat remaining in the skillet. Cook until bubbly.
Remove from heat and gradually stir in water and cook-stir until smoothe and thickened slightly.
Return meat to gravy, cover and cook over low heat for 45 minutes.

Gladys Blyth
Author & curator of the North Pacific Cannery Musuem
at Port Edward

VANCOUVER CANUCKS

Member Of
National Hockey League

100 North Renfrew Street
Vancouver, British Columbia
V5K 3N7
Telephone (604) 254-5141
Facs (604) 251-5123

BEEF AND SAUSAGE CHILI

3 Tbsp. olive oil
3/4 lb. coarse chopped onions
3 lb. ground beef
1 can kidney beans
1 lb. mix of sweet and hot sausage with casing removed (proportion each to taste)
1/4 cup cumin seeds
1/6 cup (generous) chili powder
1 1/2 Tbsp. minced garlic
1 1/8 tsp. ground pepper
2 1/4 lb. tomatoes peeled seeded and chopped or 1 large and 1 small can
6 oz. can tomato paste
3/8 cup of beer
3/8 cup chopped fresh parsley (Italian)
1/8 cup plus 2 Tbsp. chopped fresh oregano or 3/4 Tbsp. dried
1 1/2 Tbsp. lemon juice
Salt to taste

Heat oil in Dutch oven over low heat. Add onions. Cook until translucent about 10 minutes. Increase heat to medium high, add beef and both sausages. Cook until brown breaking up with a fork about 10 minutes. Add cumin, chili powder, garlic and pepper. Stir for 5 minutes. Add tomatoes, tomato paste, beer, parsley, oregano, lemon juice and beans. Simmer until chili is thick. Season with salt. Cover and refrigerate. Reheat over medium low heat.

Sincerely,
VANCOUVER HOCKEY CLUB LTD.

J. B. Patrick Quinn
President and General Manager

The PHANTOM of the OPERA™

Dear Abby,

My recipe:

Norman Roberts' Phantom Irish Stew

"You charter a plane and fly to Maxims in Paris for dinner"

But seriously folks: "Phantom Irish Stew" (Part Two) Get a lot of beef stew meat cubed cover with wine of choice (Italian type) add oregano a bay leaf basil rosemary tomato paste can of tomatoes stew for two hours thicken eat.

Thanks a lot

Love,

Norman

BEEF KOFTA CURRY

(12 meat balls)

SALT	2	tsp
GARLIC, crushed	2	cloves
BEEF, minced	225	gm
OIL	2	tbsp
CLOVES	4	
BLACK PEPPERCORNS	8	single
CINNAMON STICKS	2	pieces
BAY LEAVES	2	
CARDAMON, brown	1	clove
ONION, medium, chopped	1	
TOMATOES, quartered	2	med. size
YOGURT	1	tbsp
RED CHILLY POWDER	1/2	tsp
WATER	300	ml.
GARAM MASALA	1/2	tsp
CORRIANDER, leaves chopped	1	tbsp

Mix 1/2 tsp salt and garlic with the meat. Divide the mix into 12 parts, and roll each into a ball. Heat oil on moderate heat in a deep saucepan. Add chopped onions and saute. Add cloves, peppercorns, cinnamon, bay leaves and cardamons and stir thoroughly. When onion turns golden, add the tomatoes, yogurt and chilly powder. Water is poured in and along with remaining salt. The mix is brought to a boil. Meat balls are now dropped in and again brought to a boil. Cover the pan and allow to simmer 15 minutes or til the meat is cooked through. Sprinkle masala and corriander and serve HOT.

Recipe submitted by,
Judi Tyabji

OKAY!!! I will send in a recipe, but I waive all responsibilities for after-effects. Is it possible to get some ideas of what kind of recipes you have received to date? I was thinking of an Eastern-style dish.

Best of luck on your venture.

Sincerely,

Judi Tyabji, M.L.A.
Okanagan East

OCEAN POINTE RESORT

Königsberger Klopse (Meat Balls in a caper sauce).

Meat Balls: ① Combine: 1½ pounds of ground veal, ¼ pound of pork, and two tablespoons of melted butter. ② Soak: 2 slices of white bread in water until soft. Squeeze out water and add to meat. ③ Sauté: 2 tablespoons grated onion in 1 tablespoon butter until light brown. Add to meat mixture. ④ Add: ½ teaspoon of grated lemon rinds, 3 eggs, beaten, ½ teaspoon lemon juice, 1 teaspoon Worcestershire sauce, and 2 tablespoons of chopped parsley. Mix thoroughly and shape into 12 meat balls. ⑤ Skillet with 5 cups of beef broth, bring to boil. Place meat balls gently into boiling broth, cover, and simmer for 10 minutes.

Sauce: ① Combine: 5 tablespoons of butter with 5 tablespoons of flour (roux). Gradually stir in hot stock. Stirring until slightly thickened. Do not boil. ② Stir in 2 tablespoons of capers (chopped) with two tablespoons of chopped parsley. Season to taste with lemon juice.

Serves: Four

Enclosed find my favourite recipes which is easy to prepare and is a change of pace.

Sincerely,

Rick Stolle

F. Ulrich "Rick" Stolle
General Manager

2806 W. 30th. Ave.,
Vancouver, B.C.
V6L 1Z2.

Burnaby Chamber of Commerce,
Suite 149, 9855 Austin Ave.,
Professional Wing, Lougheed Mall,
Burnaby, B.C. V3J 1N4

Attention: Abby Anderson, C.A.E.

Re your letter of July 27, 1993 requesting a favorite recipe for your All-Celebrity Cookbook.

BEEF STEAK AND KIDNEY PIE -

1 pound kidney prepared and cut-up
1 1/2 pounds round steak, cut in small pieces
3/4 teaspoon salt
1/2 " allspice
1/2 " cinnamon
1/2 cup all-purpose flour
3 tablespoons finely chopped onion
2 cups canned consomme or bouillon, undiluted
1 bay leaf
Flaky pastry.

Cover kidney with boiling water. Let stand until white membrane shows. Remove white membrane and cut out the tubes. Mix seasonings and flour. Roll steak and kidneys in flour to coat. Place in saucepan. Sprinkle with remaining seasoned flour and onion. Add consomme and bay leaf. Simmer over low heat until tender.

Pour into deep pie plate. Place pastry covering over top. Make steam slits. Brush with slightly beaten egg yolk mixed with milk or cream to make glaze on pastry. Bake in moderate oven, 375 deg. F. for 25 to 30 minutes until golden brown. Makes 6 servings. (Canned, drained mushrooms can be added to meat before placing in baking dish.)

Sincerely,

Jim Hutchison

JIM HUTCHISON

Jim Hutchinson
BC Sports Hall of Fame
Hydroplane racing

Main Office	985-2131
Display Advertising	980-0511
Classified	986-6222
Distribution	986-1337
Subscription Sales	986-1337
FAX	985-3227

A Division of North Shore Free Press Ltd.

1139 Lonsdale Avenue, North Vancouver, B.C. V7M 2H4

July 18, 1993

Dear Ms. Anderson:

Re my favorite recipe. It used to be rumored that I liked chewing fried nails. Not true, except sometimes.

These days it is something my wife doesn't allow me to have very often, but I do it when she is out of the house.

I refer to the glories of corned beef hash. A simple dish for peasants.

Take a tin of Australian corned beef, which is said to be the least fatty. Cool in refigerator for one day. Cut into squares of about one quarter-inch or even a half-inch if you feel lazy.

Boil three average size potatoes. Allow to cool. Skin. Cut these too into small squares.

Take one average size onion. Slice thinly. Saute gently.

In a large bowl, put all three ingredients in layers. Mix thoroughly.

Using a small quantity of vegetable oil (the meat supplies much of its own fat) fry in large frying pan until the bottom of the mixture is crisp. Turn the whole in sections. Fry again. And enjoy.

Should be good for two people. But sometimes I scoff the lot myself.

Sincerely,

(Doug Collins)

Marc Diamond

610 Jackson Avenue Vancouver BC Canada V6A 3B7

Abby Anderson
General Manager
Burnaby Chamber of Commerce

Re: All-Celebrity Cookbook

Thank you for the invitation to contribute to the cookbook. Here follows my recipe:

LOATION BEEF

This simple, delicious, and possibly provocative Asian dish will, depending on your nerve, impress friends and intimidate enemies.

2 large flank steaks
5 garlic cloves
1 hot pepper (or dried hot chillies)
2 ginger toes
vegetable oil
sesame oil
oyster sauce
Chinese fish sauce
broccoli (lightly steamed)

1. Slice flank steak into thin strips

2. Prepare a marinade of crushed garlic, sliced ginger, and hot pepper or chile (to taste! - this last ingredient is where the nerve comes in, the step that impresses friends, intimidates and even makes enemies- it just depends on how far you want to go with your quantities).

3. Place marinade and beef in a large bowl. Add enough oyster sauce and Chinese fish sauce in equal parts to moisten everything. Marinate at least two hours.

4. Saute in a wok with broccoli and serve over rice.

makes 4 to 6 portions

Sincerely,

Marc Diamond
Award winning BC Playwright

THE UNIVERSITY OF BRITISH COLUMBIA

The Rick Hansen National Fellow Programme
1874 East Mall
Vancouver, B.C. Canada V6T 1Z1
Off: (604) 822-4433
Fax: (604) 822-9486

August 18, 1993

Abby Anderson
General Manager
Burnaby Chamber of Commerce
Suite #149 - 9855 Austin Avenue
Professional Wing
Lougheed Mall
Burnaby, B.C.
V3J 1N4

Dear Abby,

Enclosed is one of my favourite recipes for inclusion in the All-Celebrity Cookbook. Thank you for inviting me to contribute, I'm happy to do so.

Good luck with the venture.

Sincerely,

Rick Hansen, C.C., O.B.C.
National Fellow - Disabilities

Apple Glazed Roast Pork

4-5 lbs pork roast
1 Tbsp butter
1 small onion - grated
1 Tbsp cornstarch
1 Tbsp brown sugar
1 Tbsp soya sauce
½ tsp ginger
1 cup apple juice

Place pork fat side up on rack in shallow roasting pan. Score fat layer in diamonds and roast at 325°F ~~for~~ 1 hour

While roast in oven, prepare glaze. Melt butter in saucepan and sauté onion until soft. Thoroughly mix together cornstarch, brown sugar, soya sauce, ginger and juice. Pour into pan with sautéed onion and cook over low heat, stirring ~~always~~ constantly, until thick. Brush part of glaze over meat, then continue brushing every 15 minutes for next hour or until meat is done. Serves 8

Black Currant Pork Chops (a la Tamara)

4 pork chops

6 tablespoons black currant jelly

2-3 tablespoons dijon mustard

Lightly panfry pork chops on both sides. Remove from pan. Mix jelly and mustard, then add to juices left in pan from pork chops. Heat and stir to form sauce.

Place pork chops in a baking dish and cover with jelly sauce.

Bake for 30-40 minutes at 325°.

Really good with fresh green beans topped with chopped onions and fresh oregano, and mashed potatoes.

Tamara Jeares
U News at Six

CITY OF PORT MOODY

OFFICE OF THE MAYOR
DAVID T. DRISCOLL

CRANBERRY PORK SHOULDER ....8 to 10 servings

- 5-1/2 pound pork shoulder roast, bone-in
- 1 can (16 ounces) whole cranberry sauce
- 1 cup orange juice
- 1 teaspoon cinnamon
- 2 teaspoons salt
- 1/8 teaspoon freshly ground pepper
- Orange slices

Place roast in 4-quart casserole. Combine cranberry sauce, orange juice, cinnamon, salt, cloves and pepper; pour over roast. Cover casserole.

Bake at 325°F 3 hours, or until internal temperature reaches 170°F. Check occasionally and add a little more liquid, if needed. Slice roast and spoon cranberry sauce mixture over top. Garnish with orange slices.

or

Cook at 100% microwave power 20 minutes. Reduce power and cook at 50% microwave power 1 hour 30 minutes, or until internal temperature reaches 170°F, turning roast over once. Let stand, covered, 15 minutes before serving. Slice roast and spoon cranberry sauce mixture over top. Garnish with orange slices.

David Driscoll
Mayor

80th ANNIVERSARY
1913/1993

2425 ST. JOHNS STREET, PORT MOODY, B.C. TELEPHONE (604) 936-7211

Quails' Gate®

Spicey Pork and Peanuts

1 lb. boneless pork, loin or butt, diced

Marinade

1 tbsp. dark soy sauce
1 tbsp. cornstarch
1 tbsp. oil

---

4 cups water

---

2 tbsp. oil
4 dried chili peppers
3 quarter-sized slices peeled ginger, minced

Sauce

1 tsp. cornstarch
1 tbsp. dry sherry
1 1/2 tbsp. dark soy sauce
2 tsp. Chenkong or red-wine vinegar
2 tsp. sugar
1/4 tsp salt
1 tsp. sesame oil

1/2 cup salted peanuts

Preparations: Slice meat into thin strips or small bite sized cubes. Place the meat in a bowl then add each item of the marinade one at a time stirring in circular motions until meat is well coated. Marinate 30 minutes or longer in the refrigerator.

Bring 4 cups water to a boil in a saucepan, give the marinated meat a few big curcular stirs, then drop it into the boiling water. Stir gently to separate then cook for about 1 minute. Drain.

Prepare the sauce just prior to stir frying to assure the piquant aroma will not dissapate.

Stir frying: Heat a wok or large skillet over high heat until hot. Add the oil, swirl in pan then turn heat to low. Add the chili peppers to the hot oil and stir gently until darkened. Add the ginger, stir briskly a few times, turn the heat up to high then add the meat and stir with a tossing motion for about 45 seconds. Give the prepared sauce a quick stir then pour over the meat and stir until evenly coated. Pour meat into a dish and shower the top with peanuts. Toss once more just prior to serving.

Serve with rice and your favourite vegetable.

Sincerely,

Beverly Boudreau

Ben Stewart
President

Thank you for inviting me to participate in your upcoming All-Celebrity Cookbook.

LEILANI'S MUSHROOM GLAZED PORK TENDERLOIN

(Named after my sister who invented it!)

3 tbsp. olive oil
1 lb. whole pork tenderloin(s)
1 large clove garlic, minced
2 cups sliced fresh mushrooms
1 10 oz/284 ml can beef broth
1 tsp. Worcestershire sauce
1 tbsp. cornstarch
1/2 cup cool water

Over medium high heat, brown tenderloins in 2 tbsp. of the oil. Cook quite thoroughly.
Remove from skillet and set aside.
Add remaining oil and saute garlic and mushrooms until tender.
Pour in beef broth and Worcestershire sauce.
In a small measuring cup, mix together water and cornstarch.
Stir into broth mixture, cooking until thickened and clear.
Replace tenderloin to skillet, and gently simmer uncovered for 25 to 30 minutes until pork is thoroughly cooked.
Slice tenderloin diagonally into medallions.
Pour mushroom and broth over meat and serve.

Yours truly,

Hudson Mack
Assistant News Director
CHEK 6 Television

CHEK-TV, A DIVISION OF WESTCOM TV GROUP LTD.
780 KINGS ROAD, VICTORIA, B.C. V8T 5A2 PH. (604) 383-2435 FAX (604) 384-7766

The Corporation of the City Of
Nelson
502 Vernon Street, Nelson, British Columbia V1L 4E8
Telephone : (604) 352-5511 Fax: (604) 352-2131

From the Office of the **Mayor**

RAMSDEN'S MAPLE APPLE GLAZED HAM

1/2	(SHANK END) READY TO SERVE HAM
1 1/2	CUPS APPLE JUICE
1 TSP.	WHOLE ALLSPICE
10	WHOLE CLOVES
1	MEDIUM CINNAMON STICK
	WHOLE CLOVES
3/4	CUPS REAL MAPLE SYRUP

Place ham on rack in roasting pan.
In small saucepan combine apple juice, allspice, 10 whole cloves and cinnamon stick. Bring to a boil; simmer for 5 minutes. Spoon a little apple juice over ham surface. Roast @ 325 degrees for 1 hour - basting with apple juice mixture every 15 minutes. Remove ham from oven.
Score fat in diamonds; stud with whole cloves; drizzle with half of the syrup.
Return to oven; roast 30 minutes.
Drizzle with remaining syrup; roast another 30 minutes or until heated through.
Let stand, loosely covered with foil, for 20 minutes before serving.....

W. H. Ramsden

Celebrating our Heritage
Nelson's Centennial -- 1897 - 1997

John R. Winter
PRESIDENT

HAM BOILED IN BEER

Simmer a whole bone-in ham (20 mins. per lb) in Molson Canadian Beer (enough to cover the ham).

Add a pinch of pickling spice. When cooked, remove skin and rub in dry mustard mixed with brown sugar and stud with whole cloves.

Bake at 375 F. degrees for 3/4 hr.

It stays moist for ages.

Good luck with this venture.

Yours sincerely,

JRW/tr
encl.

MOLSON BREWERIES - WESTERN DIVISION
Suite 300 - 1681 Chestnut Street, Vancouver, B.C. V6J 4M6 Tel: (604) 737-3700 Fax: (604) 738-3492

Ms. Abby Anderson, C.A.E
General Manager
Burnaby Chamber of Commerce

Dear Abby:

I am delighted by your interest regarding my taking part in your project. I am more than happy to enclose three of my favorite Croatian recipes, just like Mamma makes them. And let me tell you, Abby, when Mamma does her stuff, I am *in Heaven!!!!*

She doesn't make these every day, but when she does, OOOOOOH! Well, here they are:

1. Bosanski Lonac (Bosnian Pot)
1/2 kg pork meat without bones, cut into bigger chunks
1/2 kg beef without bones, cut into bigger chunks
1/2 kg potato, preferably young. If potatoes are small, leave whole; bigger potatoes should be quartered
10 cloves of garlic, whole
2 medium onions, quartered
1 tomato, quartered
4 fresh green peppers; remove seeds and quarter
30 decagrams kale, cut into bigger chunks
20 decagrams green cabbage, cut into bigger chunks
2 carrots, cleaned and cut into bigger chunks
2 bunches of parsley, cleaned and cut into bigger chunks
1 bunch of celery, cleaned and cut into bigger chunks
10 snow peas, cleaned and whole
2 big spoons of sweet red pepper
15 - 20 pieces of whole black pepper
salt to taste
3 decalitres white wine (3/10ths of a litre)
water or soup stock

Prepare the above and layer it in a pot (preferably a clay pot,

but stainless steel is okay, too) in the following order: the bottom layer is mixed meat; then a layer of vegetables (a bit of various vegetables); then season the vegetable layer with a bit of garlic, salt, pepper and red pepper. Repeat this order (meat, vegetables, seasoning) until all ingredients are used; the last layer (the layer on top) will be of vegetables. Pour wine over the top. Fill the pot with either water or soup stock until it is 2/3 full. Cover the pot with parchment paper and tie the paper around the rim of the pot with a string. Cook on top of the stove until it boils. After it boils, remove from stove top and put into lightly heated oven (150 - 175 C); cook about four hours. (Serves 4 with "healthy" appetites.)

Dobar tek!! (Bon apetite),

Brano Goluza

Brano Goluza
Television Actor

Marilyn Bowering

Ribs of Pork with Chesnuts –

Soak ribs for 4 days in a mixture of white wine, salt + pepper, cloves, sliced onions, thyme & bay.

Peel & boil 2 lb. of good chesnuts with a bunch of fennel – keep hot.

Drain ribs + fry them in butter. Serve on fried croutons with a sauce made of the marinade, brown gravy & the chesnuts.

Note: The original recipe was for Wild Boar. In my first try at this recipe I soaked the ribs for 10 days, ending up with chesnuts & a plate of bones.

Good in deepest winter in an uninsulated cottage.

MARILYN BOWERING
POET

Dear Abby:

Thanks for your invitation to contribute a recipe...please find the enclosed...

By way of introducing me:

Philip Till is the host of The World Tonight -- a nightly international news and open-line programme on CKNW radio.

Try my recipe...

Philip Till's HORSEMEAT TARTAR

Raw horsemeat, ground twice, 200 grams per person...
Hefty dollop of Dijon mustard...
Big spoonful of capers...
Splash of Tabasco...
Splash of Worcestershire sauce...
Tablespoonful of tomato paste...
Portly garlic dill pickle (chopped up)...
One white onion (chopped up)...
Couple of garlic cloves (chopped up)...
Tablespoon of olive oil...
Pinch of red paprika..
Parsley, Chives (from your garden)...Chopped up...

Throw everything into a big dish...Mix it all up -- spend a long time mixing with a fork and spoon...Make sure everything is perfectly blended BUT DO NOT USE A BLENDER... Serve with french fries and butter lettuce salad and warm baguette...Drink robust Aussie Red (Bin 555)...

Get your horsemeat from Best Bi Foods, Vancouver.

If you eat meat -- don't have a hangup about horsemeat!!!

PHILIP TILL
"THE WORLD TONIGHT"

NW/98

CKNW /98 ***B.C.'S MOST LISTENED TO STATION***
BRITISH COLUMBIA ENTERPRISE CENTRE
P.O. BOX 29, 750 PACIFIC BOULEVARD SOUTH
VANCOUVER, B.C. V6B 5E7
TELEPHONE: (604) 685-4712
FAX (604) 681-5507

Entrees: Poultry Game

Sarah Sawatsky

Chicken Tortilla Casserole

2/3 cup (150 mL) salad dressing (miracle whip or Ranch)
1/4 cup (50 mL) flour
2 cups (500 mL) milk
2 cups (500 mL) grated monterey jack cheese
3½ cups (875 mL) cubed cooked chicken
1/4 cup (50 mL) mild or hot salsa
1/4 cup (50 mL) chopped parsley
10 (7-inch or 17.5-cm) flour tortillas
1/2 cup (125 mL) grated cheddar cheese
Dairy sour cream, diced tomato, salsa and chopped parsle

In medium saucepan, stir together dressing and flour until smooth. Whisk in milk and cook on medium heat, stirring frequently, until sauce comes to a boil and thickens. Remove from heat and add monterey jack cheese. Stir until cheese melts and sauce is smooth.

Set aside one cup (250 mL) cheese sauce. Into remaining sauce, stir in chicken, 1/4 cup (50 mL) salsa and 1/4 cup (50 mL) chopped parsley.

Spoon about 1/3 cup (75 mL) chicken mixture on to each tortilla. Roll up and seal overlap with a dab of reserved sauce. Place filled tortillas, seam side down in two rows, in 13x9-inch (33x23 cm) backing dish.

Spoon reserved sauce across centre of filled tortillas and top with cheddar cheese. Back at 375 F (190 C) for 25 minutes.

Garnish with sour cream, diced tomato, salsa and parsley. makes five servings.

Sarah Sawatsky
Actor in "Northwood" & "Bordertown"

COMPANY CHICKEN DISH

4 Servings   Bake at 3:50° for 40 minutes.

Take 4 pieces of chicken and take off the skin.
Roll in egg and corn flake crumbs.

Bake in the oven for 40 minutes at 3:50.

Make up a mixture of:

1/4 cup of diced green pepper.
1/4 cup of shredded yellow cheese.
1/4 cup of bacon bits.
1 tablespoon of mayonnaise (just enough to mix the above).

Spoon on the mixture on top of the baked chicken after it has baked for 40 minutes. Broil the mixture for a few minutes until the cheese has melted.

Serve piping hot with brocolli, niblets corn, and broiled tomatoe.

Arrange on a plate so that it not only looks appealing but so that the different shapes and sizes are interesting.

Claire Lovett

Claire Lovett
BC Sports Hall of Fame
Still a title winner at the Masters level after 6 decades of National badminton competition

Burnaby Chamber of Commerce
Suite #149 - 9855 Austin Avenue
Professional Wing, Lougheed Mall
Burnaby, British Columbia
V3J 1N4

Attn: Abby Anderson, C.A.E.
General Manager

In support of your All-Celebrity Cookbook, the following recipe, Lemon-Dill Chicken, is an all time favourite around our house:

LEMON DILL CHICKEN

2 boneless chicken breasts, halved and skinned
flour, salt, pepper, butter

Dust chicken with seasoned flour. Saute lightly in butter.

Add: 1/2 cup white wine
1/3 cup lemon juice
chopped fresh dill weed
1 tablespoon honey

Simmer on medium heat till chicken is done. Remove chicken to serving plate. Thicken sauce with a little cornstarch mixed in cold water.

Serve with rice and steamed fresh vegetables.

I hope you enjoy it as much as we do.

Sincerely,

Elizabeth Cull
Minister of Health

Province of British Columbia

Minister of Health and Minister Responsible for Seniors

Parliament Buildings
Victoria, British Columbia
V8V 1X4

W. T. HINTON

CAJUN CHICKEN ON PASTA

Makes 6 servings

6 quarts hot water
3 tablespoons salt
1/4 cup vegetable oil
1 1/2 pounds fresh spaghetti

Seasoning mix: 2 teaspoons dried thyme leaves
1 teasp. cayenne
3/4 teasp. white pepper
1/2 teasp. black pepper
1/2 dried sweet basil

1 pound plus 4 tablespoons unsalted butter IN ALL
1 cup very finely chopped onions
4 medium-size garlic cloves, peeled
2 teaspoons minced garlic
3 1/4 cups rich chicken stock IN ALL
For stock, use about 2 quarts cold water,
1 medium onion, unpeeled and quartered
1 large clove garlic, unpeeled and quartered
1 rib celery
chicken necks, backs, and bones (no liver)

Place all stock ingredients in a large saucepan. Bring to a boil over high heat, then gently simmer for at least four hours. Replenish water as needed to keep about 1 quart of water in the pan. Strain the basic stock, continue simmering it until evaporation reduces the liquid to 3 1/4 cups.

2 tablespoons Worchestershire sauce
two 16 oz. cans tomato sauce
2 cups very finely chopped green onions IN ALL
1 tablespoon Tabasco sauce
2 tablespoons sugar

Chicken seasoning mix:
1 1/2 tablespoons salt
1 1/2 teaspoons garlic powder
3/4 teaspoon black pepper
1/2 teaspoon dried sweet basil
1 teaspoon white pepper
1 teaspoon cayenne
1 teaspoon ground cumin

2 pounds boneless chicken--cut raw chicken into 1/2 inch cubes

Directions: Thoroughly combine the seasoning mix ingredients in a small bowl and set aside. Thoroughly combine the chicken seasoning mix in a small bowl and set aside.

In a 4-quart saucepan, combine 1 1/2 sticks of the butter, the 1 cup onions and 4 garlic cloves; saute over medium heat 5 minutes, stirring occasionally. Add the minced garlic and the seasoning mix; continue cooking over medium heat until onions are dark brown but not burned, about 8 to 10 minutes, stirring often. Add 2 1/2 cups of the chicken stock, the Worchestershire and Tabasco; bring to a fast simmer and cook about 8 minutes, stirring often. Stir in the tomato sauce and bring mixture to a boil. Then stir in the sugar and 1 cup of the green onions; gently simmer uncovered about 40 minutes, stirring occasionally.

Place cut up chicken cubes in a bowl and sprinkle chicken seasoning mix over chicken, rubbing it in with your hands. In a large skillet melt 1 1/2 sticks of the butter over medium heat. Add the remaining 1 cup green onions and saute over high heat about 3 minutes. Add the chicken and continue cooking 10 minutes, stirring frequently. When the tomato sauce has simmered about 40 minutes, stir in the chicken mixture and heat through. Serve the cajun chicken sauce over hot fresh pasta.

Tom Hinton
BC Sports Hall of Fame
Offensive guard for the BC Lions football team from 1958 - 1966, & member of the 1964 Grey Cup team.

Harbour Towers Hotel

345 QUEBEC STREET • VICTORIA, B.C. V8V 1W4
TELEPHONE (604) 385-2405 • FAX (604) 385-4453
TOLL FREE RESERVATIONS 1-800-663-5896

SESAME CHICKEN

1 chicken, 2-2 1/2 pounds (boneless breasts can also be used)
Salt, pepper and flour, mixed
2 eggs, beaten
2 tablespoons milk
1 cup flour
1/2 cup sesame seeds
1/2 tsp. salt
1/4 tsp. pepper
Peanut or safflower oil for frying
Light cream sauce

Wash and dry, then disjoint chicken. Dust with seasoned flour, then dip pieces of chicken into batter of beaten eggs mixed with milk, then roll in flour mixed with sesame seeds and seasonings. Deep fry in peanut or safflower oil at 350 F., until light brown and tender. Serve with Light Cream Sauce made of chicken broth and cream. Serves 2 to 4.

Light Cream Sauce for Sesame Chicken:

4 TBS. butter
4 TBS. flour
1/2 cup half and half
1 cup rich chicken stock
1/2 cup whipping cream
1/2 tsp. onion salt

Melt butter over low heat, add flour and blend over low heat several minutes, stirring constantly. Mix half and half, chicken stock and whipping cream and gradually add to butter and flour mixture, stirring constantly. When smooth, stir in onion salt. Add plain salt if necessary. Let cook over hot water in double boiler 15 to 20 minutes, stirring occasionally.

Alex Lindquist
General Manager

Ferguson Point,
STANLEY PARK, VANCOUVER
For reservations call (604) 669-3281

Marinated chickenbreast with Coconutsauce

Ingredients: 4 large chickenbreast wing bone on
1 can of coconut milk
1 piece of Lime

1 whole Jalapenopepper -> only if you like it hot
1 Teaspoon fresh ginger
5 cloves of garlic
1/2 bunch of fresh cilantro
small piece of lime peel
} chop very fine

1 Teaspoon Sesameoil
2 Tablespoon Oliveoil
1 Teaspoon Balsamicvinegar
1/2 Teaspoon cracked black pepper
4 Tablespoon Soyasauce
2 Tablespoon Honey
} mix well and combine with above ingredients

7501 Stanley Park Drive, Vancouver, B.C., Canada V6G 3E2 Fax (604) 687-5662

Ferguson Point,

STANLEY PARK, VANCOUVER

For reservations call (604) 669-3281

- Place 4 chickenbreast in above Marinate and store in fridge for 6-8 hours in a ziplock bag, turning it over once in a while.
- Remove chickenbreast and place on papertowels and save the Marinate
- Sear chickenbreast in a roasting pan in some oliveoie for 2 min. on each side
- set roasting pan aside
- Place chickenbreast on baking sheet and finish off in the oven with skin side up at 350°F.
- Pour the marinate in the roasting pan and add the coconut milk and the juice of 1 lime
- Simmer for approx. 10 minutes and put in blender
- blend on high for 10 sec. and simmer for another 5 minutes
- add salt to taste

Serve with wild and white mixed rice.

Bon appetite.

R. Clemens.

7501 Stanley Park Drive, Vancouver, B.C., Canada V6G 3E2 Fax (604) 687-5662

Ms. Abby Anderson
Burnaby Chamber of Commerce
Suite # 149 - 9855 Austin Avenue
Professional Wing
Lougheed Mall
Burnaby, B. C. V3J 1N4

Abby, thank you for your invitation to participate with you . . . here are two recipes favoured by guests that you might want to include in your cookbook . . .

MELON CHICKEN

Salsa:

1/2 cup watermelon - diced & seeded
1/4 cup cantelope - diced
1/4 cup honeydew melon - diced
1/4 cup red onion - diced
1/2 cup jicima - diced
1/2 cup cilentro - chopped finely
1 jalepeno pepper - diced
2 Tbsp. lime juice
1/2 tsp. salt

Mix Salsa together and refridgerate for up to 4 hours.

4 - 6 boneless and skinned chicken breasts - Bar-B-Qued over medium coals - seasoned with salt & pepper

Serves 6 and can easily be increased or decreased for the number of guests expected.

LAYERED LEMON CREME

2 envelopes unflavored gelatin
1/2 cup water
6 large eggs
1 1/2 cups sugar
1 Tbsp. grated lemon peel
2/3 cup fresh lemon juice
1 1/2 cups heavy cream
2 cups fresh fruit, such as strawberries, kiwis, or blueberries

CORPORATE OFFICE, 16TH FLOOR, 1055 WEST HASTINGS STREET, VANCOUVER, B.C. CANADA V6E 2H2 (604) 688-6764, FAX: (604) 687-2601

A RECIPE FOR FUN

HERE'S A BUBBLY SOLUTION TO BOUNCE OFF YOUR FRIENDS...

2 pkg unflavoured gelatin
1L hot water (just boiled)
50 to 70 mL glycerine
50 mL dish detergent
• dissolve the gelatin in the hot water
• add the dish detergent and glycerine
(reheat mixture whenever you use it)

SCIENCE WORLD
BRITISH COLUMBIA

SCIENCE WORLD/MAIN STREET SKYTRAIN STATION
268-6363

Sunset
Lions Gate Bridge
Vancouver B.C.
Photo Courtesy of Tourism B.C.

In a small saucepan, sprinkle the gelatin over the water. Let stand for 10 minutes and place over low heat until gelatin is dissolved. Cool. In a large mixing bowl, combine the eggs and sugar, beating until thick and pale. Combine the lemon peel and juice with the cooled gelatin. Add to the egg mixture and continue beating until well blended. Refridgerate, stirring occasionally until mixture is thick enough to mound when dropped from a spoon, about 10 minutes. Whip the cream until thick. Fold into the lemon mixture until no white streaks remain.

In a 2 quart glass bowl or 8 large wine or water goblets, place a layer of fruit and top with lemon creme - add another layer of fruit and again top with lemon creme.

Chill 2 - 3 hours before serving.

. . . hope your readers enjoy these recipes as much as we have . . .

Jim Pattison

VANCOUVER
CANADA

OFFICE OF THE MAYOR

GORDON CAMPBELL
MAYOR

CITY OF VANCOUVER
453 WEST 12TH AVENUE
VANCOUVER, B. C.
V5Y 1V4
TELEPHONE: (604) 873-7621/7622
FAX. NO. (604) 873-7685

GORDON CAMPBELL'S TERIYAKI CHICKEN

4 boneless chicken breasts
1/2 c. soy sauce
1/4 c. dry sherry
1 clove garlic finely minced
2 Tbsp. honey
1 tsp. grated fresh ginger root

Remove skin from chicken. Combine remaining ingredients and pour over chicken. Marinate for 6 - 8 hours. Remove chicken from marinade. Barbeque chicken breasts, basting frequently with the marinade.

Gordon Campbell
MAYOR

BRITISH COLUMBIA JOCKEY CLUB

CHICKEN MARBELLA

Serves 10 to 12

Ingredients:

4 Chickens - quartered (2 1/2 pounds each)
1 head of garlic - finely pureed
1/4 cup dried oregano
Coarse salt and freshly ground black pepper to taste
1/2 cup red wine vinegar
1 cup white wine
1/2 cup olive oil
1 cup pitted prunes
1/2 cup pitted Spanish green olives
1/2 cup capers with a bit of juice
6 bay leaves
1 cup brown sugar
1/4 cup fresh cilantro, finely chopped

1. In a large bowl combine chicken quarters, garlic, oregano, pepper and coarse salt to taste, vinegar, olive oil, prunes, olives, capers and juice, and bay leaves. Cover and let marinate, refrigerated, overnight.

2. Preheat oven to 350F degrees.

3. Arrange chicken in a single layer in a large shallow pan and spoon marinade over it evenly. Sprinkle chicken pieces with brown sugar and pour white wine around them.

4. Bake for 50 minutes to one hour, basting frequently with pan juices. Chicken is done when thick pieces, pricked with a fork at their thickest, yield clear yellow (rather than pink) juice.

5. With a slotted spoon transfer chicken, prunes, olives and capers to a serving platter. Moisten with a few spoonfuls of pan juices and sprinkle generously with cilantro.

6. To serve cold, cool to room temperature in cooking juices before transferring to a serving platter. If chicken has been covered and refrigerated, allow it to return to room temperature before serving. Spoon some of the reserved juice over chicken.

Charles Diamond

The Track - Exhibition Park Vancouver, British Columbia, Canada V5K 3N8 604 254-1631 Fax 604 251-0411

Our specialty is the human touch

CHICKEN DIJON

Heat oven to 350°.

3/4 cup uncooked rice
2 chicken breasts

2 cups whipping cream
3/4 cup dry white wine
2 Tbsp. Dijon mustard
1 onion, minced
1/4 tsp. salt
1/8 tsp. white pepper
1/4 tsp. tarragon

2 Tbsp. butter, melted
1/3 cup fine dry bread crumbs
1 tsp. paprika

Place uncooked rice in a baking dish. Skin and halve chicken breasts. Lay the four pieces on top of the rice.

Beat together the next 7 ingredients and pour over the chicken and rice. Mix melted butter, crumbs and paprika and sprinkle over the chicken.

Bake, uncovered at 350°F for about 1 1/4 hours or until bubbly.

Borrowed recipe - good, easy.

Yours sincerely,

N. K. Barth,
President.
NKB/mr
Encls.

3935 Kincaid Street, Burnaby, B.C. V5G 2X6 Telephone: (604) 434-4211, Fax: 434-5294

norwood group

norwood construction ltd.
norwood concrete structures ltd.
norwood project management ltd.
norwood management ltd.
norwood investments ltd.

Dear Ms. Anderson:

RE: All-Celebrity Cookbook

Thank you for you kind invitation to provide a recipe for inclusion in the Cookbook being produced by the Burnaby Chamber of Commerce.

Attached for your consideration, is my own recipe for Honey Dill Chicken which is easy to prepare and is one of our family's favourite dishes.

I wish you every success in your endeavour and look forward to seeing the All-Celebrity Cookbook in print.

HONEY DILL CHICKEN

2 lbs. Chicken
1/4 cup Dijon Mustard
1/4 cup Honey
1/3 cup Butter
1 Clove of Garlic, Crushed
2 tsp. Fresh Dill

* Brown Chicken
* Arrange in greased baking dish
* Combine remaining ingredients
* Pour Over Chicken
* Cover and Bake at 350° for 1 hour

Makes 6 Servings

****

Yours very truly,

NORWOOD GROUP

Peter M. Foreman
President

Suite #601 - 1001 West Broadway, Vancouver, B.C., Canada V6H 4B1 Tel.: (604) 733-1001 Fax.: (604) 733-0849

Thanks for asking me to participate
MiJung

SPICY LIME CHICKEN

2/3 cup soy sauce
3 tbsp honey
1/3 cup lime juice (2 limes)
1 small chopped onion
1 clove garlic minced
1 tbsp curry powder
1 tbsp chili powder
1 tbsp ground pepper
1 lb. lean chicken pieces

Combine all ingredients.
Marinate several hours or overnight.
Bake 45 min – 1 hour at 350°
or grill on skewers on barbecue.
Serve with rice.
Chicken can be replaced with beef or pork.
Enjoy!

MiJung Lee

BCTV, A Division of Westcom TV Group Ltd.
Box 4700, Vancouver, B.C. V6B 4A3 (604) 420-2288 FAX: (604) 421-9427

This is my favourite recipe, but I have to give full credit to my housekeeper, Miriam, since I rarely have time to cook. Miriam, in turn, would like to give proper credit to "The Best of Bridge" cookbook.

CHICKEN CASSEROLE

2 cups	Chicken, cooked and cubed
1 cup	Chopped Celery
3 cups	Cooked Rice
1 Cup	Mayonnaise
2 Tbsp.	Chopped Onions
1 Can	Cream of Chicken Soup
1 Can	Cream of Mushroom Soup
3/4 tsp.	Salt
3/4 tsp.	Pepper
2 Tbsp.	Lemon Juice
2 Cubes	Chicken Bouillon, dissolved in 1/2 cup water

Combine all ingredients, mixing thoroughly. Place in a casserole. Cover with crushed potato chips. Bake at 400° for 45 minutes, or until heated through.

Serves Eight.

Bill Comrie
Team Owner

SURREY TRAINING FACILITY,
10605 - 135 STREET,
SURREY, B.C. V3T 4C8
TEL: (604) 583-7747 FAX: (604) 583-7882

HEAD OFFICE

4567 Canada Way
Burnaby, B.C.
V5G 4T1

Tel: (604) 268-5000
Fax: (604) 268-5560

CHICKEN PAPRIKA

1 X 2-1/2 to 3-pound broiler-fryer, cut-up
salt
3 tablespoons paprika
3 tablespoons salad oil
1 medium onion, coarsely chopped
1 cup chicken broth
1 cup sour cream
chopped parsley for garnish
hot cooked noodles

About 50 minutes before serving:

Rub chicken pieces with 1 teaspoon salt and 2 tablespoons paprika. In 12-inch skillet over medium heat, in hot salad oil, cook chicken until browned on all sides; pour off drippings. Add onion, 1 cup chicken broth and 1/2 cup wqter; heat to boiling. Reduce heat to low; cover and simmer 30 minutes or until chicken is fork-tender.

Remove chicken to warm platter; keep warm. In same skillet over low heat, stir sour cream with one tablespoon paprika and 1/4 teaspoon salt; heat, stirring constantly, until mixture is hot. (Do not boil.) Pour sauce over chicken; sprinkle with parsley. Serve with noodles. Makes 4 servings.

Submitted by Dennis and Jean Barkman

Sincerely,

Dennis Barkman
President

Deep-Fried Marinated Chicken
"Toriniku Tatsuta-age"

4 Servings

- 2 pounds (900g) boned chicken

Marinade:

- 6 Tbsps. sake
- 3 Tbsps. light soy sauce
- 1 Tbsp fresh ginger juice
- 2 Tbsps very finely chopped green onion

- Oil for deep-frying
- 1 cup flour

To prepare:

Cut chicken into generous bite-sized pieces, with skin

Mix ingredients for marinade in a bowl, add chicken pieces, and mix thoroughly with your hands. Marinate 30 minutes.

To deep-fry:

Bring a generous amount of oil to medium temperature (340°F/170°c.) in a heavy-bottomed pot or deep-fryer. Drain the marinade from the chicken and dust the chicken lightly with flour. Use your hands to toss and coat individual pieces thoroughly. Let coated chicken rest for 2-3 minu

Slide chicken into hot oil, a few pieces at a time. Turn and separate individual pieces as they deep-fry. Skim the oil occasionally. As the chicken is finished, remove and drain on absorbent paper towel. Keep hot.

To serve:

Place 6 to 8 bite-sized pieces of deep-fried chicken on a sheet of folded white absorbent paper on individual plates or small bamboo basketwork trays

KAZUYOSHI AKIYAMA
CONDUCTOR - VSO

Canadian Broadcasting Corporation
Société Radio-Canada

NEWS ANCHOR CURRIED CHICKEN (An Evans family favorite !)

Ingredients:

* 6 chicken breast halves
* 2 cups water
* 1/2 cup butter
* 1/4 cup vegetable oil
* 2 cloves of garlic (minced)
* 2 cups of chopped onions
* 2 cups of chopped, peeled apples
* 1 cup of chopped celery
* 1/2 cup of chopped, seeded green pepper
* 2 large tomatoes (peeled and chopped)
* 1/2 cup all-purpose flour
* 3 tablespoons of curry powder (or to taste)
* 2 tablespoons of brown sugar
* 2 teaspoons of Worcestershire sauce
* 1 teaspoon of ground ginger
* 1 teaspoon of salt
* 1/2 cup raisins
* 1/4 cup desiccated coconuts

Method:

In large roasting pan arrange chicken pieces, add water, cover and bake in 350 degree F. oven for about one hour. Cool in cooking liquid, then remove chicken pieces reserving cooking liquid; remove skin and bone and cut meat into bite-size pieces. Drain chicken broth and add water if necessary to make 4 cups. Set aside.

In large skillet over medium heat, heat butter and oil with garlic. When hot, add onions, apples, celery, green pepper, and tomatoes, cook until soft stirring frequently. Add flour, curry to taste, sugar, Worcestershire, ginger, salt to taste. Cook for three minutes, stirring well.

Add reserve chicken broth, raisins and coconut. Stirring constantly, bring to boil. Reduce heat and simmer for 15 to 20 minutes. Add cooked chicken and simmer for 15 to 20 minutes longer.

Serve with rice and an assortment of condiments in separate bowls. Makes 10 to 12 servings.

Yours truly,

Kevin Evans
CBC NEWS

Classy Chicken

MOHAWK

Ingredients:

3 chicken breasts - skinned and deboned
1/4 teaspoon pepper
3 tablespoons oil
1 10oz. pkg frozen asparagus or broccoli
1 10 oz. can cream of chicken soup
1/2 mayonnaise
1 teaspoon curry powder
1 teaspoon lemon juice
1 cup grated cheddar cheese

Cut chicken into 2" x 2" pieces and sprinkle with pepper. Fry slowly in oil over medium heat until white and opaque - about 6 minutes - then drain. Cook asparagus or broccoli until tender crisp (only a few minutes), then drain and arrange in bottom of buttered casserole. Place chicken on top. Mix soup, mayonnaise, curry and lemon juice together and pour over chicken. Sprinkle top with cheddar cheese and bake uncovered at 375 degrees for 30 to 35 minutes. Serves 4-6. Serve chicken with rice, green salad.

Jambalaya

Cook in large pot:
3 strips of bacon chopped

add
3 tablespoons chopped onion
3 tablespoons chopped celery
3 tablespoons chopped green pepper
2 tablespoons parsley

add
1 large can tomatoes (28oz), juice and all
1 teaspoon salt
1 teaspoon worcestershire sauce
1 teaspoon chili powder
1/2 teaspoon cayenne pepper

add
1 cup chopped cooked ham
1 cup chopped cooked chicken

cook above for 1 hour - stir occassionally; just before serving add 1 can shrimp, heat and serve over cooked rice.

Regards. Rene

MARK DRIESSCHEN

UTV-CKVU/A Member of
The CanWest Global System
Channel 10/Cable 13
180 West 2nd Avenue
Vancouver, BC
Canada V5Y 3T9
Tel: 604-876-1344
Fax: 604-874-8225

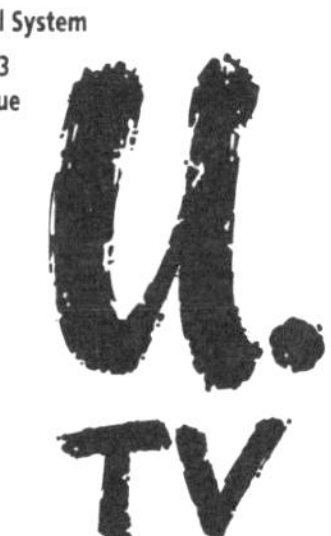

CHICKEN N SHRIMP CREOLE

1½ lb BONELESS CHICKEN
1 TBSP VEGTABLE OIL
2 ONIONS - COARSLEY CHOPPED
3 GARLIC CLOVES - MINCED
1 CAN TOMATOES 28 oz (UNDRAINED)
4 CUPS CHICKEN STOCK
1 TSP DRYED THYME
1 TSP OREGANO
1/4 TSP CAYENNE PEPPER
2 CUPS CONVERTED RICE
1 lB MEDIUM SHRIMP
1/2 CUP CHOPPED PARSLEY

- REMOVE SKIN FROM CHICKEN, CUT INTO CUBES
- COOK IN OIL FOR 3 MINUTES OVER MEDIUM HEAT IN SKILLET
- ADD ONIONS AND GARLIC, COOK FOR 3 MORE MINUTES
- STIR IN PEPPERS, ADD TOMATOES (BREAKING WITH THE BACK OF THE SPOON, OF COURSE!) (BACHELOR'S NOTE)
- ADD STOCK, THYME, OREGANO, CAYENNE - BRING TO BOIL
- STIR IN RICE, COVER, REDUCE HEAT AND SIMMER FOR 25 MINUTES OR UNTIL LIQUID ABSORBED
- COOK SHRIMP IN BOILING WATER FOR 3 MINUTES, DRAIN AND COOL 5 MINUTES, PEEL
- ADD SHRIMP AND PARSLEY TO RICE MIX
- ENJOY!!

Where U. Live

Hi Abby/Shelly

Yes, I will be more than happy to submit a couple of recipes... thousands of people just love them (well, two people).

If there is any other information you would like to know, just phone me.

Respectfully yours,

MURRAY GOLDMAN

LEMON-DIJON CHICKEN

6	Boneless Chicken Breast Halves
1/4 cup	Margarine or Butter
3 tblsp	Dijon Mustard
3 tblsp	Fresh Lemon Juice
1 1/2 tsp	Tarragon

Freshly Ground Pepper

Preheat oven to 375° F

Place Chicken in a shallow baking pan.

In a small saucepan, melt butter or margarine.

Stir in Mustard, Lemon Juice, Tarragon and pepper. Pour over Chicken.

Bake Chicken for 45 Minutes.

Spoon Sauce from pan over chicken.

Serves (6)

MURRAY GOLDMAN LTD. Head Office: 910 Richards Street, Vancouver, B.C. V6B 3C1 (604) 687-2221
MURRAY GOLDMAN BUS STOP BOYS' CO. THE CLOTHING MARKET

Hodson Manor, 1254 West 7th Avenue, Vancouver, B.C., Canada V6H 1B6
Tel.: (604) 738-6822 Fax: (604) 738-7832

Abby Anderson
General Manager
Burnaby Chamber of Commerce
#149 - 9855 Austin Avenue
Professional Wing, Lougheed Mall
Burnaby, BC
V3J 1N4

Dear Abby,

I hope it isn't too late to submit recipes for the All-Celebrity Cookbook!

I am attaching three recipes courtesy of the Vancouver Chamber Choir's Artistic and Executive Director, Jon Washburn. Jon is a "commuting conductor" as he also serves as the Artistic Director of the Phoenix Bach Choir, in Phoenix Arizona. With this in mind Jon has concocted some South of the border recipes! I have also enclosed his biography in case there is some way you can also use it.

I wish you the best of luck with this enterprise. We are pleased to take part in this publication and look forward to seeing it when it is published.

With kind regards,

Sarah Eades
Marketing & Development Manager

Hodson Manor, 1254 West 7th Avenue, Vancouver, B.C., Canada V6H 1B6
Tel.: (604) 738-6822 Fax: (604) 738-7832

Maestro's Chicken Bake

2 cups small corn chips
2 cups cooked chicken or turkey, cubed
1 10.5 oz. can cream of chicken soup
1 4 oz. can diced green chilies
2 medium tomatoes, diced
1 cup grated cheddar cheese
1 cup sour cream
1 cup guacamole (optional)

Place chips in the bottom of a glass casserole. Scatter chicken pieces on top of chips. Mix soup and chilies together and pour over all. Top with tomatoes and sprinkle grated cheese over the top. Bake at 350 degrees for 25-30 minutes or microwave for 12-15 minutes on medium. Garnish with sour cream and guacamole before serving.

Jon Washburn
Executive Director, Vancouver Chamber Choir

The Richmond Hospital

7000 Westminster Highway
Richmond
British Columbia
Canada V6X 1A2
Phone: (604) 278-9711
Fax: (604) 244-5191

CHICKEN & CASHEWS

Sauce:

- 1/2 cup ketchup
- 4 tsp. soy sauce
- 1/2 tsp. salt
- 2 tbsp. Worchestershire Sauce
- 3 tbsp. sugar
- 1 1/2 tsp. sesame oil
- 1 1/4 tsp. cayenne pepper
- 1/2 cup chicken broth

Ingredients:

- 2 tbsp. corn starch
- 1/2 tsp. sugar
- 1/4 tsp. salt
- 3 whole chicken breasts, cubed
- 1/4 cup vegetable oil
- 2 - 3 tbsp. ginger root
- 1 tbsp. garlic
- 1 small onion, chopped
- 2 red peppers
- 2 carrots
- 2 cups snow peas
- 1 1/2 cups cashews

Preparation:

1. Combine ingredients for sauce - set aside.
2. Combine corn starch, sugar and salt - toss with chicken breasts.
3. Heat WOK, add oil - hot, but not smoking.
4. Add chicken, ginger, garlic and onion.
5. Stir-fry till chicken opaque - 1 minute.
6. Add peppers and carrots - cook 2-3 minutes.
7. Add snow peas and sauce.
8. Cook - stirring until it comes to a boil.
9. Add cashews.
10. Serve immediately over rice.

Lynda Cranston
President & Chief Executive Officer

Human life is sacred

ONION PIE

the flavor of tender, sweet onions is highlighted by melted cheddar cheese

3/4 cup soda cracker crumbs
1/4 cup butter, melted
2 cups thinly sliced onions, separated into rings
2 tablespoons butter or margarine
2 eggs, beaten
3/4 cup milk
1/4 teaspoon salt
dash pepper
1/2 cup shredded cheddar cheese

Combine cracker crumbs with 1/4 cup melted butter. Press crumbs into the bottom and up the sides of an 8 inch pie plate. In a small saucepan, combine onions with 2 tablespoons butter, cover and cook over low heat until onions are soft and transparent. Spoon onions over cracker crust in pie plate. In a small bowl, beat eggs with milk, salt and pepper; pour over onions. Sprinkle cheese over all. Bake in a 350° oven for 30 minutes or until a knife inserted in the center comes out clean. Serves 4.

GREEK CHICKEN AND POTATOES

4 SERVINGS

1 3½-pound chicken, quartered
6 russet potatoes (about 3¼ pounds), peeled, quartered lengthwise
4 large garlic cloves, halved
¾ cup canned low-salt chicken broth
¾ cup olive oil
⅔ cup fresh lemon juice
2 teaspoons dried oregano, crumbled

Preheat oven to 375°F. Arrange chicken, potatoes and garlic in large roasting pan. Season with salt and pepper. Pour broth over. Whisk olive oil, lemon juice and oregano to combine. Pour evenly over chicken and potatoes.

Bake until chicken is cooked through and golden brown and potatoes are tender, basting occasionally with pan juices, about 1 hour 15 minutes.

Bob Bose

THE CORPORATION OF THE DISTRICT OF SURREY, 14245-56th AVENUE, SURREY, B.C. V3X 3A2
PHONE 591-4126 FAX 591-5175

Abby Anderson, CAE.
General Manager.
Burnaby Chamber of Commerce
Ste. 149 - 9855 Austin Ave
Professional Wing, Lougheed Mall
Burnaby, B.C. V3J 1N4

Dear Abby,
I was thrilled to be asked to submit a recipe or two for your All-Celebrity Cookbook.
I am an avid collector of cookbooks. My only problem was limiting myself to 1-2 submissions.
I have chosen two that I receive raves for from dinner guests.
The Cornish game hen is a prize winning recipe obtained from a popular fishing resort in Oregon.
The cheese wheel is simple but impressive and has always been a winner for me.
Lots of love with your project. I'll be watching for your book.

Sincerely
Marie Preisl.

CORNISH GAME HENS WITH FRUITED WILD RICE STUFFING

½ cup whole cranberries, fresh or frozen
1 cup water
⅓ cup chopped dried apricots
1 tablespoon light corn syrup
1 tablespoon dry sherry
½ cup finely chopped onion
2 garlic cloves, minced
1 tablespoon minced fresh ginger root
5 tablespoons butter
2⅔ cup chicken stock
1 6oz. pkg. long grain and wild rice (your uncle Ben's will do)
½ cup pine nuts or slivered almonds, toasted
4 Cornish game hens (about 20oz. each) rinsed and patted dry
2 tablespoons soy sauce
1 tablespoon apricot preserves
Dried apricot halves (optional)
Parsley (optional)

Combine cranberries and water in medium saucepan. Boil for 1 minute or until skins pop. Remove from heat. Add apricots. Let stand for 1 minute. Drain, reserving liquid. Stir the sugar, corn syrup and sherry into cranberries and apricots. Set aside. Heat 2 tablespoons butter over medium heat and cook onion, garlic, ginger for 1 minute. Add 2 cups broth and the rice to onion mixture. Bring to a boil. Reduce heat, cover and simmer 25 minutes. Stir reserved fruit mixture and pine nuts into rice. Place about ½ cup rice stuffing into each hen cavity. Skewer openings. Place hens on a rack in large, shallow roasting pan. Melt 2 tablespoons of remaining butter, add soy sauce and baste the hens evenly. Bake in preheated 350° oven for 1 hour. or until juices run clear when hens are pierced with a fork. Baste every 15 minutes while hens are cooking.

Remove hens from rack. Keep warm. Add reserved fruit liquid and remaining ⅔ cup chicken stock to degreased pan drippings. Bring to a boil. Continue to cook to reduce by half (or to desired thickness). Stir in the remaining 1 tablespoon butter and the apricot preserves. Serve the apricot glaze over the hens.

Garnish: Apricot halves and Parsley. Serves 4.

Marie Priessl
Actor

RICOTTA AND SPINACH STUFFED CHICKEN BREASTS
with a WHITE WINE AND DILL SAUCE

(a principal dish for four)

INGREDIENTS:

Spinach leaf	1 bunch	washed and stems removed
Olive oil	2 tbsp	
Onion	2 tbsp	minced
Garlic	1 clove	crushed
Oregano (fresh)	1/2 tsp	chopped,or 1/4 tsp dry
Dill (fresh)	1 tsp	or 1/2 tsp dry
Oyster mushrooms	1/2 lb (225 g)	sliced, regular mushrooms can be substituted
White wine	1/4 cup	Grey Monk Pinot Auxerois
Ricotta cheese	1/2 lb (225 g)	
Parmesan cheese	1 1/2 oz (50 g)	grated
Bread crumbs	2 tbsp	
Salt & black pepper	to taste	
Chicken Breasts	4 pc. (6 oz ea.)	Boneless, with 'filet' intact
Butter	2 tbsp	for browning

METHOD:

Steam the spinach for approx. 30 seconds or until wilted. Cool immediately under cold running water then drain very well, squeezing all excess water, then chop coarsely. Saute the onions in olive oil until translucent. add the mushrooms and garlic and saute until softened.Add the wine, dill and oregano and reduce liquid completely. Set aside to cool. In a bowl, combine the chopped spinach, sauteed mushrooms, ricotta, parmesan and breadcrumbs. Blend thoroughly and season with salt and pepper to taste. To stuff the chicken, hold the boneless breast like a cone, with the pointed end down, gently open the cavity behind the filet. Open the cavity with your finger and carefully stuff 1/4 of the mixture deep into the pocket. Brown the stuffed breasts in a skillet with a little butter, season with salt and pepper and bake in a 350° degree oven for 20-25 minutes Serve with a white wine-dill sauce (see recipe).

WHITE WINE DILL SAUCE

Shallots	2 medium	minced
Butter	1 tbsp (15 g)	
White wine	1/4 cup (60 ml)	Grey Monk Pinot Auxerois
Lemon juice	1/2 tsp (3 ml)	
Brown veal stock	1 cup (236 ml)	(demi glace)
Fresh dill	1 tbsp	chopped (or 1 tsp dry)
Heavy cream	1/4 cup (60 ml)	

METHOD:

In a saucepan saute the shallots in butter, add the white wine and reduce by half. Add the lemon juice and veal stock and simmer 10-15 minutes, reducing by 1/4. Add the cream, dill and salt and pepper and continue simmering until slightly thickened and shiny.

RECOMMENDED WINE: GREY MONK PINOT AUXEROIS

SUITE 100 • 999 CANADA PLACE • VANCOUVER • B.C. • V6C 3C1 • TEL.(604) 684-1339 • FAX (604) 684-7339

CITY OF COLWOOD
3300 Wishart Road, Colwood, B.C. V9C 1R1

(604) 478-5541 - ADMINISTRATION/CITY CLERK
(604) 478-5999 - ENGINEERING & BUILDING INSPECTIONS
(604) 478-5530 - FINANCE & PROPERTY TAXES
(604) 478-5590 - PLANNING & ZONING
(604) 474-4133 - PUBLIC WORKS YARD
(604) 478-7516 - FAX

Burnaby Chamber of Commerce
Suite # 149 - 9855 Austin Avenue
Professional Wing
Lougheed Mall
Burnaby, British Columbia
V3J 1N4

ATT: **Abby Anderson, C.A.E.**
General Manager

Dear Abby Anderson:

The following is one of my favourite recipes for roasting chicken. It is a simple recipe with easy accessible ingredients.

Roast Chicken -- Chinese Style

1 -- 3 to 4 lb. fryer chicken

1/2 cup soy sauce
1 tbsp. gin or sherry
1 tbsp. honey
1/2 tsp. salt
2 cloves garlic crushed
2 stalks green onion, cut in 1/2 inch lengths
chinese parsley (optional)

MIx marinate ingredients together and place into plastic bag. Add chicken and marinate 45 minutes in plastic bag. Remove chicken from bag and place in shallow baking pan on a rack. Bake in preheated 350° oven for 30 minutes on each side or until done. Cut into serving pieces and garnish with cut green onions and chinese parsley.

Yours sincerely,

Mayor Harry Chow,
City of Colwood

4949 Canada Way, Burnaby, B.C. V5G 1M2

Councillor: **LEE RANKIN**

TANDOORI CHICKEN

Preparation time:	25 minutes
Ingredients:	1/2 kg skinless chicken pieces, thighs or drumsticks 2 tbsp 'Patak' Tandoori Paste (available in the Canadian Superstores in the E. Indian section) 2 tbsp plain yoghurt
Cooking Method:	Wash, drain, pat dry the chicken pieces & set aside. Mix the tandoori paste & yoghurt in a microwave casserole dish. Place the chicken pieces in this mix & coat the pieces well with the paste. Put the lid on the casserole dish & cook in the microwave for 10 minutes at high setting. Remove it from the microwave when done. Now pick the chicken pieces & place them on a baking tray. Throw away the remaining sauce in the casserole. Place the baking tray with the chicken in a preheated oven at 325 for exactly 5 minutes. Remove it from oven & it is ready to be served.

HARRY HEINE, R.S.M.A.

TARRAGON CHICKEN.

This recipe, which I found in the Times Colonist newspaper some years ago, has long been a favourite with my family and guests.

The original recipe called for chicken breasts with bones in and skin on, but I prefer the dark meat and so I do the whole chicken, including wings.

1 whole frying chicken, cut into serving size pieces.
1 tablespoon butter.
1 tablespoon plus one teaspoon finely chopped Tarragon. (a little less if dried)
½ cup dry white wine, more if needed.
3/4 cup chicken broth.(or Chicken-in-a-mug will do.)
½ cup heavy cream.

Trim the chicken, separate thighs, drumsticks etc, leaving skin on but removing excess fat. Sprinkle with salt & pepper. Heat butter (and a little oil) in a heavy skillet large enough to hold chicken in one layer. Brown lightly on both sides. Sprinkle with Tarragon, pour wine and broth to cover and cook until done - usually about 30 minutes. (I like it well done.) Transfer pieces to a dish and keep warm. Reduce cooking liquid to about 1/2 cup, add cream and bring to a boil. The original recipe suggests straining the sauce but I don't. You can pour the sauce over the chicken but I add the chicken to the sauce to reheat for a few minutes. This serves four people.

Harry Heine
Noted BC Artist

Dear Ms. Anderson:

Recently I received your letter (via my publisher) requesting a recipe or two for your upcoming cookbook. If it's not too late, I'd like to offer my neophyte recipe for your consideration.

Roast Chicken

one chicken (deceased)
one Spanish onion (in transit)
one tablespoon paprika (powdered)
one tablespoon oregano (ground)
one tablespoon bay leaf (in tiny bits)
one quarter cup butter

1. Check the chicken's body cavity for foreign objects, such as a neck, feet, or those little bags of loose parts. Remove and simmer in a pot. Feed the soft bits to the dog. Throw the neck out or give it to grandad. Save the stock for gravy.

2. Peel the onion without crying. Cut the onion into quarters, and place in the body cavity where the other bits used to be.

3. Using a knife and surgeon-like precision, make two parallel incisions in the skin of the breast of the bird. Insert half a wedge of the butter into each cut.

4. Garnish the bird liberally with paprika, oregano and bay leaf.

5. Roast in the oven at 325 , about 25 min per pound. If you think the bird is lonely, baste once or twice.

6. Remove bird from pan. Test-nibble skin.

7. To make gravy, mix the melted fat in the bottom of the roasting pan with flour until a roux is formed. (A roux is a ball of fat and flour that looks almost dry.) You might think if you place it on the stove at low heat it will burn. It will. Place the pan on the stove at low heat anyway, and mix in some of the chicken stock the dog didn't get. Stir until the mixture thickens. Add vegetable water from boiled potatoes or carrots and mix to desired viscosity. Add salt and pepper to taste.

8. Carve and serve the chicken with vegetables, fresh rolls, white wine, and anything else whose calories you've given up counting.

I hope this will meet your needs - and that it's not too late.

Many thanks for your invitation.

Sincerely,

Don Dickinson

Don Dickinson

Don Dickinson
Award winning fiction novelist

Energy, Mines and Resources Canada

Geological Survey of Canada
Cordilleran Division
400-100 West Pender, Vancouver
V6B 1R8

Énergie, Mines et Ressources Canada

Commission géologique du Canada
Division De La Cordillere
400-100, rue Pender, Vancouver
V6B 1R8

As a field geologist who spends as much as 3 months a year out in the wilds of Canada I thought it might be nice to share a "bush" recipe with you. Critical for such a recipe is that it be simple, quick, easy to prepare and **filling**!! It is amazing how hungry you get after 10 to 12 hours of bush whacking, carrying packs that grow heavier as the day grows longer, accumulating rock sample after rock sample. This recipe comes from my mother who served it on many a camping expedition long before I even knew what the word geologist - yet alone volcanologist meant! It can be dressed up if you are close to a grocery store with fresh produce - or have lots of time to prepare the chicken both from scratch - but it is great using all those cans and dried herbs in the bottom of your grocery supply box!

Chicken and Mushroom Risotto

50 ml cooking oil/margarine/butter
250 ml long grain white rice (use brown rice if you like, but remember it will take another 30 minutes cooking time)

heat oil in a large skillet, add rice and saute until rice becomes golden brown add:

125 ml minced cooking onion (use cut up green onions if you have them, but an ordinary onion will do fine, as will reconstituted dried onion if that is all you have)

reduce heat and add:

500 ml chicken broth (use chicken bullion cubes for the speed version!)

simmer for 15 minutes. Add:

400 ml cooked chicken, cubed (for the camp version I use two or three cans of cooked chicken; turkey tastes great as well!)
125 ml grated cheddar cheese
1 can mushrooms (whole or pieces, you choose; add fresh if they are available)
pinch of:
- salt
- basil (use fresh if available - the taste difference is incredible)
- oregano (as above, you will never regret using fresh herbs!)
- pepper (fresh ground! I always take my grinder to the field with me!)

heat through and serve! This will serve two hungry geologists or four not so hungry town folk. In town serve with a crisp green salad, warm french bread and a bottle of white wine. Enjoy!

Dr. C.J. (Catherine) Hickson
Research Scientist/Volcanologist

Canada

1842-1992
Geological Survey of Canada
150 Years of Service to the Nation

1842-1992
Commission géologique du Canada
Au service de la nation depuis 150 ans

Blueberry Chicken

Takes about 5 minutes to organize and ½ an hour to cook. Gather up 2 whole chicken breasts – skinned, boned and split; ½ a cup of apricot jam, 3 tablespoons of Dijon mustard; ½ a cup of blueberries – fresh or frozen; and ⅓ of a cup of white wine vinegar.

Heat some oil – salad or olive – in a 12 inch frying pan over medium high heat. Add chicken and cook 3 minutes on either side. While this is happening stir up the jam and mustard and spread mixture over the browned chicken; sprinkle on the blueberries, reduce heat to medium low, cover and cook for about 15 minutes or until meat is no longer pink. With a slotted spoon lift out the chicken and blueberries onto a platter; keep warm.

Add the vinegar to the pan, turn up the heat and bring to a boil, stirring occasionally. When the sauce has thickened and is reduced by about a third, pour it over the chicken. Might serve 4 people about 300 calories each.

Robert Harlow.

Robert Harlow
Former CBC Radio Producer, founding department head of the Creative Writing department at UBC, well known BC novelist

CHICKEN SOPA

1 2 1/2 lb. fryer

2 cans Cream of Chicken Soup

3/4 cup Chicken Stock

1 large can Evaporated Milk

1 4-oz. can Chopped Green Chili

1/2 tsp. Salt

12 Tortillas

2 tbs. Shortening

1 Medium Onion, Chopped

1 lb. Cheddar Cheese, Grated

Colleen Nystedt

Boil fryer. (Reserve stock.) Remove meat from bone and cut into small pieces. Combine liquids and stir in chicken, chopped green chili and salt. Cut tortillas in half. Dip into hot shortening for a few seconds. Put a layer of tortillas in bottom of casserole, 9 X 13. Spoon on a layer of chicken mixture. Sprinkle with cheese and onion. Repeat until all tortillas and sauce are used. Bake at 350 degrees until bubbling, about 30 minutes. May be prepared in advance and stored in refrigerator. Allow 15 minutes longer cooking time. Serves 8 to 10.

Chicken Sopa is a popular dish throughout the Southwestern U.S. and Mexico.

Canadian Pacific Hotels & Resorts

Breast of Duck
with Saanich Gooseberry Compote

Serves 4

Ingredients

Muscovy Duck Breasts (fat scored in criss-cross pattern)	2

Gooseberry Compote

Red Gooseberries	200 grams
Golden Raisins	60 grams
Celery, diced	1 stalk
Red Onion, diced	1 small
Port	60 ml
Olive Oil	20 ml
Julienne of Spiced Basil	20 grams
Brown Sugar	50 grams
Balsamic Vinegar	30 ml

Method

This compote is best made the day before.

Boil gooseberries with golden raisins and brown sugar until berries cook down, approximately 20 minutes.

Sauté celery and onion in olive oil 3-5 minutes. Add balsamic vinegar and cook 2-3 minutes longer.

Add celery mixture to gooseberries; let cool. Add basil, salt and pepper to taste.

Final

Sear duck breast in very hot thick bottomed fry pan, fat side down (no oil in pan) to release some fat from the skin and to make skin crispy.

Roast breast in oven until breast is rare-medium rare (time depends on thickness of breast). Let stand for 10 minutes. Slice into thin slices, then fan across plates.

Serve on gooseberry compote with potatoes and fresh seasonal vegetables.

Ian Barbour
General Manager

The Empress

Chicken Marsala

1. At your supermarket purchase one package of "Tyson Gourmet Selection Seasoned Chicken Marsala".
2. Remove plate from carton and place in microwave.
3. Heat on HIGH for 6 minutes and 30 seconds.
4. Peel film from plate and serve. Bon Appétit!

Eric Wilson
Microwave Zen Master

Eric Wilson is Canada's best selling author for juveniles.

Pasta

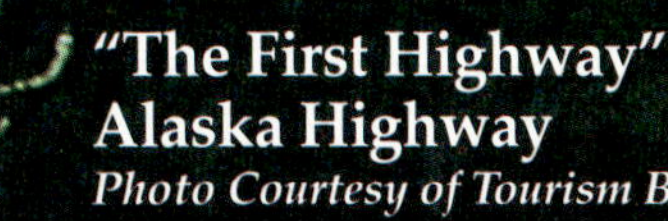

"The First Highway"
Alaska Highway
Photo Courtesy of Tourism B.C.

Spaghetti Bolonese Sauce.

1 Onion
2 cloves Garlic
1 Green Pepper
½ lb Mushrooms
1½ lbs Lean Ground Beef.
½ cup Sundried Tomatoes
2 tins Stewed Tomatoes
1 Sm tin Tomatoe Puree
1 teaspoon Oregano
1 teaspoon Basil
1 teaspoon Italian Mixed Herbs
2 Dashes Tabasco Sauce
Salt & Pepper to Taste.

Chop onions, peppers, mushrooms and saute in olive oil separately Saute Beef with crushed garlic until brown combine and add tomatoes simmer for 30 minutes

Wellington Lee
Silverwing Holidays

Spinach, Mushrooms, and Cream with Spaghetti

4 CUPS SHREDDED FRESH SPINACH LEAVES
1/2 POUND FRESH MUSHROOMS
JUICE OF 1 LEMON
4 TABLESPOONS BUTTER
1 CLOVE GARLIC, CHOPPED FINE
2 TABLESPOONS MARSALA (OR GAREM MASALA)
1 CUP HEAVY CREAM
SALT
FRESHLY GROUND BLACK PEPPER
1/2 POUND SPAGHETTI (OR OTHER PASTA)
4 TABLESPOONS GRATED PARMESAN CHEESE

1. Cook the spinach in boiling, salted water until it is tender. Drain well, and set aside.

2. Wipe the mushrooms with damp kitchen toweling and cut off stem ends. Slice thin, add lemon juice, and mix well.

3. Melt the butter in a skillet, and add the garlic and marsala. Cook for 3 minutes, then add the mushrooms. Cook an additional 5 minutes, then add the cream and bring the mixture to a boil. Add some salt, then pepper liberally. Remove from heat.

4. Cook the spaghetti until al dente. Drain and return it to the pot in which it was cooked. Add first the cooked spinach and then the mushroom mixture to the pasta. Place on individual serving plates, and top each with parmesan cheese.

Serves 2 to 4. Enjoy!

Karen Ydenberg

Dear Abby,

My favorite, quickest main meal salad, given to me by a nice nurse at Lion's Gate Hospital.

Shrimp & Feta Fettuccine

3/4 lb. cooked baby shrimp
1 lb. Feta cheese – crumbled
6 green onions, chopped up.
1 1/2 tsp. oregano
4 Tomatoes, chopped up.
salt, pepper – how much?
– whatever you like.
1/2 lb fettuccine

put everything together except the pasta.
let it stand for an hour –
cook the pasta in boiling salted water –
drain it –
mix it all together – serve it, enjoy it.

Sincerely
Mike McCardell

BCTV, A Division of Westcom TV Group Ltd.
Box 4700, Vancouver, B.C. V6B 4A3 (604) 420-2288 FAX (604) 421-0427

Toni Onley
4279 Yuculta Crescent
Vancouver, British Columbia
V6N 4A9

Dear Abby Anderson
Thank you for your letter of 22 June 93
Here is my contribution to your cookbook recently published in City Food.
Hope this is of help.

Sincerely
Toni Onley

P.S. if you need a photo let me know.
T.

Garlic Paste

Peel a garlic bulb (10 to 12 cloves) put it in the blender and barely cover with olive oil. Blend until almost a paste, and refrigerate. Use within two days.

Fettuccine and Spinach

- Garlic Paste
- One bunch spinach, well steamed
- Pinch of ground nutmeg
- 600 g egg fettuccine
- Grated Parmesan, for garnish
- 125 mL of whipping cream
- Salt and pepper, to taste
- Pine nuts, for garnish
- Parsley, for garnish

In a heavy saucepan, melt a heaping tablespoon (or more, depending on your taste for garlic) of garlic paste. Let the steamed spinach cool a bit, then place in the blender with cream and puree. Add it to the melted garlic paste and let simmer on a low heat for 10 minutes. Add nutmeg, salt and pepper to taste. Meanwhile, cook the egg fettuccine (five or six minutes if freshly made) and drain. Toss fettuccine noodles, spinach puree and pine nuts together in a bowl and serve. Garnish with grated Parmesan and finely chopped parsley. Serves four.

Pepper Salad with Capers

- 4 cups cold water
- Sesame Seed dressing, recipe follows
- 2 Tbsp caper
- 4 large, sweet yellow or red bell peppers

Preheat oven to 375°F. Pour water into a baking dish and place on the lower shelf of the oven. Put peppers on shelf above steaming water. Roast for one hour, turning three or four times. Remove peppers and immediately plunge them into a sink full of cold water. Skins should then peel off quite easily. Remove stems and seeds.

Slice peppers into thin strips and arrange on four plates. Pour on dressing, garnish with capers and serve. (Peppers can be roasted a day ahead and kept refrigerated. Slice thinly just before serving.)

Sesame Seed Dressing

Into a jar, measure equal amounts balsamic vinegar and olive oil. Add 1 tsp of sesame seeds and shake.

Toni Onley
Noted BC Artist

Dear Ms. Anderson,

What a great idea! I can't wait to see the cookbook and hope it's not too late to submit a recipe

I love to cook and always "experiment" on my husband who, fortunately, is very adventorous!

Linguine with Asparagus

This vegetarian dish is one of my husband's favorites - and it takes less than 15 minutes to make - which means it's one of my favorites too!

8 ounces (250g) egg linguine
1 tablespoon (15 ml) butter
2 tablespoons (30 ml) olive oil divided
1 garlic clove
2 cups (500 ml) sliced mushrooms
1 pound (500g) asparagus cut diagonally in 1 inch pieces
½ teaspoon (2 ml) salt
½ cup (125 ml) parmesan
1 tablespoon (15 ml) dry sherry

Cook linguine in large pot of boiling salted water until tender. Drain & keep warm.

In a large frypan or wok, heat butter and one tablespoon oil, add garlic and brown; discard garlic Add mushrooms & stir-fry until tender Remove with slotted spoon and set aside.

Heat remaining oil (15 ml) in frypan Add asparagus and stir-fry until tender crisp, 3-5 minutes.

Add mushrooms, noodles, salt, cheese & sherry to frypan; toss lightly to combine. Heat over medium heat just until hot.

Makes four servings (or 2 big ones for people like my husband!)

Bon Apetit!

Jennifer Mather

BCTV, A Division of Westcom TV Group Ltd.
Box 4700, Vancouver, B.C. V6B 4A3 (604) 420-2288 FAX: (604) 421-9427

CKNW/98
B.C.'S MOST LISTENED TO RADIO STATION
PLAZA OF NATIONS 750 Pacific Boulevard South, P.O. Box 29
Vancouver, B. C. V6B 5E7 Fax (604) 681-5507 Tel. (604) 685-4712

Abby Anderson, C.A.E. General Manager
Burnaby Chamber of Commerce,
Suite 149, 9855 Austin Avenue, (Lougheed Mall),
Burnaby, B.C. V3J1N4.

Dear Ms. Anderson:

Thank you for requesting one of my favorite recipes. I've chosen this one because its quick, easy, never fail and inexpensive. Its great for company or a quiet romantic dinner. I generally serve a salad of butter lettuce with lime and honey dressing, fresh french bread as an appetizer then:

LINGUINE ALLE VONGOLE or LINGUINE with CLAM SAUCE..(serves 4-6)

Pasta:

1lb/450g. linguine (fresh not packaged)
1tbs/mL oil (keeps pasta from sticking)
1 1/2 tbs/20g. salt
4 quarts/4L. cold water

Add oil and salt to water, bring to boil on high heat
Add pasta (cook al dente 3-5 minutes)
Drain and rinse with cold running water. Set aside.

Clam Sauce:

12 oz/350mL. canned\minced clams & liquid
1/4 to 1/2c./50mL to 100mL. dry white wine
1 small onion diced
6 tbsp./85g. butter
1 1/2 tsp. /7g. fresh garlic finely chopped/minced
3 tbsp./45g. fresh parsley finely chopped
2 tbsp. pernod

Lightly Saute' onion & garlic in butter on medium heat in large skillet...careful not to burn.
Add clams & liquid, wine & stir until well blended.
Reduce liquid by simmering on medium heat for about four minutes.
Just prior to serving...add parsley, pernod, freshly ground pepper.

Add linguini to clam sauce...toss, heat and serve immediately on warm plates. If available garnish with half a dozen each, fresh cooked clams in shell.

Bon appetite!

Shirley Stocker,
Executive Producer. DIVISION OF WESTCOM RADIO GROUP LTD.

British Columbia
Institute of Technology

Office of the President

3700 Willingdon Avenue,
Burnaby, British Columbia,
Canada V5G 3H2
Telephone (604) 432-8200
FAX (604) 434-6243

PASTA POT

Yield: Serves 8 - 10

2 lbs. lean ground beef
2 medium onions, chopped
2 cloves of garlic, crushed
2 tbsp. oil
2 c. spaghetti sauce
1 can (19 oz.) stewed tomatoes
1 tsp. salt
1 pinch of sugar
1/2 tsp. basil
1/2 tsp. oregano
1 can (10 oz.) whole mushrooms, drained - reserve liquid
2 c. shell macaroni, medium-sized
2 c. sour cream
1/2 lb. gouda cheese, grated
1/2 lb. mozzarella cheese, grated

Brown meat, onions and garlic in oil. Add spaghetti sauce, tomatoes, salt, sugar, basil, oregano and mushrooms and simmer for 20 minutes. Cook macaroni according to directions. Drain and rinse. Pour half of the cooked shells into greased casserole. Cover with half the meat sauce and then cover with half the sour cream. Top with gouda cheese. Repeat and top with mozzarella cheese.

Cover and bake at 350° for 50 minutes. Uncover and cook 10 more minutes to brown cheese.

N.B. If it doesn't seem moist enough, add some of the liquid from the canned mushrooms. It should be quite sloppy before baking.

John Watson
President

Farfalle Abruzzese
4 people

500 g. farfalle pasta (cooked)
½ cup diced sundried tomatoes
½ cup toasted pine nuts
½ cup chopped green onions
2 tablespoons minced garlic
salt & pepper

3 cups cooked & seasoned tomatoe sauce
1 bunch cooked spinach
½ cup 35% heavy cream.

6 tablespoons olive oil heated in a frying pan, add onions, garlic, pine nuts, fry 2 min. at high heat, add chopped spinach & sundried tomatoes, simmer 2 min. Add cooked tomatoe sauce until boil, add farfalle pasta & cream, simmer 3-4 min. until thick. Serve & add parmesan cheese.

552 West Broadway, Vancouver, British Columbia, V5Z 1E6, Telephone: (604) 876-3534

To Abby Anderson
GM - Burnaby Chamber of Commerce
— As Requested —

From Rafe Mair
CKNW

Rafe's four cheese Penne

1/4 LB. (125 g) Gorgonzola cheese.
1/4 LB (125 g) BRIE, DICED
1/4 LB (125 g) SWISS CHEESE
1 CUP (250 ml) WHIPPING CREAM
1/4 CUP (50 ml.) BUTTER, DICED
1/4 LB (125 g) PROSCIUTTO, DICED
1/2 TSP (2 ml) GROUND BLACK PEPPER
1/4 TSP (1 ml) NUTMEG
1 LB (500 g.) PENNE
1/2 CUP (125 ml) FRESH GRATED PARMESAN

IN A LARGE SKILLET COMBINE GORGONZOLA BRIE + SWISS & CREAM, BUTTER, PROSCIUTTO, PEPPER + NUTMEG WARM OVER LOW HEAT.
COOK PENNE DRAIN + MIX ADD PARMESAN.

Annie (Mundigel) Meraw

Burnaby.
Chamber of Commerce
Abby Anderson C.A.E.
General Manager

Dear Abby.

In answer to your letter to further enhance the growth of tourism in the Province of British Columbia in the way of an All-Celebrity-cookbook.

I feel greatly honoured to have been asked to contribute to your All-Celebrity-cookbook with such greats as those listed in your letter.

I am submitting two of my favourites.

Yours respectfully
Ann Meraw

Ann Meraw
BC Sports Hall of Fame
As a professional distance swimmer, set 7 world distance & endurance records between 1956 and 1958

Ann's
Lasagne Surprise

1½ lbs. ground beef
1½ cups chopped celery
1½ " " onion
½ " " green pepper
2 crushed garlic cloves
1 - 5½ fluid oz. tomatoe paste
1 - 27 " " tomatoe sauce
1 - 28 " " tomatoes (tin)
12 - lasagne noodles
4 cups cottage cheese (creamed)
3 cup grated old cheddar cheese
4 cups grated mozzarella "
½ " parmesan cheese
reserve ¼ cup parmesan cheese

1 tsp. dried oregano
1 " scant salt
½ " celery salt
2 tbs. chopped parsley

Method - reserve 1 cup mozzarella cheese
Brown meat in frying pan - add onion - garlic - season salt. celery salt green pepper - celery. Cook until tender.
Add.
Tomatoe paste - tomatoes - oregano parsley and spaghetti sauce.
Simmer 20 min.
Cook noodles as directed on pkg. and add 2 tsp. oil to water. Cool.
(1) Cover 13"x9"x4" pan with meat sauce.
" with layer of 4 noodles.
(2) " noodles with all cottage cheese, layer of meat sauce and ⅓ of mixed cheeses.
(3) Cover with layer of (4) noodles sauce and mixed cheeses. Repeat this layer using up meat sauce and cheeses - Add parmesan and mozzarella. Top with slices of stuffed olives - red and green pepper slices. Bake covered 45 min. Remove lid last 5 min. - 10 to 12 servings. Can be frozen

Ann (Clundegel) Theraw

Further to your letter of July 14, 1993 enclosed please find a copy of one of my favourite recipes for your All-Celebrity Cookbook.

Thank you for the opportunity to participate in this fun venture.

I would welcome a copy of the cookbook when it is published.

Yours sincerely,

Ted Nebbeling,
Mayor

MAYOR'S PASTA

1/2 lb mushrooms (sliced)
1 lb. veal or beef steak
pinch of salt
pinch of pepper
1 garlic clove (chopped fine)
4 tsps. olive oil

10 sundried tomatoes (sliced thin)
1/2 tsp. capers
6 olives (chopped) - optional
10 basil leaves (chopped)
1 tsp beef stock powder
1/4 ltr. cream

Cook Fettucini and rinse - set aside

Panfry mushrooms - set aside

Mix salt, pepper and garlic with thinly sliced beef or veal

Fry for 3 minutes in hot olive oil, add thinly sliced sundried tomatoes, capers, chopped olives and basil leaves, stir for 2 minutes, add cream and beef stock powder, add mushrooms - bring all to boiling heat.

Add Fettucini and serve when pasta is hot.

A great tasting quick lunch or dinner (enough for four).

Bon appetit from Mayor Ted Nebbeling, Whistler!

4381 BLACKCOMB WAY, BOX 35, WHISTLER, B.C. V0N 1B0
TELEPHONE (604) 932-5535 TOLL FREE 688-6018
FAX: PLANNING (604) 932-6734 FINANCE (604) 932-6217 OTHER DEPARTMENTS (604) 932-6636

Elwood N. Veitch and Associates

4762 CARSON PLACE BURNABY, B.C. V5J 2Y5 (604) 434-8315

Abby Anderson C.A.E.
General Manager
Burnaby Chamber of Commerce

Dear Abby:

As requested here is my recipe for "Pot Luck Spaghetti"

As a former politician I have given up on "eating crow" but perhaps some of the N.D.P members have a recipe in current use.

Best of fortune!

Kind regards

Elwood Veitch

Spaghetti

"POT LUCK" SPAGHETTI

— Elwood Veitch,

- 1¼ lbs. Spaghetti
- 6 oz. onions (chopped)
- 1½ garlic bulbs
- ¾ c. olive oil
- 1½ c. canned tomatoes
- ½ tbsp. Worchestershire sauce
- salt, pepper, cayenne pepper, M.S.G.
- 1 lb. mushrooms (fresh or canned)
- 4 oz. grated Parmesan cheese
- 2 cans corn (niblets)
- 1¼ lbs. chopped beef

Cook spaghetti in salt water until tender.

Fry onion and garlic in oil until golden brown.

Add tomatoes, seasonings and mushrooms and when thoroughly heated stir in one-half of the grated cheese.

When cheese is melted add spaghetti and corn.

Add one-half cup tomatoes to chopped beef mix, then add to first mixture.

Mix well and put in baking pan and sprinkle remainder of cheese on top.

Bake at 300 degrees F not more than 10 minutes. Serves 25 persons.

"COME AND GET IT"

FINANCIAL AND ADMINISTRATIVE SERVICES TO MEDIUM AND SMALL BUSINESSES

CBC Radio
P.O. Box 4600
Vancouver, B.C.
Canada
V6B 4A2

GABEREAU

Abby Anderson
General Manager
Burnaby Chamber of Commerce
Suite # 149
9855 Austin Avenue
Professional Wing, Lougheed Mall
Burnaby, B.C.
V3J 1N4

Dear Abby,

Enclosed is one of Vicki Gabereau's favorite recipes for your Burnaby cookbook.

Diane Clement gave it to her, so she would like Diane to get full credit as well. I took it over the phone, so I hope it makes sense. If you have any questions, please call me and I will try to clarify.

Just for your book information, Vicki's show is called "GABEREAU" and it airs across the country Monday to Friday, 2 to 4 pm (half an hour later in Newfoundland), on CBC AM.

If you have any other questions, please call.

Yours truly,

SPeacock
Sheila Peacock
Producer - GABEREAU

662-6985

encl.

VICKI GABEREAU BRIGHTENS WEEKDAY AFTERNOONS

One of Canada's favorite radio personalities, VICKI GABEREAU extends her celebrated interview show to weekday afternoons, starting Oct. 3 on CBC Radio. Vicki gabs with the famous, the near-famous and the should-be-famous, Monday - Friday, 2:05-4 p.m.*

* 1:05 Sask., Oct. 3-7 only;
* (3:35 and 6:35 nddt.)

CBC Radio
P.O. Box 4600
Vancouver, B.C.
Canada
V6B 4A2

GABEREAU

ONE OF VICKI GABEREAU'S ALL TIME FAVORITE RECIPES COMES FROM THE KITCHEN OF DIANE CLEMENT. DIANE IS A VANCOUVER CHEF, COOKBOOK AUTHOR, COOKING TEACHER, AND CO-OWNER OF "TOMATO FRESH FOOD CAFE" ON CAMBIE STREET. DIANE HAS ALSO BEEN A GUEST CHEF MANY TIMES ON VICKI'S RADIO PROGRAM.

PUTTANESCA (PASTA OF THE NIGHT)

INGREDIENTS:

8 - 10 MEDIUM SIZE TOMATOES
2 SMALL CANS OF ANCHOVIES - DRAINED, PATTED DRY & CHOPPED
1/2 CUP OR MORE BLACK PITTED OLIVES - CHOPPED
5 OR MORE CLOVES OF GARLIC - FINELY CHOPPED
(VICKI LIKES LOTS OF GARLIC)
1/2 TSP DRIED CRUSHED RED PEPPER FLAKES
1 CUP OR MORE OF FRESH BASIL
FRESHLY GROUND BLACK PEPPER
OLIVE OIL (SEE METHOD FOR AMOUNT)*
1 - 1 1/2 POUNDS OF DRIED SPAGHETTI, PENNE OR FETTUCCINE
1 CUP FRESH GRATED PARMIGIANO-REGGIANO OR FRESH GRATED ASAGIO CHEESE (GET EXTRA FOR ADDING AT THE TABLE IF WANTED)

METHOD:

PRE-HEAT OVEN TO 350 DEGREES. IN A LARGE LASAGNE-TYPE PAN (APPROX. 12 X 15), MAKE 2 LAYERS OF ALL THE INGREDIENTS EXCEPT PASTA AND CHEESE - START WITH THE TOMATOES AND END WITH BASIL (SAVING HALF A CUP OF BASIL FOR TOSSING IN WITH THE CHEESE LATER). * DRIZZLE BOTH LAYERS WELL WITH OLIVE OIL AND A GOOD SPRINKLING OF BLACK PEPPER.
BAKE 30 TO 35 MINUTES. IN MEANTIME, PREPARE PASTA. DRAIN AND PUT IN A LARGE SERVING BOWL AND TOSS WITH A WEE BIT OF OLIVE OIL AND HALF OF THE CHEESE. CHOP UP THE COOKED TOMATO MIXTURE AND ADD TO THE PASTA. ADD THE REST OF THE CHEESE AND THE REST OF THE FRESH BASIL.
THERE WILL BE LOTS OF JUICE, SO SERVE WITH CRUSTY ITALIAN BREAD TO MOP IT UP, AND OFFER MORE CHEESE AND BLACK PEPPER TO TASTE.

*** DO NOT LEAVE OUT THE ANCHOVIES - THE FISH TASTE DISAPPEARS WHEN COOKED AND EVEN ANCHOVY HATERS WON'T BE ABLE TO TELL - HOWEVER THE ANCHOVIES ARE AN ESSENTIAL ELEMENT.

**** IF YOU ARE IN A HUGE HURRY (AS PRESUMABLY THE SIENA LADIES OF THE EVENING WHO ARE CREDITED WITH THIS RECIPE WERE...) YOU CAN SIMPLY CHOP UP ALL THE TOMATO SAUCE INGREDIENTS AND THROW THEM INTO A LARGE, HEAVY SKILLET. SIMMER FOR APPOX. 10 - 15 MINUTES AND CARRY ON WITH THE REST OF THE RECIPE.

SERVES SIX REASONABLY HUNGRY DINERS - MORE IF YOU KEEP PUSHING THE BREAD!

PASTA WITH VODKA AND BAKED GARLIC

Ingredients

1 lb penne or other tubular pasta
5 tbsps unsalted butter (may substitute Becel margarine but should be unsalted if possible)
2/3 cup vodka
1 19 oz. can tomatoes
3/4 cup whipping cream
3/4 cup grated Parmesan cheese
2 tsps chili powder (3 chili peppers may be used as an alternate)
12 garlic cloves (peeled but whole)
1 tbsp. olive oil

Instructions

In a large non-corrodible steel pan (a large electric frying pan works very well) grill the garlic cloves in the olive oil until softened and lightly browned. Chop each in half and set aside in a bowl.

In the same pan melt the butter, increase the heat and add the vodka until simmering, add the chili powder and allow to simmer fairly rapidly for two minutes.

Blender the canned tomatoes until liquified. Add the whipping cream and blended tomatoes to the pan and simmer all ingredients together for five minutes.

Prepare the pasta al dente, drain and return to the pasta pot wet. Add the sauce and Parmesan cheese to the pasta and mix well. Provide a large serving on each plate and sprinkle chopped garlics on top. Offer freshly ground pepper when serving.

Leslie Cliff
BC Sports Hall of Fame
Silver medalist in the 400m individual medley, 1972 olympics

Veggies Side Dishes

Premium Potatoes

10 medium potatoes
salted water
1 cup cottage cheese (250ml)
1 cup sour cream (250 ml)
½ c Butter or margarine (125ml)
1 teaspoon salt 5ml
¼ teaspoon pepper 1ml
¼ teaspoon onion powder 1ml

Cook potatoes in small amount of salted water. Drain. Mash.
Add cottage cheese and mash again.
Add sour cream, butter, salt, pepper and onion powder. Mash well. Turn into 3 quart (3L) casserole. Smooth top, cover bake at 325°F (160°c) oven for 30 minutes until hot.

Serves 8.

Harold Barroby
BC Jockey Club

Ethnic cuisine, or *la plus ça change . . .*

Potato and Point: Irishtown, 1893

Boil up one potato for each who will sit to table. Garnish with rue and serve with salt.

Suspend one morsel of bacon or salt pork by a stout cord from the ceiling above the table. Entreat each diner to point at the bacon whilst eating the potato. Give thanks.

Potato and Point: any town, 1993

Save potatoes, margarine, cheddar, and bacon until the day before payday. Microwave or bake one potato for each person until fully cooked. Grate cheddar and put aside. Cook and drain bacon, then dice and put aside. Cut each potato in half lengthwise and scoop out, leaving skins with a shallow layer of potato. Put these aside. Put scooped-out potato in a large bowl and add enough milk and margarine to moisten. Powdered milk will do if you're out of liquid milk. Add bacon. Add some grated cheddar if you have enough. Add finely chopped green onion if you have it. Add salt, pepper and other spices – try sweet basil, oregano or cilantro – to taste. Stir well. Spoon this mixture back into potato shells and top with remaining grated cheddar. Microwave or grill just long enough to melt cheese. Serve with dandelion greens, nasturtium leaves, or any other vegetables on hand.

Hang your grocery bags on the front door knob so you won't forget them when you shop tomorrow. Payday! Give thanks.

Susan Mayse

Susan Mayse
Noted BC Author

Dear Abby:

Thank you for your letter of June 3, 1993, asking me to submit a recipe for your Cookbook. Here's my recipe! I'm not a very good cook, so this is an easy recipe and one dish only!

LIBBY'S SCALLOPED POTATOES PLUS
**** VERY EASY ****

Serves 4

6 potatoes, sliced, with skin on
1/2 Red pepper diced
Broccoli, about 1/2 cup - 1 Cup
2 Carrots, sliced
1/2 Red Onion, diced

1 Cup Shredded Cheese (any kind)
3 Tbsp Flour
1 3/4 cups Milk
1 Tbsp (approx) Margarine
Lots of Pepper

In a Microwave (or small saucepan):

- Melt Margarine
- Gradually add flour and milk and heat until smooth and thickened.
- Add Pepper

Then:

- Arrange potatoes/vegetables in layers in open casserole dish
- Pour sauce over casserole
- Add grated cheese
- Place in oven at 350°F for 1 hour or until vegetables are tender

NOTE: Cooking time can be decreased by parboiling vegetables in microwave for a few minutes.

Yours sincerely,

Libby Davies
COUNCILLOR

LD:emk

CITY HALL • 453 WEST 12TH AVENUE • VANCOUVER, B.C. • V5Y 1V4 • PHONE 873-7273 • FAX 873-7750

Fred Randall, MLA
(Burnaby-Edmonds)
Parliament Buildings
Victoria, B.C. V8V 1X4
Tel: (604) 356-3011
Fax (604) 356-7156

Community Office:
7671 Edmonds Street
Burnaby, B.C. V3N 1B6
Tel: (604) 521-3737
Fax: (604) 775-1101

Abby Anderson,
General Manager,
Burnaby Chamber of Commerce,
Ste. 149 - 9855 Austin Avenue
Burnaby, British Columbia
V3N 1N4

Dear Abby,

Thank you for your letter inviting me to submit favourite recipes for inclusion in the "all-celebrity" cookbook.

Enclosed are two recipes which are firm favourites with my family: Potatoes Romanoff and Papaya Seed Dressing. We have served these dishes to guests on many occasions and always received the response "delicious!". I think your readers will agree.

Again, thank you for inviting me to take part in this project. Please let me know when the cookbook is available.

Good luck!

Yours sincerely,

Fred Randall

Fred Randall, MLA
(Burnaby-Edmonds)

FR/af

Fred Randall, MLA
(Burnaby-Edmonds)
Parliament Buildings
Victoria, B.C. V8V 1X4
Tel: (604) 356-3011
Fax (604) 356-7156

Community Office:
7671 Edmonds Street
Burnaby, B.C. V3N 1B6
Tel: (604) 521-3737
Fax: (604) 775-1101

POTATOES ROMANOFF

6	goodsize	Potatoes
2	(10-ounce) cartons	Dairy Sour Cream
1 1/2	cups	Shredded Sharp Cheddar cheese, divided
1	bunch	Green Onions, chopped
1 1/2	teaspoon	Salt
1/4	teaspoon	Pepper Paprika

Cook potatoes in jackets until fork tender. Peel; SHRED into large bowl. Stir in sour cream, one cup grated cheese, onion, salt and pepper. Turn into buttered
2-quart casserole. Top with remaining cheese; sprinkle with paprika. Cover; refrigerate several hours or overnight.

Bake, uncovered, in moderate oven, 350 deg. F., about 30 to 40 minutes or until heated through. makes 8 to 10 servings.

PAPAYA SEED DRESSING:

1/2	cup	White wine vinegar
1/4	cup	Sugar
1/2	cup	Salad oil
1	teaspoon	Dry mustard
1/2	medium	Onion
1/2	teaspoon	Salt
2	Tablespoon	Papaya seed and pulp (half of a papaya)

Mix in blender on high speed; pour over butter lettuce (2 - 3) adding chopped papaya, sliced avocado and red pepper.

FORSTER FOOD SERVICES LTD.
FORSTER RESTAURANTS LTD.

Burnaby Chamber of Commerce
All-Celebrity Cookbook
Suite #149 - 9855 Austin Avenue
Professional Wing
Lougheed Mall
Burnaby, British Columbia
V3J 1N4

Dear Abby:

The following recipes are two of our family favourites. Our four sons are now married and our daughters-in-law have these recipes in their files as well. The Potato-Spinach Casserole is an excellent one to introduce children to spinach. The Seafood Casserole always gets raves from guests and family on a buffet dinner.

POTATO/SPINACH CASSEROLE

6-8 large potatoes, peeled, cooked and mashed
1 cup (8 ounces) sour cream - lite may be used
2 teaspoons salt
1/4 teaspoon pepper
2 tablespoons chopped chives or green onion tops
1/4 cup butter or margarine
1 package (10 ounces) frozen chopped spinach, thawed and dry/squeeze)
1 cup (4 ounces) shredded cheddar cheese.

Combine all the above ingredients except the cheese in a greased casserole.
Bake uncovered at 400° for 15 minutes.
Top with cheese and bake 5 minutes longer
Yields 6-8 servings.

Sincerely,

FORSTER GROUP OF COMPANIES

W. A. FORSTER
President

9547 - 152nd Street, Surrey, B.C., Canada V3R 5Y5 • Phone: (604) 588-3411

BING THOM ARCHITECTS

1430 Burrard Street (at Beach Ave.) Vancouver, BC V6Z 2A3 Tel. (604) 682-1881 Fax 688-1343

Abby,

Here's your recipe:

COLD NOODLES

measurements are per person

Mix:

1 bowl cooked blanched noodles (preferably Chinese shrimp, scallop or egg noodles, or just any noodles)

1 tsp. soya sauce (to taste)

1 tsp. oyster sauce (if unavailable, just increase the soya sauce)

1 tbsp. diced green onions

couple drops of fresh lemon or lime juice or vinegar

couple drops of sesame oil (or any cooking oil. Excepting for olive oil which is eaten raw, heat the vegetable oil to when it starts smoking to cook it) .

1 tsp. thin slivers of ginger

slivers of cooked meat or B.B.Q. pork (if carnivorous)

UNO LANGMANN LIMITED

fine arts

2117 Granville Street
Vancouver, B.C.
V6H 3E9

Tel. (604) 736-8825
Fax. (604) 736-8826

EGGPLANT SUPREME

Ingredients

4 eggplants
salt
2 litres tomatoes, skinned and chopped
tomatoe paste (approximately 2 cups)
2 green peppers, chopped (optional)
2 onions, chopped (optional)
oregano to taste
basil to taste
3 eggs
2 cups fine bread crumbs
1 litre oil for deep frying
1½ lbs cheese, such as Havarti, in 1/8" slices

Directions

1. Cut four eggplants in 1/2" slices and sprinkle lightly with salt. Spread on cookie sheet between layers of paper towel and refrigerate overnight.

2. Tomatoe sauce - Blend approximately 2 litres of skinless chopped whole tomatoes with enough tomatoe paste to make a thick sauce. Add chopped green peppers. Fry onions and add to sauce. Add oregano, basil, salt and pepper to taste. Bring to a boil and then simmer for approximately one hour. Let stand overnight.

3. Next day - Whip three eggs in shallow bowl. Dip each slice of eggplant in egg wash and then in fine bread crumbs. Deep fry in frying pan until light brown, turning once, and remove from oil. Drain on paper towels in layers on cookie sheet as before.

4. Using several casserole dishes, place a thin layer of tomatoe sauce on bottom of each dish. Follow with a layer of eggplant, a layer of tomatoe sauce and a layer of sliced cheese. Repeat with layers of eggplant, tomatoe sauce and cheese slices until casserole is full, ending with a layer of cheese.

5. Casserole may now be frozen successfully before cooking, the dish does not suffer from this at all. To cook, preheat oven to 375° F. Place dish in heated oven for approximately 45 minutes or until heated through and cheese is melted. Serve with a caesar salad and a light country red wine.

ROYAL BANK

T.W. (Terry) Kehler
Area Manager
Richmond/South Delta

Royal Bank of Canada
6400 No. 3 Road
Richmond, British Columbia
V6Y 2C2

Transit 04800
(604) 665-3200 Fax: (604) 665-3263

BAKED BEANS

1 can pork and beans drained
1 can kidney beans drained
1 can lima beans drained
1 1/2 cup chopped celery
1 1/2 cup chopped onion
1/2 tsp garlic salt
1 1/2 cup brown sugar
1 cup ketchup
bacon strips

Combine first six ingredients and put in casserole dish.
Sprinkle brown sugar over top
Pour ketchup over sugar
Lay bacon strips on top
Bake in 350 degree oven one hour.

BREAD

Combine in large mixing bowl:

1/2 cup oil
1/2 cup sugar
1/2 cup seven grain cereal
1 tbsp. salt
4 cups warm water
1 1/3 cups skim milk powder

Add: 5 cups flour

Beat for 3 minutes.

Beat in: 2 eggs
2 packages or 2 tbsp. fast acting yeast

Mix in: 6 cups flour

Knead for 5 minutes. Place in a greased bowl turning once. Cover and let rise for 1 hour. Punch down, turn over and let rise again until double in bulk. Knead a few minutes, then shape into four loaves and place in greased loaf pans. Cover with cloth and let rise until doubled. Bake at 350 for 30 minutes. Brush tops with margarine and cool.

For brown bread use whole wheat flour plus 1/4 cup molasses if desired.

MAYOR'S OFFICE
511 ROYAL AVENUE
NEW WESTMINSTER, B. C.
V3L 1H9

TELEPHONE
(604) 521-3711
FAX
(604) 521-3895

Abby Anderson, General Manager
Burnaby Chamber of Commerce
Suite #149
9855 Austin Avenue
Professional Wing
Lougheed Mall
Burnaby, B.C.
V3J 1N4

Dear Ms. Anderson:

I have received your letter explaining your cookbook project. I am flattered that you asked me. Enclosed please find two of my family's favourites. I couldn't decide which one to send so maybe you can decide what fits your needs.

Best of luck with your production, I hope it sells well.

Sincerely,

Betty Toporowski
M A Y O R

Enclosure

Red Kidney Bean Curry

Preparation time: overnight plus 15 minutes
Cooking time: 20-45 minutes
Serves: 4 people

Ingredients:

- 2 c. dried red kidney beans washed and soaked overnight in sufficient water to cover
- 2 medium onions, diced
- 4 tbsp oil (can be sautéd in ¼ c water for low fat)
- 1 bayleaf
- 1 inch piece cinnamon stick
- 6 cloves
- 6 small green cardamoms
- 2 green chilies, diced
- 3 cloves garlic, peeled and finely chopped
- 1 inch fresh ginger, peeled and finely diced
- ¾ tsp chili powder
- ¼ tsp. ground tumeric
- 2 tsp. ground coriander
- 1¼ tsp. ground cumin
- 1¼ tsp. garam masala
- 15 oz. can peeled tomatoes, chopped
- ¾ tsp salt (leave out if replacing dried beans with canned)
- 2-3 sprigs fresh parsley, chopped.

Either pressure cook the red kidney beans for 5-6 minutes, or cook them in their soaking water for 20 minutes until soft. Remove from the heat; allow to stand, covered. Sauté the onions in the oil (or ¼ c water) in a large saucepan over moderate heat until transparent. Add the bayleaf, cinnamon, cloves, and cardamoms and fry for 1 minute. Add the chilies, garlic and ginger. Sprinkle with chili powder, tumeric, ground coriander, cumin and garam masala. Stir to mix. Add tomatoes and salt. Cover and simmer 2-3 minutes. Drain the kidney beans reserving the liquid. Add beans to spiced tomatoe mixture. Stir gently and cook 1 minute. Add bean liquid and chopped parsley, cover and simmer 3-5 minutes. Serve over rice.

Elfreida Read

Vegetarian Beans

1 onion (large)
1 green pepper
1 clove garlic (or to taste)
2 Tbsps. Molasses
2 Tbsps. brown sugar
1 Tsp dry mustard
1/3 cup vinegar
1 19 oz can tomatoes
1 can Kidney beans
1 can Lima beans (drained)
1 can beans in tomato sauce (the same as Pork'n Beans without the pork)
1 Tsp. Worcestershire sauce
salt, pepper + tabasco sauce to taste.

Fry onion and pepper. Add garlic. molasses, brown sugar, mustard + vinegar and cook briefly, mixing well. Add remaining ingredients and combine all in a large casserole. Bake 2 to 2 1/2 hrs at 300°, covered. If too much liquid remains bake uncovered until sauce thickens.

Elfrieda Read
A popular author of children's & young adults books

Abby Anderson,
Burnaby Chamber of Commerce,
178 9855 Austin
Burnaby, BC.

Dear Madam
In response to your request for a recipe I send the following:

Blanche's Mustard Ring Serves 10-15

Beat
4 eggs with 1 c water and
½ c cider vinegar

Combine
¾ c sugar
4 tsp dry mustard
1 tbsp unflavoured gelatine
¼ tsp tumeric
½ tsp salt

Add to egg mixture
Cook in dbl boiler till slightly thickened
Cool till partially set.
Fold in 1½ c sour cream
¼ c finely sliced green onion
Pour into circle mold and chill

Sincerely,
(Mrs R.M.) Joan M. McLagan

Joan (Langdon) McLagan
BC Sports Hall of Fame
Set a world record for the 50yd breaststroke in 1940

JOHN MOFFAT'S "MUCHO GRANDE SPINACH CASSEROLE."

WHAT YOU NEED

1. ROASTING PAN 18"x14"
2. 2 TO 3 BAGS OF SPINACH
3. 4 EGGS
4. 2 LARGE TUBS OF DRY CURD COTTAGE CHEESE
5. 1 BRICK OF AGED CHEDDAR CHEESE
6. 1 BRICK OF MONTEREY JACK WITH CARAWAY SEEDS
7. 3 CLOVES OF GARLIC (CRUSHED)
8. 3 HANDFULS OF MUSHROOMS (SLICED)
9. WHEAT GERM (SPRINKLED ON TOP)
10. SALT AND PEPPER
11. BUTTER TO GREASE ROASTING PAN
12. A WORKING OVEN
13. A BOWL
14. GRATER

WHAT TO DO

1. PREHEAT OVEN TO 350°
2. TEAR SPINACH AND CHOP MUSHROOMS
3. GREASE ROASTING PAN. PLACE SPINACH AND MUSHROOMS IN ROASTER
4. MIX 4 EGGS AND 3 MASHED GARLIC CLOVES AND A PALMFUL OF CARAWAY SEEDS PLUS SALT AND PEPPER IN A BOWL
5. SPREAD THIS STUFF OVER THE SPINACH AND MUSHROOMS. USE HANDS TO MIX WELL
6. ADD TUBS OF COTTAGE CHEESE – MIX
7. GRATE CHEESE NOW OR EARLIER. OOPS.
8. SPREAD CHEDDAR AND MONTEREY JACK EVENLY THEN MIX
9. SPRINKLE WHEAT GERM ON TOP – NOT TOO THICK IT SHOULD FORM A VERY THIN CRUST.
10. PLACE ON MIDDLE RACK IN OVEN FOR APPROX 2 HOURS (CHECK AFTER 1½ HRS.)

THATS IT!

THIS RECIPE SEEMS TO BE A CROWD PLEASER (AT LEAST AMONG THEATRE PEOPLE. LARRY LILLO SUGGESTED ADDING GARLIC – 10 CLOVES. WE COMPROMISED AT 3.

PLEASE ENJOY

Empress Hotel
Victoria B.C.
Photo Ed Gifford
Tourism B.C.

Asparagus with Mustard Dressing
"Asparagus Karashi-Ae"

4 Servings

- 20 spears asparagus
  trimmed (and pared, if necessary)
- salt

dressing:

- 2 tsps powdered mustard
  mixed with 2 tsps water
- 1 egg yolk
- 1 tsp dark soy sauce

To prepare:

Cut asparagus spears into 1½-inch (4cm) lengths. Boil in lightly salted water. Remove while still crisp and rinse in cold water to improve colour.

Prepare the mustard in a large mixing bowl. Beat in the egg yolk and mix well. Add the soy sauce and mix. (You may add flavor to the dressing by including 1/4 cup ito-kezuri-Katsuo" dried bonito thread-shavings" after finishing with the dressing and before adding the asparagus.)

Put the asparagus in the large mixing bowl with the dressing. Toss.

To serve:

Serve in small individual dishes. Arrange asparagus lengths in a neat pyramid. Serve at room temperature.

Kazuyoshi Akiyama
A Conductor for the Vancouver Symphony Orchestra

B.C. FEDERATION OF LABOUR (CLC)

4279 Canada Way
Burnaby, B.C. V5G 1H1

TEL (604) 430-1421
FAX (604) 430-5917

Kenneth V. Georgetti
President

Angela Schira
Secretary-Treasurer

May 17, 1993

Abby Anderson, C.A.E.
General Manager
Burnaby Chamber of Commerce
149 - 9855 Austin Avenue
Professional Wing, Lougheed Mall
Burnaby, B.C.
V3J 1N4

Dear Ms. Anderson:

Enclosed please find my recipe for the Burnaby Chamber of Commerce all-celebrity cookbook, as requested in your letter of April 27, 1993.

I would appreciate it if you could let me know when the cookbook is completed so I can obtain a copy.

Thank you for inviting my participation.

Yours truly,

KENNETH V. GEORGETTI
President

KVG/ljn
c:recipe

oteu-15

B.C.
FEDERATION
OF LABOUR
(CLC)

4279 Canada Way
Burnaby, B.C. V5G 1H1

TEL (604) 430-1421
FAX (604) 430-5917

Kenneth V. Georgetti
President

Angela Schira
Secretary-Treasurer

SPINACH CHIEF

INGREDIENTS

2 lbs. fresh spinach
4-5 strips lean bacon - chopped
1 small onion - chopped
3 cloves garlic - chopped
2 tablespoons fresh parsley
1 tablespoon olive oil
Salt
Pepper
1 14 ounce tin plum tomatoes - chopped

DIRECTIONS

Blanch spinach. Rinse in cold water and set aside.

In large frying pan, add olive oil. Fry bacon, onions, garlic and parsley until onions turn golden brown. Add tomatoes, salt and pepper to taste.

Add spinach. Cook on low heat until most liquid is gone.

Serve immediately.

Kenneth V. Georgetti
President
B.C. Federation of Labour

oteu-15

BURNABY
CHAMBER OF COMMERCE

MACADAMIA NUT RICE

- 2 tbsp. olive oil
- 1 oz. whole butter
- 1/2 cup diced onions
- 1 medium red pepper, diced
- 1 medium yellow bell pepper, diced
- 1/2 cup button mushrooms, diced
- 1/2 cup shiitake mushrooms, diced
- 1 tsp. garlic, minced
- 1 medium egg plant, diced
- 1 medium carrot, diced
- 1 tsp. ginger, chopped
- 1 cup rice
- 1 cup wild rice, cooked
- 1 3/4 cup boullion
- 1/2 tsp. hot bean sauce
- 1/2 tsp. ancho chili paste
- 1 cup macadamia nuts, chopped
- 1 cup azuki beans, cooked

Saute onions, pepper, mushrooms, garlic, eggplant, carrots and ginger in butter until lightly browned. Add white rice and saute until heated through. Add boiling stock, hot bean sauce and anch chili paste. Cover & simmer gently for 20 minutes. Mix in wild rice, macadamia nuts, and azuki beans and adjust seasoning.

ENJOY!

Carl de Jong
President

Suite #149 - 9855 Austin Avenue, Professional Wing, Lougheed Mall, Burnaby, BC V3J 1N4 • Ph: (604) 421-0084 • Fx: (604) 421-3630

W.P. KINSELLA

Dance Me Outside

Scars

Shoeless Joe Jackson Comes to Iowa

Born Indian

The Moccasin Telegraph

The Thrill of the Grass

Shoeless Joe

The Iowa Baseball Confederacy

The Alligator Report

The Fencepost Chronicles

Red Wolf, Red Wolf

The Further Adventures of Slugger McBatt

The Rainbow Warehouse

The Miss Hobbema Pageant

Two Spirits Soar

Box Socials

The Baseball Wolf

The Winter Helen Dropped By

Magic Time

Houghton Mifflin Literary Fellowship
Books in Canada First Novel Award
Canadian Authors Association Prize for Fiction
Stephen Leacock Medal for Humor

PEPPERS TRIESTE
(from my Baba Drobney's recipe)

X 3 large green bell peppers
1 Lb lean hamburger

Halve peppers vertically, clean out pulp
Microwave pepper halves for about 5 minutes.
Season hamburger with A-1, pepper, salt (fine chopped onion, garlic, optional)
Place seasoned meat on plate and microwave until brown, interrupting to drain off liquid.

Stuff pepper halves with browned meat.
Microwave again for about three minutes.
Place a thick slice of cheddar cheese on each pepper half, microwave until cheese melts. Serve.

Bill Kinsella

☆Maggie O'Hara's Vegetarian Recipe☆

· Indian Baked Avocadoes ·

Ingredients

4 Avocadoes
1/2 Cup Green Peas
1 Cup Firm tofu or Paneer* (cubed)
2 tbs. Ghee or Olive Oil
1/4 tsp. Hing*
1 Chopped Fresh Ginger
1 tsp. Sesame Oil
1 tbs. Hot Chili sauce
1 tbs. Soy Sauce
3 tbs. Creamed Coconut
1 tbs. Lemon Juice
1/2 Tsp. Salt
Chopped Cilantro (to taste)

Cut Avocadoes in Half.
Scoop out Pulp, Leaving 1/2 inch bordes
Heat Ghee or Oil in Frying Pan
Add Hing & Ginger
Add tofu or Paneer and stir to Golden brown.
Add Sesame oil, Chili sauce and Soy Sauce.
then Add Creamed Coconut and mix to melt over Low heat.
Add Lemon juice, fresh Cilantro, Salt and Peas
Finally Stir All together with the Avocado pulp
and Warm through. Stuff Avocadoes with mixture.
Place in Glass Baking Dish
Grill for a few minutes till Golden Brown on top
And... Voila! Serve and Enjoy!

* Available at East Indian Stores

STU'S BROCCO-FLOWER CHEESE PIE

Crust:

2	cups	packed, grated raw potatoes	
1/2	tsp.	salt	
1		egg, beaten	
1/4	cup	grated onion	Heat oven to 400

Set the freshly grated potato in a colander over a bowl. Salt & leave for 10 minutes. Squeeze out excess water, & add it to the remaining ingredients. Pat it into a well-oiled 9-inch pie pan, building up the sides of the crust. Bake 40-45 minutes until browned. After the first 30 minutes brush the crust with a little olive oil to crispen.
Turn down to 375.

Filling:

1 1/2	cups	cheddar cheese, grated
1	small	cauliflower, broken into flowerettes
1	cup	broccoli, pieces
1	large	garlic clove, crushed
1	cup	onion, chopped
2	tbsp	olive oil
1/4	tsp	thyme
3/4	tsp	basil
1/2	tsp	salt

Custard:

2		eggs
1/4	cup	milk, beaten together
1/4	tsp	paprika
pinch		cayenne pepper

In skillet saute onion and garlic in olive oil for 5 minutes. Add cauliflower, broccoli & herbs. Cook covered about 10 minutes stirring occasionally. Spread 1/2 of the cheese on to the baked crust, then the saute, then the rest of the cheese. Pour custard over and dust with paprika. Bake 35-40 minutes, until set.

STU JEFFRIES -

PLAZA OF NATIONS 750 Pacific Boulevard South, P.O. Box 29
Vancouver, B. C. V6B 5E7 Fax (604) 681-5507 Tel. (604) 685-4712

FANNY KIEFER'S CAULIFLOWER ITALIANO

ONE HEAD OF CAULIFLOWER

ONE RED ONION

TWO CLOVES GARLIC

TWO OUNCES SUN DRIED TOMATOES

ONE CUP CHICKEN OR VEGETABLE BROTH

ONE HALF CUP OR LESS OLIVE OIL

TWENTY LARGE PITTED GREEN OLIVES CHOPPED

CHOPPED ITALIAN PARSLEY

SALT AND PEPPER TO TASTE

DIRECTIONS:

BREAK UP CAULIFLOWER INTO FLOWERLETS, PUT IN A BOWL, BLANCH WITH BOILING WATER FOR ONE MINUTE, DRY WITH CLEAN TOWEL AND SET ASIDE.

IN A HEAVY FRYING PAN OR CASSEROLE DISH PUT IN OLIVE OIL AND TURN ELEMENT TO MODERATE HEAT. FINELY CHOP GARLIC, ONION, TOMATOS AND SAUTE FOR FIVE MINUTES. ADD CAULIFLOWER AND ONE HALF CUP OF STOCK, COVER AND COOK FOR TEN MINUTES AT LOW HEAT. ADD SALT, PEPPER TO TASTE AND EXTRA STOCK IF NEEDED. FIVE MINUTES BEFORE DISH IS DONE, ADD CHOPPED OLIVES. SERVE IMMEDIATELY OR LET COOL AND SERVE LATER.

AS MARK TWAIN ONCE SAID "TRAINING IS EVERYTHING: THE PEACH WAS ONCE A BITTER ALMOND; CAULIFLOWER IS NOTHING BUT CABBAGE WITH A COLLEGE EDUCATION.

DIVISION OF WESTCOM RADIO GROUP LTD.

William & Lillian Van der Zalm

VANDER ZALM'S "CABBAGE DELIGHT"

1 Cabbage (Danish Baldhead variety much preferred)
Put in pot - add salt to taste and water.
Boil for 25 minutes.

When you poke with a fork and it feels soft, drain off the water, add butter and mash.

Now serve and sprinkle ground nutmeg over top to taste.
(I like it generously sprinkled with nutmeg).

Bill Vander Zalm

"Normandy Manor"

"Sarmele with Mamaliga" is being offered courtesy of Doubleday and as such it is necessary to credit the title of the book, the author and the publisher.

Kitchen Classics from the Philharmonic by June LeBell
DOUBLEDAY, a division of Bantam, Doubleday,
Dell Publishing Group Inc.

Sarmele with Mamaliga
(Romanian Stuffed Cabbage)

Serves 8 to 10

1 large green cabbage (about 2 pounds) cut in half and cored, leaves separated

2 pounds ground round beef
1 (11 ounce) can onion soup
3 tablespoons of uncooked rice
2 large eggs, lightly beaten
2 tomatoes, chopped
1 teaspoon salt
1 teaspoon pepper
1/4 cup chopped Italian parsley
1 (16 ounce) package sauerkraut, rinsed, drained and squeezed dry
1 (16 ounce) can tomato sauce
1 (16 ounce) can stewed tomatoes
1 cup water

MAMALIGA

7 cups cold water; 2 teaspoons salt; 2 cups cornmeal

1) Bring a large pot of water to a boil and add cabbage leaves, Stir and cook until tender, about 3 to 4 minutes. Drain well and set aside until leaves are cool enough to handle.

2) Meanwhile, in a large mixing bowl, combine meat, onion soup, rice, eggs, chopped tomatoes, salt, pepper, and parsley. Mix well. Fill each cabbage leaf with about 2 tablespoons of the stuffing, wrapping each leaf around filling to form a roll. Place seam side down in a large (6 to 8 quart) saucepot and spread sauerkraut on top. Pour tomato sauce, stewed tomatoes and water on top, cover and bring to a boil over high heat. Lower heat to a simmer and cook for one hour. Let cool and refrigerate overnight. The next day, remove from refrigerator and let stand 30 minutes.

3) Preheat oven to 350.

4) Bake Sarmele covered for 30 minutes or until hot. Serve with Mamaliga

5) To make the mamaliga, bring 6 cups water to a boil in a medium saucepot. Add salt. Mix the cornmeal with the remaining 1 cup cold water and slowly add, stirring constantly, to the boiling water. Cook, stirring, 12 to 15 minutes or until smooth and thickened.

Maestro Sergiu Comissiona
A conductor for the vancouver Symphony Orchestra

Joan M. Sawicki, M.L.A.
(Burnaby-Willingdon)

Polish-style Sauerkraut Pirogi

Filling

1 can or jar of sauerkraut
Approximately 1/2 cup each of bacon
mushrooms
onions

- Parboil sauerkraut. Strain and squeeze out extra moisture.
- Stir fry chopped bacon, mushrooms and onion.
- Add sauerkraut. Season with salt and pepper. Fry until moisture is gone.

Dough

4 cups flour
1/2 tsp salt
warm water

- Add warm water in small amounts just until flour is taken up.
- On a large, floured board or table top, knead dough until smooth. (Dough should be soft but not sticky.)
- Roll out fairly thin. Cut out circles of about 3 inch diameter using a regular kitchen glass.
- Forming a small 'cup' in the palm of your hand, add about 1 tablespoon of filling. Fold over filling and pinch edges together. (Make sure the seam is closed or pirogi will fall apart during cooking.)
- Place on floured teatowel.

Freezing

Freeze individually on floured tray before putting into bags.

Cooking

- Place fresh or frozen pirogi in pot of salted, boiling water. Cook until dough is tender, about 7 - 10 minutes.

- Drain. Layer in bowl with melted butter and sauteed diced onion.

- Serve as is with sour cream **or** cool for a few hours then fry until crispy, golden brown, and serve with sour cream.

Dear Abby Anderson

I Love Shepherd's pie, of course being in show-biz — I gotta watch my diet — right? & so here is a Kenny Colman "Keep Thin" Shepherd pie —

2½ lbs minced turkey / 2 eggs
4 oz. tomato sauce / ½ cup
bread crumbs — 1 teaspoon salt —
¼ tsp pepper — a dash of cayenne —
2 cloves of minced garlic —
5 sprigs of parsley (chopped)
10 large potatoes — 1% milk —
"I can't believe it's not butter"
2 large onions — sunflower oil
to fry onions —

Fry 2 large onions untill crispy — (set aside)
Pre-heat oven to 350° —
Mix 1st 9 ingredients together —
Place in oblong pyrex dish & bake
in pre-heated oven for 15 min.
Remove from oven, drain excess liquid, —
mash meat mixture with fork &
return to oven for another 15 min —
Remove and set aside —

Boil potatoes in salted water untill very soft. Drain and mash with 1% milk (or skimmed) + "I can't believe it's not butter" until very creamy — Add fried onions to potatoes ——

Place potatoes over meat mixture and add a dash of pepper and paprika. Return to 350° oven for ½ hr — untill top is golden!!

Voila

"You are now a thin person"!

However, being on the road most of my life — I can really order "Room Service" a lot better —

Thanx
Kenny Colman

July 17/93 / Vegas Kenny Colman + some singer?

Peter C. Toigo

Suite 300 - 4088 Cambie Street
Vancouver, B.C.
V5Z 2X8

RISOTTO WITH RADICCHIO ROSA (RED CHICORY)

1 large head radicchio
8 1/2 oz. italian rice
2 cubes Knorr chicken cubes
1/2 C. white wine
80 grams of butter
2 Tbs. olive oil
1/2 large onion, chopped
6 oz. cream
salt & pepper to taste
plenty of parmesan cheese

Sauté onion in half butter & oil, add raddicchio, sauté. Add rice, stirring together until well blended. Add the wine & keep stirring. Dissolve Knorr cubes in 4 cups of hot water for the stock. Keep adding the stock as the rice keeps drying. Keep stirring and adding the stock, don't let it dry. Add remaining butter and stock. If needed add a little extra butter. When the rice is aldente add the parmesan cheese & the cream, keep stirring it. It will become a creamy texture, do not over cook. Serves 4 people.

*Italian ladies measure - 1 fistful of rice per person.

SHATO HOLDINGS LTD.

per: Peter C. Toigo
Chairman of the Board

UMBERTO MANAGEMENT LIMITED 1380 HORNBY STREET, VANCOUVER, BRITISH COLUMBIA, V6Z 1W5 TEL.: (604) 669-3732 FAX: (604) 669-9723

RISOTTO CON ASPARAGI
Risotto with Asparagus

Serves 4-6.

2cups/500 ml arborio rice (short grained)	Wash rice in cold water and set aside.
3/4 lb/350 g fresh asparagus	Blanch asparagus in a saucepan of boiling water for 3-4 minutes. Drain asparagus and set aside. Keep warm. Reserve 8-12 asparagus tips for garnish.
2 shallots, finely chopped 2 tbsp/25 ml olive oil	Saute shallots in olive oil in a skillet for 1 minute until soft and transparent.
1/2 cup/125 ml dry white wine	Put rice, shallots and white wine together in a pot and stir with a wooden spoon for 1-2 minutes. Begin to cook rice on medium heat.
4 cups/1 L chicken consomme (see recipe)	Using a ladle, add chicken consomme to rice every time rice becomes dry. Add chicken consomme a little at a time, always keeping rice moist and gently stirring after each addition. Cook rice for a total of 15-18 minutes.
	Approximatley 2 minutes before rice has finished cooking, add asparagus and gently stir. Add chicken consomme to rice throughout cooking time, but add carefully at end of cooking time as rice absorbs more liquid then than at beginning. Rice is done when it is tender, but firm. Rice should always be creamy not runny or sticky.
3 tbsp/50 ml unsalted butter 4 tbsp/60 ml Parmesan cheese, freshly grated	When rice is done, add butter and Parmesan cheese and stir.
salt white pepper	Season with salt and pepper to taste.
8-12 asparagus tips (reserved above)	Put rice in a warm serving dish or on warm plates. Garnish with aspargus tips.Serve immediately.

RISOTTO ALLA TOSCANO
Risotto With White Wine (6)

Of the several risotto, this is the plainest and most delicate, and therefore the most easy to make badly. The rice must be Italian Arborio rice for the proper outer creaminess and inner firmness, and both the stock and the wine must be of good quality. For preference, use Toscano Bianco, a flavourful white wine. Be lavish, the risotto should taste of wine, not water.

1	Medium onion, finely chopped
1 1/2 oz./40 G.	Butter
12 oz./350 G.	Italian Arborio Rice
1 1/2 pt./900 ml.	Chicken stock (approx.)
6 fl. oz/175 ml.	Toscano Bianco (White)

Melt the butter in a medium sized pan. Saute the onion until a pale brown and then add the rice, stirring until glistening and semi-transparent. Meanwhile, heat the stock in a saucepan. Turn up the heat under the rice and pour in the wine; when it has almost disappeared, add about 1/2 pint (300 ml) hot stock and, when absorbed, add more stock (or wine for a stronger flavour) a spoonful at a time as it is absorbed by the rice (the rice will become noticeably flat on top when it needs more liquid). It should take about 20-30 minutes to cook. Stir frequently while adding liquid and just before serving stir in some butter and several tablespoons of grated pecorino or parmesan cheese.

Keith Davis
President of Bright's Wines

Suite 200 – 4370 Dominion Street, Burnaby, BC V5G 4L7 • Fax: (604) 451-9522 • Telephone: (604) 451-9511

TONI CAVELTI LIMITED MAKER AND DESIGNER OF FINE JEWELRY

565 WEST GEORGIA STREET, VANCOUVER, B.C., CANADA V6B 1Z5 TEL: (604) 681-3481 FAX: (604) 688-2577

CAPUNS

Filling:

1	medium onion, chopped
½ cup	parsley, chopped
½ cup	chives, chopped
2	Landjager sausage, finely chopped
½ cup	sliced pastrami meat, finely chopped
½ cup	sliced ham, finely chopped

Mix all ingredients above in a bowl. Add ingredients below and let rest for ½ hour at room temperature.

150g	flour
	salt and pepper to taste
3 tbsp.	milk
2	eggs

While filling is resting, prepare the chard leaves:

20 mangold or swiss chard leaves

Cut out white stem. If leaf is very big cut in half lengthwise. Blanch leaves in boiling water for about 10 seconds. Plunge them into cold water to stop the cooking process, drain and lay to dry on paper towels.

Fill each leaf with one spoon of filling and roll it up. Tie with cotton string. Brown capuns lightly in butter, set aside.

Sauce:

2dl	whipping cream or milk
5dl	bouillon

In a large pot, bring to boil, simmer and add capuns, simmering for approx. 20 minutes. Serve with Parmesan cheese if desired.

WINNER DIAMONDS INTERNATIONAL AWARD

Sincerely,

Toni Cavelti
Toni Cavelti Ltd.

JACK DIAMOND, O.C.

SWEETBREADS

Obtain a quantity of **calf sweetbreads.**

Boil in water for approximately 3 minutes.

Peel off any obvious membrane and split in half.

Saute onions and sliced mushrooms in butter.

Dip sweetbreads in beaten egg and coat with breadcrumbs.

Place on a deep baking pan and cover with onions and mushrooms.

Bake at 350° F. for 1 to 1 1/2 hours, basting as needed.

Jack Diamond, O.C.

Jack Diamond
BC Jockey Club

ROBERT BATEMAN

BOB BATEMAN'S SUCCOTASH & CRACKERS

SUCCOTASH

2 cups dried white navy beans
5 cups water
pinch of salt
pinch of sage
1 large onion
1 clove garlic
4 pieces bacon
2 tins cream style corn
3 cups skim milk

Wash beans, soak overnight. Rinse. Bring to a boil in 5 cups of water, cook until tender being careful to make sure beans are covered. Add a generous pinch of salt. Chop onion and garlic. Lightly fry in safflower oil until pale golden. Sprinkle in a liberal pinch of sage. Fry or microwave 4 pieces of bacon until crisp. Dispose of fat. When the beans are cooked, add onions, garlic and bacon, plus 2 tins of cream style corn. Add 3 cups skim milk. Bring to boil. Turn down the heat. Add salt and pepper to taste.

CRACKERS

1 cup wheat bran
1 cup oat bran
1 cup rolled oats
generous pinch of salt

Heat an empty stainless steel saucepan on a stove - turn to "high". Put all dry ingredients in the hot saucepan and stir vigorously with a wooden spoon until they begin to smell "toasty". Add sufficient hot water to make a fairly stiff porridge - the water of course will sizzle and boil instantly when added to the hot mixture. Stir vigorously. If you wish, eat a little of this as porridge.

Add oat bran until the mixture becomes much stiffer and "doughy". Take a Teflon type cookie sheet and liberally sprinkle with oat bran. Roll dough mixture into balls. Using fingers, flatten out as thin as possible into wafers. Put the cookie sheet with the wafers on top of the woodburning stove or in a very low oven. Continue heating until they are dry and crisp. Bake until they are light brown. Do not overbake. A more flavourful variation may be obtained by adding grated cheese, possibly old cheese or smoked cheese, or adding a teaspoon or two of onion soup mix at the porridge stage. It should be tasty and healthy.

Good luck with your project!

Desserts

FRENCH UNBAKED CAKE

Another "quick & easy" recipe. Great for either entertaining or just for a family treat. Warning: it goes pretty fast!*() denotes doubling of recipe

(1) ½ cup margerine
(4) 2 tbsp. cocoa
(1) ½ cup brown sugar
(2) 1 egg slightly beaten
(2) 1 tsp. vanilla extract
(1½) 3/4 cup walnuts
(32) 16 double graham wafers roughly broken

Melt margerine. Mix sugar, cocoa , and egg together and add to margerine. Stir and bring to boil then turn to low heat. Remove from heat and add vanilla, nuts, and graham wafers. Put in greased pan and press flat. Put in fridge or freezer. Cut in squares and serve.

DAPHNE GOLDRICK
EXECUTIVE COMMITTEE

Canadian Conference of the Arts
189 LAURIER AVENUE EAST, OTTAWA, ONTARIO K1N 6P1
TEL: (613) 238-3561 FAX: (613) 238-4849

BRITISH COLUMBIA JOCKEY CLUB

June 15/93.

Dear Abby

Thank you for the opportunity to contribute to your celebrity cookbook. Please find enclosed a couple of recipes from home which the "boys" on the roof enjoy. I have signed the bottom of the recipes, but if you want to block it out please feel free to do so.

Dan Jukich

The Track - Exhibition Park Vancouver, British Columbia, Canada V5K 3N8 604 254-1631 Fax 604 251-0411

BRITISH COLUMBIA JOCKEY CLUB

SWEETS FROM HIGH ATOP THE GRANDSTAND

ORANGE POPPYSEED CHEESECAKE WITH LEMON GLAZE

CRUST

3/4 cup graham wafer crumbs
3/4 cup ground almonds
1 Tbsp sugar
1/4 cup butter or PARKAY MARG,melted

Combine crust ingredients; press mixture onto bottom and 1 inch (2.5 cm) up sides of a 9 inch (23 cm) springform pan. Bake at 350 F (180 C) for 8 minutes. Cool.

FILLING

2 pkgs (250 g) PHILADELPHIA LIGHT OR REGULAR CREAM CHEESE, softened
1 cup sugar
4 eggs
1 tsp grated orange rind
3 Tbsp All-Purpose flour
1/4 cup orange juice
3/4 cup whipping cream
2 Tbsp poppyseeds

In a large bowl, using an electric mixer, beat cream cheese and sugar until very smooth. Beat in eggs, one at a time, until just blended. Beat in remaining filling ingredients. Pour into pan. Bake at 450 F (230 C) for 10 minutes- reduce heat to 250 F (120 C) and continue baking 35-45 minutes or until centre is just set. Remove from oven and run a knife around rim of pan to prevent cracking. Cool thoroughly at room temperature. Chill overnight.

GLAZE

2 eggs
3/4 cup sugar
1 tsp grated orange & lemon rind
1/4 cup lemon juice
2 Tbsp orange juice
2 Tbsp butter

In a small saucepan whisk eggs until foamy. Combine with sugar, rind, juices and butter in saucepan. Cook over low heat, stirring constantly until smooth and thickened. Cool. Just before serving, spread evenly over cheesecake.

Enjoy
Dan Jukich

The Track - Exhibition Park Vancouver, British Columbia, Canada V5K 3N8 604 254-1631 Fax 604 251-0411

BARBARA COPPING, M.L.A.
(Port Moody-Burnaby Mountain)
Legislative Buildings
Victoria, B.C.
V8V 1X4

POPPY SEED CAKE

1	Yellow Cake Mix
1 Pkg.	Instant vanilla pudding mix
1 cup	Sour Cream
4	Eggs
1/2 cup	cooking oil
1/2 cup	Sherry
1/3 cup	Poppy Seeds

Put all above together in a bowl. Beat all for 5 minutes. Grease tin. Bake 1 hour at 350 degrees.

ROYAL BANK

Brad H. Lambert
Vice-President - Corporate Banking
British Columbia & Yukon

Royal Bank of Canada
1055 West Georgia Street
Vancouver, B.C. V6E 3S5

Tel.: (604) 665-6783
Fax: (604) 665-6465

RASPBERRY CAKE

CAKE:

1 Cup	Flour
3/4 Cup	Sugar
1/2 Tsp.	Baking Powder
1/4 Tsp.	Baking Soda
1/4 Tsp.	Salt
1	Large Egg
1/3 Cup	Buttermilk
1/3 Cup	Melted Butter ... cooled to room temperature
1 Tsp.	Vanilla
1-1/4 Cups	Fresh Raspberries

CRUMB TOPPING:

1/2 Cup	Brown Sugar
1 Tbs.	Butter
2 Tbs.	Flour

For cake, combine flour, sugar, baking powder, soda, salt in large bowl.

In another bowl, beat together egg, buttermilk and vanilla until smooth.

Pour mixture into flour mixture and stir until dry ingredients are moistened.

Spread batter evenly in greased 8 inch square baking pan.

Place raspberries evenly on top .... sprinkle crumb topping over berries.

Bake at 375 degrees for 35 to 40 minutes or until well browned. Let cake cool on rack until warm.

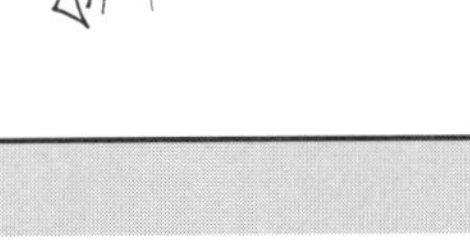

Business Council of British Columbia

Suite 810
1050 West Pender Street
Vancouver, BC V6E 3S7
Telephone (604) 684-3384
Facsimile (604) 684-7957

Jerry L. Lampert
President and Chief Executive Officer

Ms. Abby Anderson, C.A.E.
General Manager
Burnaby Chamber of Commerce
149--9855 Austin Avenue
Professional Wing
Lougheed Mall
Burnaby, B.C. V3J 1N4

Dear Ms. Anderson:

Thank you for your letter of June 2, 1993 inviting my participation in Burnaby Chambers' All-Celebrity Cookbook. Congratulations on an interesting and entertaining idea. I am pleased to enclose my contribution to the cookbook, "Sherry's Rum Cake."

Please accept this letter as an order for a copy of the cookbook when it is published.

Best wishes for every success in this endeavour.

Yours sincerely,

Jerry L. Lampert

/bam
encl.

Jerry L. Lampert

SHERRY'S RUM CAKE

CAKE

INGREDIENTS:

1 Duncan Hines Yellow Cake Mix
1 Small Package Instant Vanilla Pudding
1/2 Cup White Rum
1/2 Cup Oil
1/2 Cup Water
4 Eggs

METHOD:

Mix cake mix and pudding together. Add rum, oil and water. Mix well. Add one egg at a time (total: 4), mixing well each time. Pour into greased/floured bundt pan and bake for one(1) hour at 350F.

SAUCE:

INGREDIENTS:

1/4 lb Unsalted Butter
1 Cup Sugar
1/4 Cup Water
1/4 Cup Rum

METHOD:

Bring all ingredients, **except rum**, to a boil. Let boil for one (1) minute. Take off heat. Add rum. Poke holes in cooled cake and pour sauce over. Before serving, sprinkle icing sugar over cake.

Serve and enjoy! A great dessert when entertaining at home or an enjoyable conversation cake for pot-luck occasions.

Submitted by: Jerry Lampert
President and Chief Executive Officer
Business Council of British Columbia

To maintain the vision and principles of Terry Fox while raising money for innovative cancer research in an annual event known as The Terry Fox Run.

Mission Statement of
The Terry Fox Run

Puffed Wheat Cake

1 cup Brown Sugar
1/2 cup Syrup (Beehive)
1/4 cup Butter or Margarine
2 tablespoons Cocoa

Boil the above for 3 minutes.
Remove from heat

Add: 1 tsp. Vanilla
6 to 7 cups puffed wheat
Mix well put into a large cake pan.

This cake was a favorite of Terry's

Betty Fox

CORPORATION OF THE
DISTRICT OF MAPLE RIDGE

Office of the Mayor

11995 Haney Place
Maple Ridge, B.C. V2X 6A9
Telephone (604) 463-5221
Fax (604) 467-7329

CHOCOLATE ZUCCHINI CAKE

1/2 c. butter/margarine 1/2 c. oil 1 3/4 c. white sugar	Cream together
2 eggs 1 tsp. vanilla 1/2 c. sour milk	Add to above mixture & Beat well.
2 1/2 c. white flour 4 tbsp. cocoa 1 tsp. soda 1/2 tsp. cinnamon 1/2 tsp. ground cloves	Add to above

Stir in 2 c. grated zucchini. Sprinkle top with 1/2 c. chocolate chips.

Bake in 9 x 12 greased pan. 325 Degrees for 45 to 55 minutes.

Submitted by:

Belle Morse, Mayor

BOARD of PARKS
and RECREATION
CITY OF VANCOUVER

2099 BEACH AVENUE
VANCOUVER, B.C.
CANADA V6G 1Z4
PHONE (604) 681-1141
FAX (604) 643-2877

WHEAT FREE CHOCOLATE CAKE

Day before: Cook potatos in skins. Cool, peel and grate or mash.

175 grams sugar
4 egg yolks
1 orange or lemon juice and zest
100 grams chocolate squares (or powder)
50 grams walnuts (grated)
50 grams fruit peel
2 tspn baking powder
4 egg whites
pinch salt
250 grams grated or mashed potatos

Mix sugar and egg yolks until fluffy. Add juice and zest. Melt chocolate in top of double boiler and add water. Cool slightly and add to sugar mixture.

Mix together the rest of the dry ingredients and slowly add to sugar and chocolate mixture a little at a time.

Beat egg whites with 3 tspns (approx) of sugar until stiff and fold carefully into mixture.

Put mixture in greased pan. Bake for 45 minutes at 360 degrees. Check with tooth pick. Bake a little longer if necessary.

Hans Halbheer
Vancouver Parks Board

from H.H.

Sailing off Kitsilano
Vancouver B.C.
Photo Courtesy of Tourism B.C.

District Of Stewart
Post Office Box 460
Stewart, British Columbia
V0T 1W0
Tel (604) 636-2251
Fax (604) 636-2417

August 25, 1993

Abby Anderson
Burnaby Chamber of Commerce
Suite 1490 9855 Austin Avenue
Professional Wing
Lougheed Mall
Burnaby BC V3J 1N4

Dear Abby:

What an original project you have taken on. Enclosed is a chocolate lovers recipe and easy. How I came by it is tourism related.

Stewart is located on the Alaska border our neighboring community being Hyder. Groups visiting the area are catered to by a lady in Hyder and she serves the Cherry Chocolate Cake. I was fortune to get the recipe after having the opportunity to share in one of her feasts.

Perhaps you will give us the opportunity to purchase copies of your publication.

Sincerely,
Darlene Cornell
DARLENE CORNELL
MAYOR

CHOCOLATE CHERRY CAKE

1 pkg Devils Food Cake Mix
21 oz can Cherry Pie Filling
1 tsp almond extract
2 eggs beaten

Heat oven to 350. Grease and flour 9" x 13" pan. In large bowl combine all above ingredients. Stir by hand until well mixed. Pour into prepared pan, bake 25 to 35 minutes.

FROSTING

1 cup sugar
5 tbls butter or margarine
1/3 cup evaporated milk
2 eggs beaten
6 oz pkg (1 ciup) semi sweet choc chips

In small saucepan, combine sugar, butter, and milk-boil 1 minute stirring constantly. Remove from heat-stir in chocolate chips until smooth. Pour over warm bars. Cool completely.

Abby Anderson,

Dear Abby,

Many thanks for your letter of July 27 1993.

Enclosed is a short Recipe which has always been a favorite of mine. It has originally been one of my mothers, and one of my sisters favorites. My sister was a professional chef, and personal chef to Mrs John Prentice, and the late Mr. John Prentice, of Canada Forest Products.

Best wishes to you in your upcoming endeavor. Many thanks for including me among your many participants.

Yours sincerely,

George D. Athans
M.D

Pound Cake

1 Lb. Butter
2 cups sugar
2 tsp. almond Extract
9 eggs
3 cups Flour
1 tsp. Baking powder
½ tsp salt

Cream butter and sugar + almond Extract.

Add 1 egg at a time beating well.

Add flour, baking powder and salt.

Bake in angel food pan (Grease pan) for 1 Hr. 15 min at 325° oven

George Athans, Sr.
BC Sports Hall of Fame
Ten-time Canadian diving champion between 1936 & 1950

TO THE BURNABY CHAMBER OF COMMERCE
RE ALL-CELEBRITY COOK BOOK.

DEAR ABBY ANDERSON, C.A.E
GENERAL MANAGER,

ENCLOSED ARE TWO RECEPIES; MY FAVORITES,
GOOD LUCK WITH THE BOOK.

BERT LOWES,
BOXING
B.C. SPORT HALL OF FAME.

From the kitchen of... Bert Lowes House

Applesauce Cake

1/2 cup shortning	Cinnamon
1 " sugar	1/2 tsp each of
1 " applesauce	allspice, nutmeg
2 " flour	and ginger
1 tsp each of	1/4 tsp cloves
salt, soda,	1 cups raisins
Baking Powder,	3/4 " chopped nuts

Cream shortning, add sugar egg and applesauce Blend dry ingredients mix into creamed mixture. Stir in raisins and nuts
Bake in 8-inch pan at 350° about 50 or 60 min Cool in pan

From:

Linda Moore

Cheesecake

Crust

1 cup flour
½ cup margarine
¼ cup finely chopped pecans
¼ cup icing sugar

Mix flour, pecans and sugar. Cut in margarine. Press into 9" pie pan.

Bake 12-15 minutes at 400°.

Filling

1 cup whipping cream
¼ cup icing sugar

Whip cream and fold in sugar.

8 oz cream cheese
¼ cup icing sugar
1 tsp. vanilla

Beat together. Fold in whipped cream. Pour into crust. Chill.

Top with fruit.

---

* Make the day ahead. Great with blueberries, kiwis, etc.

Maxine Miller Ltd.

16.09.93

Cheese Cake

Base
1 6oz. Pkg. Zwieback [crushed}
1 cup Sugar
1 teaspoon Cinnamon
1/2 cup melted Butter
Butter Spring Form Pan ..... Press mixture into pan, saving 1/4 cup Base to sprinkle on top of filling.

Filling
[1] 1 1/2 lbs [3Pkgs] Philadelphia Cream cheese
1/4 cup flour [blend together in large bowl]
[2] 1 cup Sugar, 1/8 teasepoon salt, 1 tsp vanilla
4 eggs ..... beat together in smaller bowl
Add 1/2 Lemon juice and rind
Add 1 cup Whipping cream to 1st mixture, beat until smooth.
Pour 2nd mixture into 1st and beat with electric hand mixer until smooth. Pour into form. Sprinkle top with Base mixture.
Cook 1 hour at 300 - 325 or until set. Open door for 1 hour. Cool.
Top sometimes cracks. You can cut cake on Spring base or move to separate plate. Top with any fruit in season, pureed or serve plain.

ENJOY

Thank you for the invitation Abby. All success for your Burnaby Chamber of Commerce All-Celebrity Cookbook.

Maxine Miller

Maxine Miller
Actor, Singer, Voice Specialist

DISTRICT OF CHILLIWACK
OFFICE OF THE MAYOR

August 18, 1993

Burnaby Chamber of Commerce
#149 - 9855 Austin Avenue
Burnaby, BC
V3J 1N4

ATTENTION: Abby Anderson

Dear Ms. Anderson:

Thank you for your letter about your recipe book project. I am impressed with your list of contributors to date.

I am pleased to enclose a recipe to be included in your book, and I thank you for allowing me this opportunity.

Yours truly,

John Les
Mayor

JL:isr

RHUBARB COFFEE CAKE

1/2 c butter or margarine
1 1/2 c granulated sugar
2 eggs
1 c sour cream
1 tsp vanilla
2 c flour
1 tsp baking soda
2 c finely cut rhubarb

Preheat oven to 350 F (180 C). Cream butter and sugar together in mixing bowl. Beat in eggs one at a time. Stir in sour cream and vanilla. Mix flour and baking soda together and fold into batter. Stir in rhubarb. Turn into greased 9x13 pan.

TOPPING:
1/2 c brown sugar, packed
1 Tbsp flour
1 tsp cinnamon
1 Tbsp butter or margarine softened

Mix all four ingredients together until crumbly. Sprinkle over top. Bake in oven for 30 to 40 minutes until an inserted wooden pick comes out clean.

8550 Young Road, Chilliwack, British Columbia V2P 4P1
Phone: (604) 792-9311 Fax: (604) 792-2561

TAYLORE T. FOX
Blake Enterprises/Starmaker Productions Ltd.
1512 West 3rd Ave., 2nd Floor
Vancouver, B.C. V6J 1J7
(604) 732-0188 Fax (604) 572-9818

EASY FRUIT CAKE

This East Coast recipe came from Doris Headley when her husband Frank Headley was a Senator and Judge in the state of New Jersey in the 1950's.

Ingredients

1 lb dates	1 lb pecans	1 cup flour	1/2 lb candied cherries
1/2 tsp salt	1 cup sugar	4 beaten eggs	1/2 lb candied pineapple
2 tsp vanilla			

Method

Cut dates in half, but leave pecan nuts whole. Sift flour and salt together, then add to dates and nuts. Sift sugar into beaten eggs and then add date/nut mixture. Combine cherries and pineapple to mixture adding vanilla last.

Pour into 3 small loaf pans lined with wax paper on very well greased, brown paper. (The new non-stick pans are good). Place a flat pan filled with water in the bottom of the oven. Bake for 1 1/2 hours at 275°. **Yield: 3 small loaves or 1 large loaf**

Abby Anderson,
General Manager,
Burnaby Chamber of Commerce.

Your recipe project sounds quite exciting. Your categories for contributors are listed as Entertainment, Arts, Government and Commerce. Since any claim to fame that I have is in the realm of Sport do I really qualify? Just in case I do I will enclose a favorite of the family recipe.

THE PUMPKIN PIE.

This is not a recipe for the meticulous measurer, but it always turns out well regardless.

1&1/2 cups cooked pumpkin. (If there is a bit more in the can just put it in)
1 dessert spoon of flour.
1 cup of sugar.
1 tsp each of ginger, cinnamon.
1/2 tsp mace, nutmeg.
Salt 1 tsp or more.
3 eggs
1/2 cup milk.
Mix pumpkin flour, sugar ,salt and spices together. (Here I taste and usually add a bit more spice and salt)
Beat eggs well, add milk to beaten eggs then add to pumkin mixture and stir all well.
Pour into an unbaked pie shell (should be a deep one) and bake in a moderate oven (350) till the filling is firm.
Serve with whipped cream or ice cream .

Donalda M. Smith (Mrs.)

Donalda Smith
BC Sports Hall of Fame
Synchro swimming coach, judge, & committee chair

CRAN-APPLE PIE

For one 9-inch pie, you will need:

Crust:
- 2 cups all-purpose flour
- 1 tsp. salt
- 2/3 cup shortening
- 5 to 7 tbsp. cold water

Filling:
- 3 cups peeled and chopped apples
- 2 cups cranberries
- 1 cup sugar
- 2 tbsp. all-purpose flour
- 3/4 tsp. ground cloves

Preparation:

1. Mix together flour and salt. Cut in shortening until crumbly.
2. Mix in water by tablespoons until a dough is formed.
3. Roll out half of dough on a floured board. Place into a 9-inch pie pan.
4. Mix filling ingredients. Turn into crust.
5. Roll out other half of dough on a floured board. Place on top of pie or cut into circles.
6. Trim edges and crimp with fork tines or place circles on top of filling.
7. Bake pie at 400°F to 425°F for 40 to 45 minutes.

Recipe submitted by:

BRIAN MINTER
President
MINTER GARDENS

52892 BUNKER ROAD, ROSEDALE, B.C. • MAILING ADDRESS: P.O. BOX 40, CHILLIWACK, B.C. V2P 6H7
PHONE (604) 794-7191 • OFF-SEASON: COUNTRY GARDEN LTD. (604) 792-3919 • TELEX 04-361540 (COUNTGARD)

Raisin Cream Pie

B.C. Credit Union Centre
1441 Creekside Drive
Vancouver, B.C. V6J 4S7
Telephone: (604) 734-2511
Fax: 737-5055

BC Central Credit Union

Pre-bake one 9" pie shell

1 cup raisins
- boil until tender and drain

Add:
1/4 cup sugar
2 tbsp. cornstarch
1 tsp. vanilla
1 cup of half and half
- cook until thick

Add:
2 eggs
- well beaten

Place in baked pie shell
Cover with meringue
Brown until golden

To make meringue

3 egg whites
- room temperature
1/4 tsp. cream of tartar
3 tbsp. granulated sugar
Method
- beat egg whites and cream of tartar until soft peaks form.
- beat in sugar gradually until stiff.
- pile on pie filling, spread to edge, covering pie completely

Bake at 400°F
Allow to cool

BON APPETIT!

Sincerely,

Denise McDermott

for Wayne A. Nygren,
President and
Chief Executive Officer

Province of
British Columbia

Commission of
Inquiry into the
Public Service and
Public Sector

600, 1125 Howe Street
Vancouver, British Columbia
V6Z 2K8
Telephone: (604) 660-0324
Fax: (604) 660-0681

BLUM'S COFFEE TOFFEE PIE

Pastry Shell

8 oz Piecrust mix
1 1/4 oz brown suger
1 oz Guittard bittersweet chocolate - grated
3 oz Walnut, finely chopped
1 Tbls Water
1 tsp Vanilla extract

Combine piecrust mix with brown sugar, chopped walnuts and grated chocolate. Add 1 tbsp. water and 1 tsp. vanilla. Using a fork, mix all ingredients together well. Mix will be crumbly and slightly moist in texture.

Transfer piecrust mixture to well greased 9" pie plate. Firmly press crust mixture against the sides and bottom of pie plate.

Bake in 350^0 over for 10 minutes. Cool pie shell on wire rack at room temperature.

Filling

4 oz. Butter, softened
5 1/2 oz. Granulated sugar
1 oz Guittard bittersweet chocolate, melted and cooled
2 tsp. Instant coffee granules
2 Eggs, large

Beat butter using electric mixer until white and creamy, about 2 minutes. Gradually add granulated sugar, beating about 4 minutes. Scrape bowl. Add 1 egg, beat 5 minutes. Add remaining egg, beat 5 minutes. Spoon filling into complete cooled baked pie shell.

Coffee Topping

16 fl. oz Whipping cream
2 Tbsp. Instant coffee granules
2 1/4 oz Confectioner's sugar

Combine cream, instant coffee granules, and confectioner's sugar. Mix together to dissolve coffee and sugar. Cover bowl and refrigerate for 1 hours to allow coffee granules to dissolve.

Beat cream until it forms stiff peaks. Spoon topping onto pie. Top with grated Guittard Semi-Sweet Chocolate.

Judi Korbin

Dee Daniels

Dear Abby,

Thank you very much for providing me with the opportunity to participate in the All-Celebrity Cookbook. What a fun idea!

I wish you and the Burnaby Chamber of Commerce much success with this project.

All the best,

Dee

DEE'S SWEET POTATOE PIE

3 medium or 2 large yams
2 eggs
3/4 cup milk
3/4 cup sugar
1/2 cup butter or margerine
1 tsp. vanilla extract
1 tsp. allspice
1/2 tsp. cinnamon
1/2 tsp. salt
1/4 tsp. nutmeg

Peel and cut up yams. Place in sauce pan with enough water to barely cover yams. Cook over medium high heat until tender.
Drain excess water from cooked yams and mix in all other ingredients one at a time. (Use more or less sugar depending on personal taste). For best results use an electric beater at low speed.

Preheat oven to 350 degrees. Pour mixture into an uncooked pie crust and bake for 45 minutes or until crust is golden brown. Let cool and serve alone or with whipped cream or vanilla ice cream.

PIE CRUST

1 cup sifted flour
1/2 cup Crisco shortening
2 tsp. ice water
1/2 tsp. salt

Combine flour and salt in mixing bowl with pastrry blender until mixture is uniform and resembles large peas. (Do not overmix). Slowly sprinkle in water mixing lightly with a fork. Add just enough water to form dough into a firm ball with a minimum of handling. Flatten ball into a circle and roll to a uniform thickness. Dust lightly with flour if dough sticks. Transfer dough to pie pan. Trim dough to 1/2" beyond edge of pan. Fold under and flute edge. (Frozen deep dish pie shells may also be used).

Dear Ms. Anderson:

I consider it an honour to have been asked to submit one of my favorite recipes for the All Celebrity Cookbook. To be honest, I have to thank my sister Carmen Opsal for this dessert recipe. It has been a favorite of mine for many years.

Yours very truly,

F. E. Opsal

Frank E. Opsal

CARMEN'S ANGEL LEMON PIE

Meringue Shell:

5 Large Egg Whites
1 cup Sugar
1/2 tsp. Baking Powder
Pinch of Salt

Beat egg whites and salt until frothy. Add sugar mixed with Baking powder a little at a time, until mixture stands in stiff peaks. Pour into a pyrex pie plate which has been greased with butter. Bake in a slow oven (275 degrees) for one hour. Turn off heat and leave the oven door ajar until shell is completely cool.

Lemon Filling:

5 Egg Yolks
1/2 cup Sugar
Juice of tow Lemons (1/2 cup)
Rind of Lemon

Cook in top of double boiler over boiling water until thick. cool completely.

Whip 2 1/2 cups whipping cream with 1/2 cup sugar and 1 tsp. vanilla. Add one large scoop of whipped cream to cooled lemon mixture and fold in.

Pour into cooled meringue.
Refrigerate overnight.

Before serving, decorate top with remainder of whipping cream and tiny pieces of maraschino cherries.

Frank Opsal
BC Sports Hall of Fame
One of the first Canadians to shoot trap and skeet internationally, winning more than 300 tournaments over 40 years of competition

D. NEEL STUDIO

43 E. 7th Ave. - 2nd Floor, Vancouver, BC V5T 1M4
(604) 970-2121 / 286-9971 (Fax)

Italian plum pie

1 lb. italian prune plums	11/1 C. Flour
1 tsp sugar	1/2 tsp salt
1/2 C oil	2 tblp. milk

Wash, half, pit plums. Mix flour, salt, and sugar. Combine oil and milk in a cup, Pour over the flour mixture. Mix until damp. Turn into pie tin and pat out to cover the bottom and sides. Arrange plums and sprinkle stresel over top.

STRESEL: Mix 3/4C sugar,2 tblp. butter until clumbly. Bake at 400' for 40 - 45 min.
2 tbsp. flour, 1/4 tsp. salt

HINT Even though the recipe calls for 1 lb. plums I add extras as I like the looks and taste of the extra fruit.

This is an different and easy dessert and one that get great comments

D. Neel

Bill Parnell

I got this recipe out of the Sun paper a couple of months ago. It was so good that I doubled the recipe as given in the paper. So this is the recipe as I made it.

Mock Rhubarb Pie

500 ml (2 cups) finely diced rhubarb.
250 ml (1 cup) sugar.
250 ml (1 cup) flour. (all-purpose)
10 ml (1 tsp) double-acting baking powder.
1 ml (1/4 tsp) ground cinnamon
250 ml (1 cup) chopped walnuts or pecans
2 large eggs, lightly beaten.
10 ml (2 tsp) vanilla.

Place rhubarb in a large bowl. Add sugar, flour, baking powder, cinnamon, and nuts. Pour the lightly beaten egg and vanilla mixture over the rhubarb mixture. Stir the mixture until all ingredients are well combined. Spread mixture into a greased (use butter) 25 cm (10 in.) pie plate.
Bake at 180C (350 F) for 25-30 minutes.
Best served warm with topping of ice cream or whipped cream.
Makes several servings depending on size of each portion. Refrigerate left over portions.

This recipe is for a topping for a pie using a frozen pie shell.

Topping Mixture

175 ml (3/4 cup) rolled oats
125 ml (1/2 cup) brown sugar
75 ml (1/3 cup) whole wheat flour
75 ml (1/3 cup) canola oil

Combine all ingredients in a medium bowl and mix well. Sprinkle topping over fruit in pie shell and press gently. Bake in a 180C (350F) for 45-50 minutes. Doubled recipe can be used as a Crisp topping.

Bill Parnell
BC Sports Hall of Fame
Won the Gold medal in the mile at the 1950 British Empire Games in Auckland, New Zealand

BRITISH COLUMBIA
AMATEUR SPORTS COUNCIL

INCORPORATED 1959

Organized to Encourage and Promote the Participation of British Columbia Athletes in National and International Competition

August 6, 1993.

Burnaby Chamber of Commerce,
Suite #149, 9855 Austin Ave.
Lougheed Mall,
Burnaby, B.C. V3J 1N4

With reference to your letter of July 27, 1993 I am pleased to enclose one of my favorite recipes.

It sounds like a novel and interesting undertaking and I am sure the dedication of the Burnaby Staff will insure a real success.

Best wishes to a successful project.

Sincerely

Merv. Ferguson

from the kitchen of:
Merv Ferguson

recipe for: "Old Fashioned Ginger Cookies"

ingredients: 1½ cups shortening (1/2 butter; 1/2 marg)
1 tablespoon ginger 4 cups flour 1 egg 1 tsp. salt
1 cup molasses 1½ cups brown sugar
1 teaspoon soda dissolved in 3 tbsps. hot water

METHOD Mix dry ingredients. Blend in shortening. Add egg and molasses, soda and hot water. Mixture will be sticky.
Roll into oblongs and place in frig. Leave overnight.
Slice thin while dough is cold.
Bake at 350 deg. F. 10 - 15 min. Makes 5 doz. cookies.

THE CANADIAN GAMES · OLYMPIC GAMES · PAN AMERICAN GAMES · BRITISH COMMONWEALTH GAMES FEDERATION

CITY OF BURNABY
OFFICE OF THE MAYOR

HERE'S THE COOKIE RECIPE. IT MAKES LOTS. 10-12 DOZEN.

BEAT TOGETHER:

2 CUPS OF MARGARINE
2 CUPS OF BROWN OR YELLOW SUGAR
2 CUPS OF WHITE SUGAR
4 EGGS

ADD:

2 1/2 CUPS OF FLOUR
1 TEAS. SALT
2 TEAS. BAKING SODA
4 TEAS. VANILLA

THEN STIR IN:

2 CUPS RICE CRISPIES
4 CUPS ROLLED OATS
2 CUPS RAISINS
2 CUPS CORN FLAKES
2 CUPS FINE COCONUT
2 CUPS CHOCOLATE CHIPS

DROP FROM SPOON ON GREASED COOKIE SHEET.

BAKE AT 350 DEGREES FOR 8-10 MINUTES.

ENJOY!!!

Bill Copeland
WILLIAM J. COPELAND
MAYOR

4949 Canada Way, Burnaby, British Columbia, V5G 1M2 ❖ Telephone (604) 294-7340 Facsimile (604) 294-7724

DAVID FOSTER'S FAMOUS

SHORTBREAD

1 LB BUTTER (NOT MARGARINE)

1 CUP ICING SUGAR

2 TABLESPOONS CORNSTARCH OR RICE FLOUR

3 1/2 TO 4 CUPS ALL PURPOSE FLOUR

WORK SUGAR INTO THE BUTTER AND MIX WELL. ADD FLOUR A BIT AT A TIME.

KNEAD SLIGHTLY FOR ABOUT 2 MINUTES- NO MORE

NEXT FORM ROLLS WITH THE DOUGH AND REFRIGERATE FOR 2 TO 3 HOURS (OR OVERNIGHT)

SLICE AND BAKE 30-40 MINUTES OR UNTIL SLIGHTLY BROWN IN 300 OVEN

R. DOW REID GALLERY-1560 PANDOSY ST., KELOWNA, B.C. V1Y 1P4 – 763 6714

Dear Abby:

Thank you for your letter of July 13, regarding your All Celebrity Cookbook, and requesting my participation with this endeavour.

Whatever talent I may possess I am afraid little, if any, is channeled towards the culinary arts!!!

However, I have an old recipe which I brought with me from Scotland, many years ago for the best Scottish shortbread. I have enclosed this recipe and trust it may be worthy of inclusion in your cookbook.

Good luck with your project, best regards.

Yours sincerely,

R. Dow Reid.

SCOTTISH SHORTBREAD.

Ingredients;

12 Heaped Tblsp. All Purpose Flour

4 Heaped Tblsp. of Berry Sugar

6 ozs. Butter.

Method:

Put ingredients into a bowl and using two knives or a pastry blender cut and blend until breadcrumb like. Then using hands, knead mixture until mixture holds together in one lump (important to knead three to four mins.)

Place mixture into a 10" pie plate and using the palm of your hand evenly flatten out mixture . Prick all over with a fork and bake in a 250° oven for 2 hours. Remove from oven and while hot cut into wedges and allow to cool. Sprinkle the top with a little berry sugar.

OFFICE OF THE PRESIDENT & C.O.O.

- Burnaby
- Calgary
- North Edmonton
- South Edmonton
- Duncan
- Prince George
- Prince Rupert
- Kitimat
- Vernon
- Washington
- Fort McMurray
- Campbell River
- Whitehorse
- New Westminster
- Dawson Creek
- Sparwood
- Kamloops
- Red Deer
- Oregon
- California
- Winnipeg
- Peace River
- Hinton
- Grande Prairie
- Tumbler Ridge
- Nanaimo
- Saskatoon
- Mackenzie
- Montana
- Arizona
- Mexico
- Singapore

Abby Anderson, C.A.E.
General Manager
Burnaby Chamber of Commerce
Suite 149 - 9855 Austin Avenue
Professional Wing
Lougheed Mall
Burnaby, B.C. V3J 1N4

Dear Ms. Anderson:

In response to your request of June 29th for a terrific recipe, I am pleased to submit this one:

PEANUT BUTTER, WHITE CHOCOLATE & MACADAMIA NUT COOKIES

1 cup ccarsley chopped macadamia nuts (toast in medium skillet for 5 minutes until fragrant)
1 cup flour, 1/2 tsp baking soda, pinch of salt
1/2 cup chunky peanut butter
1 stick (4 oz) unsalted butter (room temperature)
1/2 cup light brown sugar
2 tsps white sugar
1 egg, 1 tsp vanilla, 6 oz white chocolate (chopped)

Toss together flour, salt, soda and set aside. In large bowl cream peanut butter, butter, sugars until smooth and light (approx. 3 minutes). Add egg and beat 3 minutes, add vanilla and beat until incorporated. Using wooden spoon, stir in flour mixture and stir in nuts and chocolate. Spoon heaping tablespoon of dough 1" apart on ungreased sheet. Flatten dough mounds slightly with fingers. Bake 12 - 15 minutes at 375 degrees. (Do not overbake or they will be dry)

Yours sincerely,

B.C. BEARING ENGINEERS LIMITED

R.S. (Robby) MacPherson
President and C.O.O.

CHOCOLATE CHIP COOKIES: Dr. Egon Nikolai

1-1/4 c. sifted flour
1/2 tsp. salt
1/2 c. margarine
1/2 c. brown sugar (packed)
1/3 c. granulated sugar
1 egg unbeaten
1/2 tsp. vanilla
1/2 tsp. soda
1 tb. hot water
1 c. semi-sweet chocolate chips
1/2 c. chopped nuts (optional)

Set oven at 350^0 to preheat. Sift together flour, salt. Cream shortening, sugars, egg, vanilla. Combine soda and water. Add to batter. Also add chocolate chips, nuts and sifted mixture. Beat. Drop by 1/2 tsp. on greased cookie sheets. Bake about 10 min. and cool. Makes about 3 dozen, so you may want to double recipe.

THE FRASER INSTITUTE

HEAD OFFICE: 626 Bute Street, Vancouver, British Columbia V6E 3M1 Canada □ □ □ (604) 688-0221
Fax: (604) 688-8539

Dear Ms. Anderson:

Thanks for the opportunity to submit two recipes to your proposed cook book. The first recipe for chocolate chip cookies was given to me by Mrs. Rose Friedman, the wife and collaborator of Nobel Prize winning economist Milton Friedman. It produces crunchy chocolate chip cookies that are among the best I have ever tasted.

1 cup butter
3/4 cup white sugar
3/4 cup brown sugar
1 teaspoon vanilla
2 eggs
2 1/4 cups white flour
1 teaspoon baking soda
1/2 teaspoon salt
12 ounces chocolate chips
1/2 cup nuts (optional)
2 cups grapenuts

Cream butter and sugar. Add vanilla and eggs. Combine flour, baking soda and salt and add to mixture. Fold in chocolate chips, nuts and grapenuts and drop by teaspoonfuls onto ungreased cookie sheet. Bake at 375° for 8 to 10 minutes. (For crispy cookies, bake 12-15 minutes.)

Sincerely,

Mike Walker

Michael A. Walker
Executive Director

Suite 2550 - 55 King Street West, Toronto Dominion Centre, Toronto, Ontario M5K 1E7 (416) 363-6575 Fax: (416) 601-7322

Mikes All Time Favorite . . .

CHOCLATE CHIP COOKIES

Refrigerate dough, don't use black cookie sheets, us(ice cream scoop, oven 290 - bake 18 min. Transfer to cold plate immediately, store with slice of white bread to keep moist. U.S. measurements.

2 1/4 cups unsifted all-purpose flour
1 teaspoon baking soda
1 cup softened butter
1 cup light brown sugar
1 pkg. (4 serv. size) INSTANT vanilla pudding
1 teaspoon vanilla pudding
2 eggs
1 pkg. bitter-sweet chocalate chips (12oz.)
1 cup chopped nuts

Mix flour with baking soda. Combine butter, the sugars, pudding mix and vanilla in large mixing bowl, beat until smooth and creamy. Beat in eggs. Gradually add flour mixture, then stir in chips and nuts. (Batter will be stiff) Refrigerate to cool. Drop unto ungreased baking sheet, using ice-cream scoop, about 2 inches apart. Bake at 290 18 minutes. Makes 7 dozen.

Michael Harcourt
Premier

Province of British Columbia | Office of the Premier | Parliament Buildings, Victoria, British Columbia V8V 1X4

Dear Ms. Anderson:

Further to your letter of June 2, 1993 to Mr. Ron Bremner, attached is his recipe for "Chocolate Loaf" for inclusion in the All-Celebrity Cookbook. Mr. Bremner is out-of-town just now and asked that I forward this to you.

On behalf of BCTV, may I wish you the best of luck with this cookbook and thank you for inviting Mr. Bremner to contribute.

MAKE THIS THE DAY BEFORE YOU PLAN TO SERVE IT!

CHOCOLATE LOAF
"LOW-FAT"

BAKE AT 350° FOR 45-50 MINUTES
MAKES 1 LOAF (12 SLICES)

INGREDIENTS:

1 3/4 cups all-purpose flour
1/2 cup unsweetened cocoa powder
1 teaspoon baking soda
1/2 teaspoon salt
1 Tablespoon instant espresso powder
1 egg, slightly beaten
1/4 cup (1/2 stick) unsalted butter, melted
1 cup buttermilk
1 cup sugar
2 teaspoons vanilla
1/2 cup pecans, toasted & chopped
1/2 cup golden raisins

1) *Preheat oven to moderate (350°).*
Grease 9"x5"x3" loaf pan.

2) *Combine flour, cocoa, baking soda & salt in a medium sized bowl.*

3) *Beat together espresso powder, egg, butter, buttermilk, sugar & vanilla in large bowl. Add dry ingredients, stir just until evenly moistened. Fold in pecans & raisins. Spoon into prepared pan; smooth top.*

4) *Bake in preheated oven for 45 to 50 minutes or until wooden toothpick inserted in centre comes out clean. Cool in pan on rack for 10 minutes. Remove from pan to rack. Cool completely before serving.*

BCTV, A Division of Westcom TV Group Ltd.
Box 4700, Vancouver, B.C. V6B 4A3 (604) 420-2288 FAX: (604) 421-9427

JOSEPH KUYEK
Vice President & General Manager

4260 Still Creek Drive
Burnaby, B.C. V5C 6C6
Tel. (604) 268-4579
Fax (604) 298-4421

Abby Anderson, C.A.E.
General Manager
Burnaby Chamber of Commerce
Suite #140 - 9855 Austin Avenue
Professional Wing, Lougheed Mall
Burnaby, B.C. V3J 1N4

Dear Ms. Anderson,

In response to your request for recipes for your cookbook, I am enclosing a copy of one that has been provided to me by our receptionist, Mrs. Gayle Foster.

I would consider this recipe to be one of my favourites because I often have the pleasure of enjoying the Chocolate Mallow Fudge whenever she brings it in to the office to share with our staff.

Sincerely,

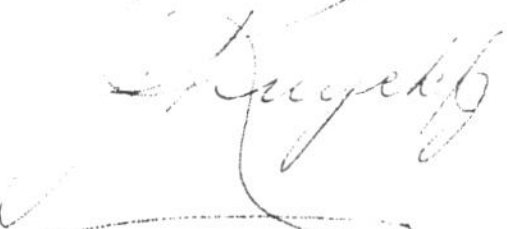

Chocolate Mallow Fudge

Kids in the kitchen? Stormy weather? Try fudge in 10? You'll be a winner....trust us!

4	squares Baker's Unsweetened Chocolate, chopped	4
3 tbsp.	butter	50 ml
3 cups	icing sugar, sifted	750 ml
1/4 tsp	salt	1 ml
1/3 cup	hot milk	75 ml
1 tsp	vanilla	5 ml
1 cup	Kraft Miniature Marshmallows	250 ml
1 cup	chopped walnuts	250 ml

Melt chocolate and butter over hot water or in large microwaveable bowl on "medium" 2 minutes, or until melted. Stir in icing sugar, milk and vanilla; mix well. Fold in the marchmallows and nuts. Spread into a waxed paper-lined 9" x 5" (2L) loaf pan. Chill until firm.

Helpful Hint: Recipe may be doubled and spread in 9" (23 cm) square pan. Cut and store fudge in airtight container in the refrigerator.

August 4, 1993

Abby Anderson, CAE, General Manager
Burnaby Chamber of Commerce
Suite 149 - 9855 Austin Avenue
Professional Wing
Lougheed Mall
Burnaby, B.C.
V3J 1N4

Dear Ms. Anderson:

Thank you for your letter of August 14, 1993 requesting a recipe to be included in your All-Celebrity Cookbook. Mayor Joy Leach has asked me to forward a copy of the official *Nanaimo Bar Recipe* to be her contribution on behalf of Nanaimo.

This is the official recipe which hangs in City Hall. Thousands of copies are given away each year to people all over the world. Good luck with your venture.

Yours sincerely,

Connie Thompson

Connie Thompson
Secretary to the Mayor & Council

CITY HALL, 455 WALLACE STREET, NANAIMO, BRITISH COLUMBIA, CANADA V9R 5J6
TELEPHONE (604) 754-4251 FAX (604) 754-8263

THE ULTIMATE

NANAIMO BAR RECIPE

And now the search is over! Hidden (probably in the back of a drawer or high on a shelf in a Nanaimo kitchen) was the ultimate Nanaimo Bar recipe. Here it is for the world, and you, to munch, savour, and enjoy. Smooth, scrumptious, and delectable! Cheers and Bon Apetit!

Bottom Layer:

1/2 c. unsalted butter
1 3/4 c. graham wafer crumbs
1/2 c. finely chopped almonds
1 c. coconut
1 egg, beaten
1/4 c. sugar
5 tbsp. cocoa

Melt first 3 ingredients in tope of a double boiler. Add egg and stir to cook and thicken. Remove from heat. Stir in crumbs, coconut and nuts. Press firmly into an ungreased 8 x 8 pan.

Second Layer:

1/2 c. unsalted butter
2 tbsp. vanilla custard powder
2 c. icing sugar
2 tbsp. and 2 tsp. cream

Cream butter, cream, custard powder and icing sugar together well. Beat until light. Sprcad over bottom layer.

Third Layer:

4 sq. semi-sweet chocolate (1 oz each)
2 tbsp unsalted butter

Melt chocolate and butter over low heat. Cool. When cool, but still liquid, pour over second layer and chill in refrigerator.

submitted by Mayor Joy Leach

TAYLORE T. FOX
Blake Enterprises/Starmaker Productions Ltd.
1512 West 3rd Ave., 2nd Floor
Vancouver, B.C. V6J 1J7
(604) 732-0188 Fax (604) 572-9818

Recipe from Maestro Bamboshek - Conductor at the Metropolitan and Philadelphia Opera, my coach and conductor, 1950's.

BROWNIES DELUXE

Ingredients

4 squares chocolate	2/3 cup margarine	2 cups sugar	4 eggs
1 1/2 cups flour	1 tsp baking powder	1 tsp salt	2 tsp vanilla
1 cup chopped walnuts			

Method

Melt chocolate and margarine together. Mix sugar in with well beaten eggs and combine to chocolate and margarine. Sift flour, salt, and baking powder together and add to egg mixture. Finally add nuts and vanilla. Spread brownie mixture onto greased cookie sheet and bake for 15 minutes at 350°. When brownies have cooled cover with frosting recipe noted below:

CHOCOLATE FUDGE FROSTING

3 oz chocolate
2 1/4 cups sugar
3/4 cup milk
9 tbsp margarine
1/2 tbsp corn syrup
1/2 tsp salt
1 1/2 tsp vanilla

Method: Bring slowly to a full rolling boil. Stir continually and let boil briskly for 2 minutes. Cool to lukewarm temp. Add vanilla and beat until creamy.

"CHOCOLATE DELIGHT"

CRUST: 1½ c. graham cracker crumbs
¼ c. white sugar
¼ c. melted butter

FILLING: 1 pkg. (8 oz.) cream cheese
¼ c. white sugar
2 tbsp. milk
1 large container of "Cool Whip"
2 pkg. (4 oz. each) of instant chocolate pudding
3½ c. cold milk

- combine crust ingredients
- press into 9 x 13 greased pan
- beat cream cheese, sugar & 2 tbsp. milk until smooth
- fold in ½ c. "Cool Whip", then spread over crust
- prepare pudding & spread over cream cheese
- spread the rest of the "Cool Whip" over pudding
- chill until ready to serve.

P.S. For this delicious dessert recipe, I thank my grandmother!

Brenna Quan

CANADIAN PREMIERE - MAY 26TH, 1993

Brenna Quan
Actor, Singer, Specializing in Stage Productions

2910 Pacific Centre South
P.O. Box 10064,
700 West Georgia Street
Vancouver, B.C.
Canada V7Y 1B6

Peter H. Thomas

CHOCOLATE SOUFFLÉ

2/3	Cup Unsweetened Cocoa Powder	3/4	Cup Sugar plus extra for preparing soufflé dishes
4	Tsp. Corn Starch	1	Cup Skim Milk
1/8	Tsp. Cinnamon	7	Large Egg Whites at room temperature
2	Tsp. Vanilla Extract		Pinch of Salt
1/4	Tsp. Cream of Tarter		Confectioners Sugar for dusting on top
1/2	Oz. Unsweetened Chocolate grated		

In small heavy sauce pan, blend cocoa, 1/4 cup sugar, corn starch and cinnamon. Whisk in milk bring to a boil. whisking constantly, continue stirring and cook for 1 minute or until thickened. Remove from heat and stir in vanilla. Let cool to room temperature.

Position oven rack in the lower third and preheat oven to 350°F. Lightly coat soufflé dishes with Pam. Sprinkle with sugar. Tap out excess.

In large bowl beat egg whites with an electric mixer on medium speed until foamy and opaque. Add cream of tarter and salt, gradually increase speed to high and beat until soft peaks form. Gradually add the remaining 1/2 cup sugar and beat until stiff.

Stir the cocoa mixture well. Whisk about a quarter of the egg whites into the cocoa mixture. Sprinkle mixture with grated chocolate. With rubber spatula fold in the remaining egg whites.

Place dishes in roasting pan filled with hot water to come 2/3's up the soufflé dishes. Bake for about 25 minutes for individual dishes - 40 minutes for large soufflé dish.

Serves 6.

OFFICE OF THE MAYOR

DISTRICT OF KITIMAT
270 City Centre
Kitimat, British Columbia
Canada V8C 2H7

Phone (604) 632-2161
Fax (604) 632-4995

Attention: Abby Anderson, General Manager

Dear Madam:

Re: All Celebrity Cook Book

Further to your request, please find enclosed one of my favorite dessert recipes. It was passed down to us by my wife's family who came to Canada from Switzerland - the land of chocolate. The original recipe was handwritten in French and it has been translated into English for your cookbook. I am certain your cookbook readers will enjoy this dessert, I know I do!

Best Wishes,

Richard W. Wozney,
MAYOR

Suave de Chocolat for 8 persons

(Originated in Basel, Switzerland - copied word for word from the handwritten original)

250 grams good, dark chocolate
250 grams butter
250 grams sugar
4 eggs (entire)
1 tsp. of white flour

Butter well a timbale-mold (or any heat-proof cooking bowl with a tight-fitting cover)

Melt chocolate and sugar slowly in a double boiling pan. Put in butter and stir well. Separately dissolve in a bowl the flour with a drop of water, add the 4 eggs, mix it well and add this carefully into the chocolate, stir very quickly until the mass gets smooth. (I keep it on a tiny fire, the pan still in the hot water bath)

Then put the whole preparation into the timbale-mold, cover tightly, put it in a big pan with simmering, nearly boiliing hot water and let it simmer 3/4 of an hour. Then look inside. It ought to be a little liquid in the middle. Let it cool of a night, then turn it over on a dish and decorate with whipped cream.

FRESH FRUIT BROCHETTES WITH A WARM RASPBERRY SABAYON

2 BROCHETTES PER PERSON:

- 1 BASKET OF STRAWBERRIES
- 2 PLUMS
- 2 NECTARINES — FOR BROCHETTES
- 2 KIWIS
- 1 CANTALOUP MELON
- ½ PINEAPPLE

- 1 BASKET OF PURÉED AND STRAINED RASPBERRIES
- 1 WHOLE EGG
- 3 YOLKS
- ½ LEMON SQUEEZE
- 30 GR ICING SUGAR
- 2 OZ RASPBERRY BRANDY
- 3 OZ SWEET DESSERT WINE

TAKE YOUR CUT UP FRESH FRUIT AND MAKE TWO BROCHETTES PER PERSON.

FOR THE SABAYON, COMBINE THE PURÉED AND STRAINED RASPBERRIES AND THE REST OF THE INGREDIENTS IN TO A MIXING BOWL. PLACE BOWL IN A HOT WATER BAIN-MARIE AND WHISK UNTIL MIXTURE IS NICE AND FOAMY. THEN POUR THE SABAYON ON A PLATE AND PRESENT THE BROCHETTES ON TOP.

EXEC. CHEF

THE HART HOUSE ON DEER LAKE
6664 DEERLAKE AVE.
BURNABY BC.
V5E - 4H3

J. Bleuler

Barkerville B.C.
Heritage Properties Branch

BANANAS BUCKLEY

Dear Abby,

As requested, I have attached my favourite and most "fattening" dessert recipe I could find.

Best wishes for this exciting project.

Sincerely,

per: Warren Buckley
President & CEO
B.C. PAVILION CORPORATION

INGREDIENTS:

4 to 6 Scoops	Vanilla Ice Cream
1/4 Cup	Butter
1/2 Cup	Light Brown Sugar
1/4 Tsp.	Cinnamon
3 to 4	Firm Bananas (sliced in half - lengthwise)
1/2 Cup	Banana Flavoured Liqueur or Grand Marnier
1/2 Cup	Dark Rum

METHOD:

1. Use 4 to 6 dessert dishes and fill each with ice cream.

2. Melt butter in a large skillet, preferably a copper frying pan. Stir in brown sugar and cook until dissolved. Stir in cinnamon. Add bananas, then stir in liqueur.

3. In a separate pan, warm rum on low heat. Ignite it carefully, then pour flaming rum over the bananas and sauce. Stir quickly, and spoon over ice cream.

Yield: 4 to 6 Servings

Suite 600, 375 Water Street, Vancouver, B.C. Canada V6B 5C6 (604) 687-3800 FAX (604) 681-9017
A Crown Corporation of the Province of British Columbia, operating: B.C. Place Stadium,
Fraser Valley Trade & Exhibition Centre (TRADEX), Robson Square Conference Centre, The Bridge Studios, Vancouver Trade & Convention Centre

PAMELA MARTIN'S FRUIT TORTE

1/2 CUP BUTTER
1/2 CUP SUGAR
2 EGGS
1 CUP FLOUR
1 TSP. BAKING POWDER
1/2 TSP. SALT
FRESH WHIPPING CREAM
SUGAR & CINNAMON TO TASTE

FLUTED 2" DEEP FLAN PAN
(REMOVABLE BOTTOM)

CREAM BUTTER AND SUGAR. ADD EGGS AND FLOUR. MIX BAKING POWDER AND SALT. POUR INTO PAN. LOAD TOP OF DOUGH WITH SLICED FRUITS (AT LEAST 2 VARIETIES). BALANCE FRUIT FLAVOURS WITH A MIXTURE OF SWEET & TART. USE FRUITS THAT COOK WELL OR CHOOSE FROM:

NECTARINES, PLUMS, RHUBARB, PEACHES, STRAWBERRIES, APPLES,

KIWI, ALL BERRIES.

SPRINKLE WITH 1/4 CUP CINNAMON & SUGAR TO TASTE.

350 DEGREES FOR 1 HOUR.
REMOVE FROM PAN, WHIP CREAM & ADD SUGAR. SPREAD WHIPPING CREAM OVER TORTE. GARNISH.

ENJOY!

BCTV, A Division of Westcom TV Group Ltd.
Box 4700, Vancouver, B.C. V6B 4A3 (604) 420-2288 FAX: (604) 421-9427

CITY OF
QUESNEL

405 BARLOW AVENUE
QUESNEL, B.C. V2J 2C3
PHONE (604) 992-2111
FAX (604) 992-2206

OFFICE OF THE MAYOR
- STEPHEN D. WALLACE -

LEMON FRUIT FREEZE

Serving Size: 12
Keywords: Frozen Dessert, Lemon, Fruit, Easy

Qty	Measurement	Preparation	Ingredient
1			graham cracker crust
14	oz.	sweetened condensed	milk
½	c.		lemon juice
21	oz.		lemon pie filling
17	oz.	drained, canned	fruit cocktail
2	c.	whipped	topping

1. Make crust and cool.
2. In a large bowl mix milk, lemon juice.
3. Stir in pie filling and fruit.
4. Pour over crust.
5. Top with whipped topping.
6. Freeze for four hours. Remove twenty minutes before cutting.

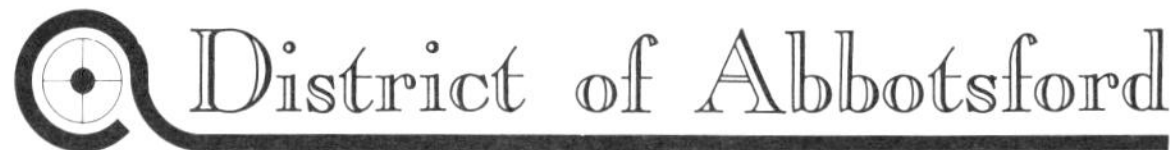

34194 MARSHALL ROAD, ABBOTSFORD, B.C. V2S 5E4
TELEPHONE (604) 853-1155

Office of the Mayor

August 18, 1993

Ms. Abby Anderson, C.A.E.
General Manager
Burnaby Chamber of Commerce
Suite #149 - 9855 Austin Avenue
Burnaby, B.C. V3J 1N4

Dear Ms. Anderson:

Thank you for your letter dated August 13, 1993, requesting recipes for a celebrity cookbook you are compiling. Enclosed is a copy of one of my favourite recipes for inclusion in this book.

I wish you well with this project and would be pleased to know when the cookbook is available for purchase.

Yours very truly,

George F. Ferguson
Mayor

RASPBERRY JELLO DESSERT

Base: 1¼c. crushed graham wafers
3/8 c. melted butter
¼ c. sugar

Mix together and press into 10 x 10 pan. Refrigerate and top with the following:

3 oz. pkg. raspberry Jello
1 pkg. frozen raspberries - slightly thawed
1 sml. carton whipping cream, whipped
½ c. milk
20 marshmallows, quartered

Mix Jello powder with 1 c. boiling water and add frozen raspberries. Put in refrigerator until partially set, then spread on top of base.

In top of double boiler, put milk and marshmallows. Heat till blended, then cool (but don't let it set) and add stiffly whipped cream. Spread over Jello layer and then refrigerate for 24 hours.

OKANAGAN UNIVERSITY COLLEGE

3333 College Way, Kelowna, B.C., Canada V1V 1V7
Telephone (604) 762-5445

September 3, 1993

Ms. Abby Anderson
General Manager
Burnaby Chamber of Commerce
Suite 149, 9855 Austin Avenue
Professional Wing
Louheed Mall
Burnaby, B.C.
V3J 1N4

Dear Ms. Anderson:

Your letter regarding your cookbook arrived while I was on holiday. I have no culinary talents whatsoever. However, I do enjoy eating tasty dishes prepared by others, and I particularly enjoy Okanagan peaches. My administrative assistant, Ms. Arluene King, is talented in these arts, and she has kindly provided the attached recipe which you will note includes peaches although other fruits from the Okanagan can be substituted.

Yours truly,

W.D. Bowering
President

Okanagan Peach Squares

Combine and beat until smooth:

1 cup sugar
1 cup margarine
1 egg

Mix together then add to above:

2 cups flour
1.5 tsp. baking powder.

Pat onto jelly roll pan (for squares) or into an 11 X 13" cake pan (for cake).

Place sliced fruit (apples, cherries, or peaches) on top.

Make a crumble topping (brown sugar, butter, flour), sprinkle over top and bake for about half an hour at 350 degrees.

Great served hot with ice cream!

Armstrong Kelowna Keremeos Oliver-Osoyoos Penticton Princeton Revelstoke Salmon Arm Summerland Vernon

PINEAPPLE SQUARE — MARGE ANDERSON

Base:
2 cups all-purpose flour
1 cup margarine
2. tblsp. sugar (granulated)

Filling
1 14-15 oz. Can crushed pineapple (undrained!)
1/4 cup granulated sugar.
2 tbsp cornstarch
1/4 cup water
3/4 maraschino Cherries

Topping
2 egg whites
2 tbsp Sugar
1/2 c shredded coconut
1/2 tsp Almond flavouring

Preheat Oven to 350°F

Base.
Cut margarine into flour that has been sifted together with the sugar. Should create a dry pastry like consistency. Press dough into a 9"x12" pan. Bake at 350°F for 20 minutes.

Filling
Cook pineapple, sugar, cornstarch and water in a saucepan on medium heat until thick. Cool. Add maraschino Cherries. Set aside.

Topping
Beat egg whites until stiff. Add sugar, Almond extract

To Complete
Spread filling on cookie base, Layer topping over filling and sprinkle with Coconut. Bake at 350°F until meringue is golden. Set on a rack to cool.

Marge Anderson
competitive swimmer

Canadian Pacific Hotels & Resorts

Hotel Vancouver

Dear Ms. Anderson,

Further to your letter of June 14th, herewith two recipes which we're serving in the hotel and which I particularly like and have added to my own repertoire. For the Mille Feuille, I often use black cherry jam, without the cherries.

With kind regards,

Michael M. Lambert
Regional Vice-President/General Manager

MILLE FEUILLE SLICES

10 portions

INGREDIENTS:

Puff Pastry

500 g	Flour
500 g	Butter
1/4 ltr	Milk
1 tbsp	Water
1 tbsp	Lemon Juice
1 tbsp	Rum
10 g	Salt
2	Eggs, beaten to egg wash

Creme Patissiere or Custard

10	Egg yolks
250 g	Sugar
120 g	Flour
1 ltr	Milk
1/2	Vanilla Pod
1/2 ltr	Whipped Dairy Cream
50 g	Red Currant Jelly
Fondant or Icing Sugar	

METHOD:

Make the puff pastry and thin out to a rectangle, 4-5 mm thick (about 1/4 inch). Cut into strips about 4-5 cm wide (about 2 inches). Arrange on a baking sheet. Prick with a fork and brush with egg wash. Bake in a hot oven until golden.

For the custard, mix the egg yolks with the sugar and flour. Boil with milk with the vanilla pod, pour over the egg mixture. Put back on the fire and cook for 10 minutes, stirring constantly. The custard should be smooth and thick. Allow to cool. Remove the vanilla and fold in the whipped cream.

Spread half the strips very thinly with sieved red currant jelly. Cover the other half to a thickness of 2 cm (about 3/4 inch), with custard. Place the jelly coated strips on top and ice with a thin film of fondant. Mask the edges smoothly with custard and cut the strips into slices 3 cm wide (1 1/4 inch), using a sharp knife.

Note: At Hotel Vancouver we use icing sugar instead of fondant and do a marking with a red iron.

Canadian Pacific Hotels Corporation, 900 West Georgia Street, Vancouver, British Columbia, Canada V6C 2W6 Tel: (604) 684-3131
Sales/Catering Fax: (604) 662-1907, Business Centre Fax: (604) 662-1929, Administration Fax: (604) 662-1937

MAKE IT AHEAD. YOU'LL WANT TO STEAL SPOONFULS BEFORE SERVING TIME.

CRUST

1½ CUPS CRUSHED CHOCOLATE WAFERS	375 mL
¼ CUP BUTTER	60 mL
¾ CUP CRUSHED PECANS OR ALMONDS	175 mL

MOUSSE

¾ CUP CHOCOLATE CHIPS	175 mL
8 OZ. CREAM CHEESE	250 g
¼ CUP SUGAR	60 mL
1 TSP. VANILLA	5 mL
2 EGGS, SEPARATED	
¼ CUP SUGAR	60 mL
1 CUP WHIPPING CREAM	250 mL
CHOCOLATE CURLS	

TO MAKE CRUST: PREHEAT OVEN TO 325°F. COMBINE CHOCOLATE CRUMBS AND BUTTER AND PRESS INTO A 9" SPRINGFORM PAN. SPRINKLE NUTS OVER TOP OF CRUST AND BAKE FOR 10 MINUTES.

TO MAKE MOUSSE: MELT CHOCOLATE CHIPS AND SET ASIDE TO COOL. BLEND CREAM CHEESE, SUGAR AND VANILLA. BEAT EGG YOLKS, ADD AND STIR. MIX IN COOLED CHOCOLATE.

BEAT EGG WHITES UNTIL SOFT PEAKS FORM. ADD SUGAR SLOWLY AND BEAT UNTIL STIFF. FOLD INTO CHOCOLATE MIXTURE.

Thank you for including me in your publication.

Yours truly,

Red

Red Robinson

RED ROBINSON MANAGEMENT LTD.
401-68 Water Street, Vancouver, B.C., Canada V6B 1A4 Telephone (604) 684-2382 Fax (604) 688-7118

VanDusen Botanical Garden

Operated by the Board of Parks and Recreation, City of Vancouver

5251 Oak Street
Vancouver, B.C.
V6M 4H1
Administration 266-7194
Education 263-1707
Membership 263-4769
Fax 266-4236

Curator Roy Forsters Recipes

When I'm out gardening or visiting gardens I like to have a Ploughmans Lunch of fine cheeses, crusty bread and lots of butter . Pickled onions are an essential part. All washed down with my home brew beer or scrumpy. [Cider]. Here is the recipe for the onions.

Use small size onions whole.Remove skins,and cover with brine[salt and water for 24 hours].Drain and rinse.Pack in jars, cover with spiced vinegar containing mace, allspice, cloves,stick cinnamon, and peppercorns
Seal tight and keep cool until aged for a few weeks

For dessert I like the noble grape or cherries in season.Out of season one of my favourite desserts is Coconut Cherry Squares. Here is the recipe.

Coconut Cherry Squares

Crumb bottom 1/2 cup Butter
1/2 cup sugar
1 cup flour

Press in to buttered square pan . Cook ten minutes.at 350
Then beat

2 eggs
1 cup sugar
2 tsp flour
1 tsp baking powder
1 cup coconut
1 tsp almond

Spread over previously baked bottom. Sprinkle with 2/3 cup candied cherries. Cook for 20 minutes at 350 degrees
Cut in to squares while still warm

I hope you enjoy my garden lunch, on warm summer afternoons but do not eat too much and fall asleep under the Mulberry Tree.

Sincerely,

R. Roy Forster

R. Roy Forster
Curator

TL'AZT'EN NATIONS
P.O. Box 670
Fort St. James, B.C. V0J 1P0
Phone: (604) 648-3212
Fax: (604) 648-3266

Recipe for Tl'azt'en Soapberries

Ingredients:

- 1/4 cup water
- 1/2 cup soapberries
- 1 egg white
- 1/2 cup sugar

Add 1/2 cup soapberries to 1/4 cup boiling water, boil for five (5) to ten (10) minutes. Let it cool for five (5) minutes then squeeze berries and remove the pulp.

Mix the juice of the soapberries with one (1) egg white and 1/2 cup of sugar and beat until it forms a peak when egg beater is lifted.

ENJOY !

Chief Edward John
Tl'Azt'en Nations
P.O. Box 670
Fort St. James, BC V0J 1P0

Apple Devon

4 Tart apples
2 Peaches, fresh or frozen
1 cup sugar
1 Tablespoon chopped crystalized ginger
1/2 Tea. cinnamon
1 Tea. lemon juice
1 Tea. Grand Marnier
3/4 cup all purpose flour
1/8 Tea. salt
6 Tab. Butter
1/4 cup nutmeats

Whipped Cream or Ice Cream

- Preheat oven to 350°
- Peel, Core, Slice the apples into a bowl with the peaches and add one half cups of the sugar, ginger, lemon juice, grand marnier. Mix lightly and pour into 1½ litre buttered baking dish
- Blend the remaining sugar, flour, salt and butter to a crumbly consistency. Add nuts and sprinkle over the apple mixture.
- Bake 45 min. or until the apples are tender and crust is nicely brown.
- Serve w/ whipped cream or Ice cream.

Brian McGugan
BC Actor & writer

BOWEN ISLAND CRUMBLE

Base

2 cups pitted prune plums or apricots or blackberries and apples
2 tsp cornstarch
1/4 cup sugar

Topping

1 cup flour
1/2 cup marg or butter
1/2 cup sugar

Method

1. Mix fruit with cornstarch and 1/4 cup of sugar and place in an ovenproof dish

2. Rub marg or butter into flour with the palms of your hands until it is thoroughly mixed

3. Place crumble mixture on top of fruit and pat down

4. Bake for 25 mins at 350°

5. Serve with English custard, yoghurt, ice cream, whipped cream or unadorned

Maria Tippett
Author & winner of the Governer General's Award for Emily Carr's Biography

The Vancouver Sun A Southam newspaper
2250 Granville Street, Vancouver, B.C. V6H 3G2 Telephone (604) 732-2111

VERY ENGLISH, VERY RICH, VERY FATTENING — VERY GOOD!

THIS IS FROM DELIA SMITH, ENGLAND'S MOST POPULAR TV CHEF. I'VE TRIED THIS A NUMBER OF TIMES — IT'S EASY TO MAKE AND REHEATS WELL. KIDS LOVE IT!

IAN HAYSOM
EDITOR-IN-CHIEF

RICH BREAD AND BUTTER PUDDING

- 6 slices bread (from small loaf), buttered
- 1 tablespoon candied lemon, orange or mixed peel, chopped fine
- ⅓ cup currants
- 1¼ cups milk
- 5 tablespoons whipping cream
- ¼ cup granulated sugar
- ½ teaspoon grated lemon rind
- 3 large eggs, lightly beaten
- Freshly grated nutmeg

Cut each slice of bread in half, leaving crusts on. Arrange one layer of bread, buttered side up, over bottom of well-buttered 8-inch square baking dish. Cut bread to fit, if necessary. Sprinkle with peel and half the currants. Cover with another layer of bread, buttered side up; sprinkle with remaining currants.

Combine milk and whipping cream. Stir in sugar and lemon rind, then whisk in eggs. Pour milk mixture over bread and sprinkle with nutmeg.

Bake at 350 F for 25 to 30 minutes or until puffed and golden. Serve warm.

Makes four to six servings.

CITY OF VICTORIA
BRITISH COLUMBIA

OFFICE OF THE MAYOR
NO. 1 CENTENNIAL SQUARE,
VICTORIA, VANCOUVER ISLAND,
B.C. V8W 1P6 (604) 385-5711
File Number: 0220-03

ENGLISH SHERRY TRIFLE

1	plain sponge cake OR
1 pkg	ratafia biscuits
1/2 cup	raspberry jam
2 cups	fresh raspberries
1 1/2 cups	prepared custard
1/2 cup	sherry
1 cup	whipping cream

Cut sponge cake in half and spread with raspberry jam.
Put halves back together.
Cut sponge cake into small pieces and place in bottom of large bowl.
Add 1 cup of fresh raspberries and pour sherry over both.
Add prepared custard.
Beat whipping cream and spread evenly on top of mixture.
Garnish with 1 cup of raspberries.

David Turner
MAYOR

attachment

John Cherrington
BARRISTER & SOLICITOR

NUNDAL, CHERRINGTON, EASINGWOOD & KEARL

20570 - 56TH AVENUE
LANGLEY, B.C.
V3A 3Z1
TEL: 530-2191
FAX: 530-6282

9067 CHURCH STREET
BOX 580, FORT LANGLEY, B.C.
V0X 1J0
TEL: 888-5811
FAX: 888-6565

These are two of my favourite dessert treats
John Cherrington

FROZEN GRAND MARNIER SOUFFLE

6	6 egg whites
1 ml	1/4 tsp cream of tartar
375 ml	1 1/2 cups sugar
357 ml	1 1/2 cups whipping cream
	cream
	red and yellow food colouring (optional)
5 ml	1 tsp vanilla
	grated zest of 3 oranges
50 ml	1/4 cup Grand Marnier
Garnish	chocolate curls

In large mixing bowl, beat egg whites with cream of tartar until frothy. Add sugar gradually and continue to beat until stiff but not dry. Place whipping cream in another bowl, and add 4 drops of red food colouring and 12 drops of yellow. Add vanilla and beat until thick. Fold in orange zest and grand marnier. Gently fold in beaten egg whites to whipped cream mixture. Pour into glass serving bowl, cover with plastic wrap. Freeze at least overnight. Remove from freezer 15-20 minutes before serving. Garnish with chocolate curls.

DOWN HOME BREAD PUDDING

1 qt milk
3 cups bread cubes
1 cup sugar
1/4 tsp salt
3 egg yolks, beaten
3 Tbsp melted butter
1/2 tsp vanilla
1/2 cup tart jelly, any flavor
3 egg whites, beaten

Scald milk. Pour over bread cubes. Add 1/2 cup sugar and the salt. Add egg yolks, slightly beaten, butter and vanilla. Mix well. Pour into a 1 1/2 quart casserole. Set casserole in a baking pan. Pour in hot water to depth of 1". Bake in moderate oven (325°F) for 45 minutes or until set. Spread jelly over top. Whip egg whites still, fold in remaining 1/2 cup sugar gradually. Swirl this meringue on jelly. Bake 20 minutes longer or until brown. Chill. Makes 6 to 8 servings.

DESSERT INTERNATIONALE

WHEN VISITING RUGBY BIG-WIGS ARRIVE BEFORE PREPARATION IS POSSIBLE, TRY THIS SURE-FIRE WINNER.

- One scoop vanilla ice-cream in a glass.
- Sprinkle no more than $\frac{1}{4}$ teaspoon chocolate cocoa mix.
- Sprinkle no more than $\frac{1}{4}$ teaspoon instant coffee.
- Add one or two ounces of Triple Sec (substitute Drambuie or Grand Marnier if stock is low... actually we have substituted a lot of things for rugby types.

THE TASTE IS DELICIOUS. A GUARANTEED HIT.

TED HUNT

Ted Hunt
BC Sports Hall of Fame
Captained the BC rugby team that held the Canadian National title from 1958 - 1969

THE CORPORATION OF THE DISTRICT OF OAK BAY
MUNICIPAL HALL - 2167 OAK BAY AVENUE - VICTORIA, B.C. V8R 1G2
PHONE (604) 598-3311 FAX (604) 598-9108

OFFICE OF THE MAYOR

Dear Ms. Anderson:

Thank you for your invitation of July 14, 1993 to participate in the creation of an All-Celebrity Cookbook, featuring recipés from a variety of individuals throughout the province.

I look forward to the publication of this Cookbook, and to experimenting with the recipés submitted by the other contributors. Please accept my best wishes for a successful project. I am sure that your efforts will indeed succeed in enhancing the growth of tourism in British Columbia.

Yours very truly,

Diana Butler

Diana M. Butler, Mayor
District of Oak Bay

Sour Cream Dessert

1 envelope gelatin
¼ cup cold water
2½ cups heavy cream
1 cup superfine sugar
2 cups sour cream
1 teaspoon vanilla
raspberries/strawberries/blueberries or other fruit of choice

Dissolve gelatin in water. Heat (**do not boil**) cream, sugar and gelatin while stirring gently. Cool. Fold in sour cream and vanilla. Chill.

Serve in dessert bowls with fresh fruit.

Concord Pacific Developments Ltd.

Suite 900
1090 West Pender St.
Vancouver, B.C.
Canada V6E 2N7
Tel: (604) 681-8882
Fax: (604) 681-8086

Dear Ms. Anderson:

Re: Burnaby Chamber of Commerce - All-Celebrity Cookbook

I am most pleased to help enhance tourism in British Columbia by contributing to your cookbook. Enclosed herewith please find a recipe for one of my favorite Chinese deserts, **Red Beans and Coconut Pudding.** Enjoy!

Yours truly,
CONCORD PACIFIC DEVELOPMENTS LTD.

Per: Terry Hui
President & C. E. O.

Red Beans and Coconut Pudding

Ingredients:

6 oz. red beans
3/4 cup evaporated milk
12 oz. coconut juice
5 oz. cornflour
1 1/3 cup sugar
30 strips agar agar

Method :

1. Blend cornflour, coconut juice and evaporated milk together.
2. Soak agar agar for 1/2 hour and then drain.
3. Wash red beans and boil with 6 cups of boiling water. Simmer over low heat for 1 1/2 hr. until beans soften. Drain and save boiling water afterwards.
4. Boil agar agar in the saved boiling water (approx. 5 cups of red bean water) until agar agar dissolves. Add sugar, then gradually pour in cornflour mixture blended in step 1 and keep on stirring until it thickens. Put in red beans and bring to boil again.
5. Pour final mixture into nonstick pan or container that has been previously rinsed with cold water.
6. Cool and chill pan in the refrigerator. Cut into pieces before serving.

Sauces Relishes Jams

NORA PATRICH

CHIMICHURRI

this is a sause used in my home country Argentina to flavor meat, specially barbique. or on Milanesa or steak.

- ½ cup oil
- 1 cup warm water
- 1 cup vinegar or ½ cup vinegar and ½ cup wine
- 1 teaspoon salt or to taste
- 2 cloves of garlic. (minced)
- 2 tablespoons parsley, finely chopped or silantro
- 1 green onion (choped)
- 1 small tomato (peeled, seeded and chopped)
- 1 small sweet pepper, (finely chopped)
- 1 teaspoon paprika
- ½ teaspoon ground cumin
- ½ teaspoon ground pepper or chili powder
- ½ teaspoon ground oregano leaves
- 2 bay leaves, (broken in small pieces.

these ingredients should be finely chopped, but in no case reduced to a smooth paste. put all ingredients together in a bottle and then shake the bottle lit sit. it keeps in the fridge for a long time. It is superb on barbeque meet or steaks if you prefer it hoter just add more chili pepers.

NORA PATRICH

Hodson Manor, 1254 West 7th Avenue, Vancouver, B.C., Canada V6H 1B6
Tel.: (604) 738-6822 Fax: (604) 738-7832

Washburn's Wicked Barbeque Sauce

1 stick margarine
1 cup sliced onion
1 cup ketchup
1 cup commercial barbeque sauce (hickory is great for this)
1 tablespoon dijon mustard
1/4 cup worchester sauce
Tabasco sauce, to taste
Salt & Pepper
1/4 cup white vinegar
1/4 cup Log Cabin syrup

Mix and heat. Can be stored in refrigerator for a month or more, using as needed. Great to add 1/2 cup to a can of baked beans, also!

Continuing Studies

515 West Hastings Street
Vancouver, British Columbia
Canada V6B 5K3

Tel: 604/291.5100
Fax: 604/291.5098

Grandma's Chili Sauce

1 large can tomatoes (or equivalent amount of fresh)
three-quarters cup sugar
1 cup vinegar
1 large onion
1 teaspoon cinnamon, 1 teaspoon nutmeg, three-quarters teaspoon allspice, 3 teaspoons chili powder, 1 teaspoon salt

Put tomatoes, sugar, and vinegar into large pot. Add finely chopped onions and spices. Bring to boil and simmer for a couple of hours. Pour into sterilized jars and seal. Will keep for months. Can be made in any quantity--just keep the proportions the same. Note: This is a sweet and spicy sauce, not a hot one. It can be made as hot as you like by the addition of lots of jalapeno or other hot peppers.

Christine Hearn

THE CORPORATION OF THE CITY OF WHITE ROCK

CITY HALL
15322 BUENA VISTA AVENUE
WHITE ROCK, B.C.
V4B 1Y6

Admin. DEPARTMENT

TEL: 531-9111
FAX: 538-6049

1993 July 26

Abby Anderson, C.A.E.,
General Manager,
Burnaby Chamber of Commerce,
#149 - 9855 Austin Ave.,
Professional Wing, Lougheed Mall,
Burnaby, B.C.
V3J 1N4

Dear Ms. Anderson:

Further to your letter of 1993 July 14 regarding the All-Celebrity Cookbook, please find enclosed Mayor Hogg's recipe for his world famous Antipasto.

Mayor Hogg has asked me to convey his sincere best wishes for the success of this venture and, further, to commend yourself and those at the Burnaby Chamber of Commerce for taking a leadership role to enhance the growth of tourism in our province.

Sincere best wishes.

Yours truly,

D. Taylor

per Donna Obermeyer
Secretary to the Mayor
and Administrator

ANTIPASTO

Gordon Hogg
Jim Garnett

8 - oz. Olive Oil

1 - 16 oz. tin of broken green olives chopped

1 - very large cauliflower, chopped

2 - 12 oz. jars pickled onions, chopped

2 - tins ripe olives, chopped

ADD:

1 - 15 oz. bottle Heinz Ketsup (hot)

1 - 48 oz. jar mixed pickles, chopped

2 - 10 oz. tins mushroom stems & pieces

2 - large green peppers, chopped

2 - 4 oz. tins pimento, chopped

4 - 15 oz. bottles Heinz Ketsup

1 - 28 oz. jar "Hot" Salsa

Generous portions of Tabasco Sauce (to taste)

Stir and simmer for 10 minutes. Drain, then rinse the following with boiling water:

3 - 7 oz. tins solid tuna, chopped

3 - tins small shrimp

2 - tins anchovies, chopped

Mix everything together and place in sterilized jars.

documentary productions ltd.

THE CHOLESTEROL FIX

Feeling a little nutritionally deprived after all those lentil soups and celery sticks? How about a mess of pure butter and eggs with .01% "other"?

It's my purloined-and-ad-lib instant (40 second) Hollandaise Sauce for the strong-hearted...so good you'll want to lick the osterizer right down to the blades.

Simply gather in a heap near the sink, the blender and the microwave:

- 3 egg yolks
- 1\2 cup of butter
- a lemon
- a pepper grinder
- a salt shaker
- a pinch of cayenne

While the butter is melting to hot (not warm), drop the yolks in the blender, add about a tablespoon of lemon (my friend James Barber uses one hand as a sieve to strain the seeds) the cayenne pepper and salt. Fire up the blender at high speed for three seconds and then start adding the butter (it actually "cooks" the eggs to thicken the sauce) for 30 seconds or so.

Stop the blender and stick your index finger in the finished work of art. Ecstasy guaranteed.

Of course, the piece de resistance. Pour it generously over poached eggs on buttered toast.

Jack,

Jack McGaw

BURNABY ARTS CENTRE CAPITAL CAMPAIGN

Randy Salad Dressing

1/3 balsamic vinegar
(or vinegar of choice)

1/3 olive oil

1/3 honey

2 large tablespoons
of Dijon mustard.

Michael Harding

6450 Deer Lake Ave.
Burnaby, B.C.
V5G 2J3, Canada
Phone: (604) 291-7479
Fax: (604) 291-7841

Aug 10th/93.

Ruth Wilson

Dear Abby,

Your request for a favorite recipe from me for your Burnaby Chamber of Commerce "Cook Book" was a surprise.

Unfortunately I have never done much cooking. My mother, Mrs. Lily Plant Wilson, was a superb cook and consequently I had no need to learn beyond the basics.

However I did hunt up my mother's ancient personal recipe book. Inside was a well worn loose page of a very old recipe for "Pickled Damsons".

I remember this recipe — it was a favorite with my father.

Thank you for including me in this project.

Sincerely,

Ruth Wilson.

Ruth Wilson
BC Sports Hall of Fame
Won 4 consecutive Canadian basketball championships with the Vancouver Hedlunds, and coached the Vancouver Eilers to 2 National titles

[illegible]led Damsons

6 quarts Damsons
1 " Vinegar
6 lbs Sugar
$\frac{1}{4}$ oz of Cloves
$\frac{1}{4}$ oz Cinnamon

Prick the damsons well and all over before using them; boil the vinegar, sugar & spice well together.

Pour the liquor over the fruit, three days successively & the last time give them a scald let the damson be free from bruises & be sure to prick them well or they will burst do not scald them much the last time.

Lychgate House
Chaddesley, Sep. 13. 1918

Province of British Columbia

With My Compliments

Honourable Tom Perry
Minister of Advanced Education,
Training and Technology

PERRY'S (DEVILISH) MANGO CHUTNEY

INTRODUCTION

This chutney recipe comes from the far south of India (Nagercoil) via the peripatetic Dr. Don Lovely, presently of Saanich, British Columbia. The recipe may be varied to taste. I always find the quantity is hard to believe, so I underdo the vinegar and sugar. On the last batch I did not have time to soak the Mangoes overnight in salt and I am not sure why it makes any difference, but I put in less salt than called for in the recipe. A good size case of large Mangoes these days can be had for less than $10.00 in summer and may be enough to make as much as a threefold recipe. If you like the chutney "devilish", add some extra chili powder and/or some curry spice or tikka paste, or something similar. If you don't soak the Mangoes overnight, you will need to add less water than called for in the recipe since that water gets discarded in the original. The chutney will keep for at least several years. It seems to even keep well in the jar in the refrigerator once opened. I have had some opened for as long as a year without any apparent deterioration, but that may be pushing it.

Aspiring politicians take note: This chutney can be used to satisfy the incessant demands for fund raising auction items from constituency associations. If you have that in mind, make many small bottles so that you can keep some for yourself to eat, or give to your special friends.

Parliament Buildings
Victoria, B.C. V8V 1X4
Telephone: (604) 387-5202
Fax: (604) 356-1232

PERRY'S (DEVILISH) MANGO CHUTNEY

Ingredients:

1.5 kg	(3 lbs.)	green mangoes (4 cups or 8 medium) peeled, halved, stoned
6 tbsp	(6 tbsp)	salt
1.75 L	(4 pints)	water
0.5 kg	(2 *Cups)	sugar (*C)
0.6 L	(2 1/2 C)	vinegar
75 g	(3 oz)	fresh root ginger, peeled & finely chopped
10	(10)	garlic cloves, finely chopped
2 tsp	(2 tsp)	"hot" chili powder
1x10 cm	(4 in)	cinnamon stick
125 g	(2/3 C)	raisins
125 g	(2/3 C)	stoned (pitted) dates, chopped

* I usually use less, especially if mangoes are sweet

Method:

Cut Mangoes into cubes. Dissolve salt in the water in large bowl. Stir in the mango cubes. Cover and set aside at room temperature for 24 hours. Drain cubes in a colander and set aside. (This step can be omitted going directly to the cooking. In that case, use less salt, because some of the salt would have been thrown away in the rinse water)

Dissolve the sugar in the vinegar over low heat. stirring frequently. When dissolved, bring mixture to a boil. Add the mango cubes, ginger, garlic, chili powder, cinnamon, raisins and dates (and other spices if desired) and bring back to boil, stirring occasionally. Reduce heat to moderate low and simmer the chutney for 1 1/2 to 2 hours or until thick. Remove from heat. Remove the cinnamon sticks. Spoon into clean, warmed, jam or preserve jars. Cover with vinegar resistant paper or use regular canning jar covers, label and store in a cool dry place until ready to use.

NOTE: Cooking time varies depending on quality of fruit used and yield, therefore, cooking time is approximate. Chutney improves with keeping after three to four weeks.

CITY OF PORT ALBERNI

PHONE (604) 723-2146
FAX (604) 723-1003

GILLIAN TRUMPER
Mayor

CITY HALL, 4850 ARGYLE ST., PORT ALBERNI, B.C V9Y 1V8

July. 19. 1993

Dear Mr. Anderson.

I am just leaving on holiday tomorrow, so I felt I should send this recipe off to you. What a great idea. I am enclosing one of my chutney recipes. It is very popular, and is great with meat, chicken and, or, cheese.

Fruit Chutney.

- 3 cups peaches.
- 3 cups pears.
- 3 cups plums.
- 3 cups apples
- 2 cups onions.
- 2 cups celery.
- 1 cup raisins
- $\frac{1}{2}$ cup preserved ginger.
- 1 tablespoon salt.
- 2 teaspoons each allspice, & cinnamon.
- 1 tablespoon chili powder.
- 1 teaspoon cloves.
- 1 tablespoon Angostura bitters
- 4 cups brown sugar.
- 3 cups dark vinegar.
- 2 cups tomato sauce.

Chop fruit etc. into chunks. Put all ingredients into large saucepan. Heat to boiling point, and then simmer until thick and dark, stir occasionally. Seal in sterilized jars.

Enjoy.

Gillian Trumper

Capilano Suspension Bridge
North Vancouver B.C.
Photo Courtesy of Tourism B.C.

A. TED EWACHNIUK & ASSOCIATES

TRIAL LAWYERS

A. TED EWACHNIUK

GEORGE KINCAID - ASSOCIATE COUNSEL

TELEPHONE: (604) 273-1844
FAX (604) 273-5625

MARINA PLACE
8331 RIVER ROAD
RICHMOND, B.C.
V6X 1Y1

OUR FILE NO.

MOM'S SPECIAL CANTALOUPE MARMALADE

INGREDIENTS:
4 medium-sized ripe cantaloupes
3 oranges
3 lemons
2 cans (15 oz) crushed pineapple
granulated sugar (quantity described below)

METHOD:
Peel cantaloupes, remove seeds and put through a mincer
Wash oranges and lemons, remove seeds (but not rind) and put through a mincer
Add crushed pineapple (including the juice).

Measure the fruit combination: To every 10 cups of fruit mixture, add 7 cups of sugar.

Cook for 2 hours at a light boil, stirring frequently.

Place immediately in sterilzed jars and seal.

Submitted by: A. Ted Ewachniuk, Lawyer

Yours truly,

A. TED EWACHNIUK & ASSOCIATES

A. TED EWACHNIUK

/ann
enclosures

A. TED EWACHNIUK & ASSOCIATES

TRIAL LAWYERS

A. TED EWACHNIUK

GEORGE KINCAID - ASSOCIATE COUNSEL

TELEPHONE: (604) 273-1844
FAX (604) 273-5625

MARINA PLACE
8331 RIVER ROAD
RICHMOND, B.C.
V6X 1Y1

OUR FILE NO.

SOPHIA'S OLD-FASHIONED STRAWBERRY JAM

INGREDIENTS:
6 heaping cups whole strawberries, washed and hulled
6 cups sugar

METHOD:
Place 2 heaping cups of strawberries in a heavy dutch oven.
Crush berries with a potato masher.
Add 2 level cups of sugar; boil mixture for 10 minutes (stir constantly)

Then add:
2 cups of whole strawberries (do not mash)
2 cups of sugar, and boil mixture another 10 minutes (stir constantly)

Next, add:
2 cups of whole strawberries (do not mash)
2 cups of sugar, and boil mixture another 10 minutes (stir contantly).

Immediately place in sterilized jars and seal.

Submitted by A. Ted Ewachniuk, Lawyer

Yours truly,

A. TED EWACHNIUK & ASSOCIATES

A. TED EWACHNIUK

/ann
enclosures

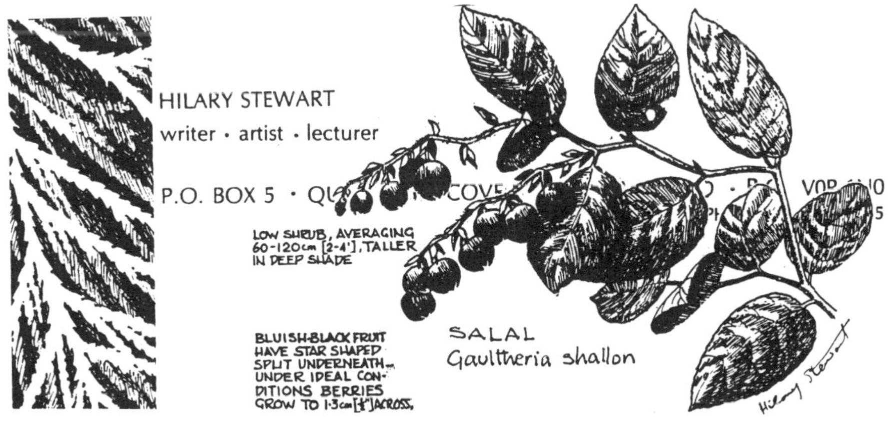

SALAL BERRY JAM and FRUIT LEATHER

Here are two recipes that take you outdoors and into the country at the height of summer. The main ingredient is SALAL BERRIES - those small black berries that often edge B.C.'s forests, trails and clearings, those berries that you always thought were poisonous because of their colour. Salals are very edible, tasty, abundant and FREE.

The berries are ready for picking (late July or August) when they are quite black and readily come off the stem with a twist of fore finger and thumb. With several kilos (or pounds) you can now make a delicious jam and/or fruit leather. Both start out the same way:

* Spread out the berries and remove any stems, fir needles etc., then rinse.

* Place the wet berries in a large saucepan over medium heat, and keep crushing with a potato masher as they cook. Continue crushing until no berries remain whole and the juice makes the whole thing sloppy. Add sugar to taste, also vanilla or almond essence, about 1/2 teaspoon per pound.

* Let the mashed berries cook for 15 - 20 minutes, and keep stirring.

JAM. Spoon the berry mash into sterilized jars. When cooled, cover with liquid parafin wax or cover with plastic wrap and freeze.

FRUIT LEATHER. Cover a cookie sheet with plastic wrap, then spread out the berry mash to a thickness of about 6cm (1/4 ") You can sprinkle with finely chopped nuts for added nutrition.

* Dry the mash in the sun for several days, less in very hot weather. Or, put in the oven (100°) and the door partly open, until the fruit is firm.

* Now roll up the salal berry leather, peeling back the plastic wrap as you go. Cut the long roll in thirds, wrap and store in the fridge.

** If you wish, you can also add chopped apples (peeled and cored) to the berries - for both the jam and the fruit leather.

MOM'S SECRET

"MADE FROM THE SHELF"

SPAGHETTI SAUCE

1.5 lbs	ground beef
1	onion
2	Hot Italian Sausages
1/2 bag	Money's Mushrooms
6 oz	Sommet Rouge
1 can	tomatoes (stewed)
1/2 tin	tomato paste
1 jar	spaghetti/mushroom sauce (Prego)
1 can	tomato soup

oregano, pepper, sweet basil, bay leaves, spaghetti seasonings - and lots of 'em.

Easy to make and delicious! Brown meat, sausage, onions, and mushrooms. Add all canned ingredients and the jar of spaghetti/mushroom sauce. Season aggressively. Cook for 3 hours and enjoy Calona Chardonnay.

Open a bottle of Calona Cabernet Sauvignon while you broil/bake garlic toast and toss your green salad with oil and vinegar dressing and add spaghetti (of course).

Ian Tostenson
President

Suite 214 - 1285 West Broadway, Vancouver, British Columbia, Canada V6H 3X8 Telephone (604) 738-9463 Fax (604) 738-0182

BURNABY
CHAMBER OF COMMERCE

Abby,

Who would have thought that an idea discussed over coffee all those months ago would have turned into the slick publication you see before you. The work involved in putting this publication together exceeded our expectations. The enthusiasm from all involved has been tremendous from the start and I'm looking forward to begin work on Volume II.

I have to credit the following recipe to a very dear friend, Diana Bishop, in Connecticut. I had the opportunity to try this recipe when my wife, Josette, arrived home with 30 pounds of cucumbers from a cousin's garden. It was very easy to make and I hope you enjoy it.

DI'S BREAD AND BUTTER PICKLES

7 cucumbers, sliced
5 white onions, sliced
1 green pepper, chopped
1 small red pepper, chopped
1/4 cup salt
cracked ice

Pickling Solution:
2 1/2 cups white vinegar
2 1/2 cups sugar
1 tablespoon mustard seed
1 teaspoon celery seed
3/4 teaspoon turmeric
1/4 teaspoon powdered cloves

Prepare vegetables, mix in salt and cracked ice, put in cool place and let stand for at least 3 hours; drain.

Mix pickling solution. Add to drained vegetables in pot. Bring mixture to boiling point, remove vegetables to jars immediately and pour hot liquid over; seal. Makes about 6 pints.

CAUTION: If mixture is allowed to boil, pickles will become soft. Be sure mixture is only brought to a boil.

Enjoy pickles after cooling in the fridge overnight.

Sincerely,

Shane Nagel
Sales Manager

Suite #149 - 9855 Austin Avenue, Professional Wing, Lougheed Mall, Burnaby, BC V3J 1N4 • Ph: (604) 421-0084 • Fx: (604) 421-3630

BOWZER BONES

4	cups	whole wheat flour
1/2cup		wheat germ
1	cup	powdered skim milk
1/2tsp.		garlic powder
2	tbsps.	brewers yeast
1/4tsp.		salt
12	tbsps.	olive oil (or other healthy oil)
2		eggs
2	tbsps.	molasses
2	100 ml	jars of baby food (beef, chicken, lamb)

Combine all dry ingredients in large bowl. Blend in olive oil, eggs, molasses and baby food. Knead all together.

Roll dough to about 1/4" thick and cut out into shapes. (bones, birds, cats)

Place on cookie sheet and bake for 20 to 25 minutes at 375.

STU JEFFRIES

INDEX

BREAKFAST/BRUNCH

APPETIZERS

SOUPS/SALADS

ENTREES: FISH/SEAFOOD

ENTREES: MEATS

ENTREES: POULTRY/GAME

PASTA

VEGGIES/SIDE DISHES

DESSERTS

SAUCES/RELISHES/JAMS/ETC.

B.C. All-Celebrity Cookbook
Burnaby Chamber Of Commerce
Suite 149-9855 Austin Avenue
Burnaby, B.C. V3J 1N4

Please send me ________ copies of the B.C. All-Celebrity Cookbook .... @ $23.95 each ____________
Add 7% Goods and Services Tax .... @ 1.68 each ____________
Postage and handling .... @ 3.00 each ____________

Enclosed is my Cheque or Money Order in the amount of .... $ ____________

Make cheque(s) payable to the Burnaby Chamber of Commerce

Please charge to my MasterCard or Visa No. ____________
Expiration date ____________ Signature ____________

NAME ____________
ADDRESS ____________
CITY ____________ PROV. ____________ POSTAL CODE ____________

(PLEASE PRINT)

B.C. All-Celebrity Cookbook
Burnaby Chamber Of Commerce
Suite 149-9855 Austin Avenue
Burnaby, B.C. V3J 1N4

Please send me ________ copies of the B.C. All-Celebrity Cookbook .... @ $23.95 each ____________
Add 7% Goods and Services Tax .... @ 1.68 each ____________
Postage and handling .... @ 3.00 each ____________

Enclosed is my Cheque or Money Order in the amount of .... $ ____________

Make cheque(s) payable to the Burnaby Chamber of Commerce

Please charge to my MasterCard or Visa No. ____________
Expiration date ____________ Signature ____________

NAME ____________
ADDRESS ____________
CITY ____________ PROV. ____________ POSTAL CODE ____________

(PLEASE PRINT)

B.C. All-Celebrity Cookbook
Burnaby Chamber Of Commerce
Suite 149-9855 Austin Avenue
Burnaby, B.C. V3J 1N4

Please send me ________ copies of the B.C. All-Celebrity Cookbook .... @ $23.95 each ____________
Add 7% Goods and Services Tax .... @ 1.68 each ____________
Postage and handling .... @ 3.00 each ____________

Enclosed is my Cheque or Money Order in the amount of .... $ ____________

Make cheque(s) payable to the Burnaby Chamber of Commerce

Please charge to my MasterCard or Visa No. ____________
Expiration date ____________ Signature ____________

NAME ____________
ADDRESS ____________
CITY ____________ PROV. ____________ POSTAL CODE ____________

(PLEASE PRINT)